T0067912

Reflections of a Police Psychologist

Primary Considerations in Policing

Third Edition-R

Reflections of a Police Psychologist

Primary Considerations in Policing

Information for police officers and those that would like to better understand the worlds of policing and police psychology

Jack A. Digliani, PhD, EdD

To order additional copies of this book, contact:
Xlibris
844-714-8691
www.Xlibris.com
Orders@Xlibris.com
843531

Contents

Acknowledgements

I would like to thank my colleagues and those police officers, deputy sheriffs, state troopers, park rangers, and other law enforcement officers who have contributed to this book by sharing their thoughts, feelings, and experiences. I owe a debt of gratitude to the spouses of officers and the civilian employees of police agencies that also helped to shape the ideas presented.

I am grateful to Bruce Glasscock, the Fort Collins, Colorado Police Services (FCPS) Chief of Police from 1984 to 1990. It was under his administration that in 1986, the first FCPS peer support team was created. Thank you to Howard "Bud" Reed, Sherri Wagner, and Dave Wilson, the police officers who joined me in comprising the first FCPS peer support team (Appendix C).

Special thanks to Tim Brown and (A.S.) Bryce Griffin for their enduring support, assistance, and professional contributions. Both are certified instructors of the Police Peer Support Team Training program and continue to advance the principles of law enforcement peer support.

I would like to especially thank Lorie, my wife of many years for her unwavering support, faith, and love. Now and forever.

TaLkD35aEpS

This book includes ideas, information, and documents created by the author and others. In cases where the source of specific information is known, the source has been cited. The author acknowledges the countless contributions of those persons whose thoughts have been so completely incorporated into general knowledge that they are no longer readily identified.

Foreword

The streets are protected each and every day by cops who feel, cops who love, cops who need and want—just like you. They are sometimes single, sometimes married, sometimes moms and dads. All have bills to pay, yards to mow and a life away from the job. Yet even off duty, they carry the emotional baggage and mental strain of what they sometimes have to do to stay alive and make it home. Occasionally, the bucket in their mind reserved for miserable memories and pictures gets full and threatens to overflow. When that happens, there is no one more valuable—more indispensable— than a competent police psychologist. He or she can literally save the life of a hero worth saving. A gallant soldier we pay to protect our community.

Dr. Jack—Jack Digliani—does this like few others. He knows, like few police psychologists can, because before he was a shrink, he was a cop. While attending university to become a leading expert in this highly specialized field of psychology, he worked as a police officer in Wyoming and Colorado, learning first-hand the trials and tribulations with which he would one day be called upon to help his brothers and sisters—the men and women still on the street.

Those who first come to him as his patients ultimately discover that Dr. Jack is a peer, a friend, a brother, and a trusted confidant. I did. I still do.

Trooper Jim Geeting, Wyoming Highway Patrol, Retired.

Author of: *The Badge - Thoughts from a State Trooper*
Shots Fired Shots Forgiven, The Steve Watt Story
The Badge Part Two - More Thoughts from a Retired State Trooper
Truckers and Troopers
Cops and Kids - A Very Special Friendship
The American Trucker

Author's Notes

I have chosen to write in a style that I feel is conducive to easier reading. For the most part, I have taken the liberty of using the masculine pronoun in sentences that require a pronoun. This permits the avoidance of the more descriptive yet cumbersome phrases like *he or she, himself or herself,* and *they or themselves.* Unfortunately, the English language does not have a single pronoun that is inclusive of all persons. Rest assured that unless otherwise specified, the information applies equally well and is intended to include everyone. I hope that this style of writing, selected only for ease of reading, is viewed as nothing more than convention. Certainly, it is so intended.

The use of the terms *officer* and *police officer* are intended to include civilian personnel of law enforcement agencies, deputy sheriffs, state troopers, park rangers, and other law enforcement or peace officers at all levels of government.

Although many issues and concepts are presented and discussed in terms of police officers and policing, most are equally applicable to those outside of police work.

Reflections of a Police Psychologist, Third Edition-R includes changes made in the earlier Revised Edition (2010), Second Edition (2015), and Third Edition (2022). For greater comprehensiveness, the Third Edition-R incorporates some information previously published in Contemporary Issues in Police Psychology (Digliani, 2015) and the Law Enforcement Peer Support Team Manual (Digliani, 2022).

The Third Edition-R, like those before it, includes several references to the Colorado Revised Statutes (C.R.S.). These are used only to illustrate a point, clarify a concept, or demonstrate an option. Therefore, most of the discussion involving the C.R.S. applies equally well to all states and the federal level of government.

The various chapters of this book may be read independently of one another. References to other chapters are indicated when appropriate.

Introduction

General Psychology and Police Psychology

Police psychology differs from general psychology in its emphasis of interest. The major areas of interest in police psychology are those that are inclusive to the profession of policing. These range from the psychological assessment of police candidates to retirement and life after a police career. Because the fundamental principles of psychology apply equally well to the profession of policing as they do any occupation, it makes sense to think of police psychology as the study and application of fundamental psychological principles as they relate to the profession of policing.

A psychologist that works in the area of police psychology is called a *police psychologist*. Currently there is no legal definition or title protection for the use of this designation, although use of the title "psychologist" is regulated in all states.

Police psychologists are professionally associated through a number of organizations, including the International Association of Chiefs of Police (IACP) and the American Psychological Association (APA). The APA recognizes police psychology as a specialty within the field of psychology in Division 18, *Psychologists in Public Service, Section: Police and Public Safety* (n.d., para.,1).

Police psychology is not criminal psychology. Police psychologists work with police officers. Criminal psychologists work with criminal offenders. Professionally, there is no prohibition against a psychologist working with police officers and criminal offenders, or criminal psychologists consulting with police agencies, so long as established ethical standards of conduct and statutory requirements are maintained. However, most police psychologists limit their practice to police officers, civilian employees of law enforcement agencies, and their families. This is the focus of concern and the true realm of police psychologists.

Law Enforcement and Policing

It is more accurate to use the term *policing* than it is to use the term *law enforcement* because police officers in modern society do much more than enforce the law. Although law enforcement is a major responsibility of police officers, police officers serve their communities in a variety of additional ways. Police officers function as peacekeepers, negotiators, teachers, individual and family counselors, security consultants, problem solvers—the list goes on and on. One thing is certain, policing in America today has become a multifaceted profession which brings with it an increased demand for the acquisition of special knowledge and unique skills.

Most people would agree that policing looks quite different today than it has in the past. The advances in policing technology over the last several decades were not likely foreseeable by police officers of the mid-twentieth century. Some of the more obvious changes in policing include the use of cell phones and other devices, dashboard and body cameras, ballistic vests (policing in America years ago was regularly conducted without such protection), high-capacity semiautomatic pistol magazines (many police departments historically prohibited the carrying of semiautomatic handguns citing their unreliability), global positioning and navigation equipment, and in-vehicle computers.

The development of policing technology has not been limited to that mentioned. Research into the realm of alternative weaponry has produced an array of less-lethal technologies, including rubber baton weapons, beanbag rounds, chemical weapons, and electrical stun devices. Additionally, scientific advances now allow police officers to solve cases based on nearly imperceptible trace evidence, DNA, and the results of increasingly sophisticated gene-related and gene-tracing laboratory procedures.

Police training has also evolved. Police academies have expanded their curriculum to include courses in stress management, officer wellness, and police officer family dynamics. Courses not seen in the police academies of previous generations, such as crisis intervention, de escalation of violence, and assisting persons with mental illness, have now become common.

Specialized police training has likewise advanced. One of the most visible areas of specialized training is crisis negotiation. Officers trained in crisis negotiation are called upon to communicate with persons involved in any number of circumstances, including the holding of hostages. Crisis negotiators regularly work with Special Weapons and Tactics (SWAT) units to resolve difficult and dangerous situations. Even the on-scene assistance of police psychologists during SWAT operations has become more prevalent. This is very different from the days when "beat cops" were expected to handle any situation, no matter how dangerous or complex.

Dangerous Environments, Police Officers, and the Community

It is a sad commentary that American communities must be considered dangerous environments; nonetheless, this is a fact for police officers. For a glimpse into the police world, think about a job where every one of your clients must continually be evaluated for the risk that they pose to your safety. This is not to say that everyone represents a risk, but only that their potential risk must be continually evaluated. This is true even in "safe" neighborhoods. Many police officers have been killed or injured in safe neighborhoods by "good" people. This is the reality of policing.

Remaining mindful that even initially cooperative persons may become violent with an intention to harm is a component of every police officer's psychological reality. It does not matter what gender, whether a person is young or elderly, verbal or silent, intoxicated or sober, all can become a threat. This compels police officers to live in an occupational world of *assumption of possible threat*. It is much different than most other workers, who live in an occupational world of *assumption of safety*. It is the psychological *assumption of safety* that is shattered when bad things happen in historically safe work environments. The same is true for historically safe non-work environments.

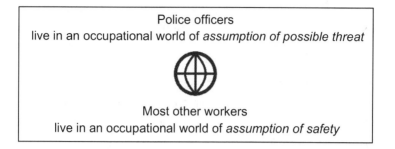

Police officers
live in an occupational world of *assumption of possible threat*

Most other workers
live in an occupational world of *assumption of safety*

Risk in Policing

There is inherent risk in policing. Due to differences in political views, personal values, patterns of thoughts and beliefs, and the ultimately unpredictable nature of human beings, this risk will never be zero. Police officers counterbalance the risk inherent in policing by applying the three T's of policing—Training, Tactics, and Technology. While the three T's of policing change over time, they are designed to reduce the risks confronted by police officers.

Acceptance of risk

The truth of the matter is that American society accepts a degree of risk for its police officers. This is expressed in the societal acceptances of what constitutes appropriate police behavior. Consider the case of an escaping bank robber who shot a bank employee during the robbery. Once the police locate and stop the getaway vehicle, no one would object to police officers taking a guns-drawn approach. In police terminology this is called a *felony* or *high-risk* stop. In such vehicle contacts, police officers take cover positions, prepare themselves to use deadly force, and order the suspect out of the car. In this bank robbery scenario, engaging the high-risk car-stop procedure is the best that police officers can do to protect themselves and the public. (Note: for those unfamiliar with police terminology, *cover* differs from *concealment* in that objects of cover will likely stop a bullet, while objects of concealment will only keep officers from being seen.)

Now think of police officers taking a similar approach with *all* vehicle stops. Keep in mind that any vehicle contact may represent an *unknown* danger (and therefore an unknown risk) to officers. Because officers cannot know the unknown, it would be safer for them to routinely utilize the high-risk vehicle-stop procedure. But is this policing strategy too aggressive? Maybe not, when you consider that several police officers are killed and many more are injured each year by the driver or a passenger of a vehicle that has been stopped for reasons no more serious than a traffic infraction. However, there is a problem.

The problem with this kind of universal, defensive police behavior, albeit safer for officers, is that it is unacceptable to the vast majority of citizens. In fact, it is unacceptable to the vast majority of police officers. High-risk defensive tactics are used by police only upon justifying cause. During vehicle stops, even though there may be an actual unknown danger, without such knowledge or other indications of threat, officers will approach the vehicle and greet the driver. Although this places officers at greater risk, (officers are without cover, can easily be watched, and can be surprised by the unanticipated actions of vehicle occupants) it is an accepted risk. There is not a community or police agency in America that would endorse the high-risk vehicle stop procedure as a common practice. In law, policy directives, and in societal acceptances, police officers are expected to assess risk and act accordingly. If their assessment is incorrect or if there is unknown malicious intent, officers suffer the consequences.

Police authority in America is intentionally limited

In America, police authority and options for police action are intentionally limited. The limits of police authority are known and acknowledged by police officers. In order to protect the constitutional liberties of citizens and to better serve the community, police officers willingly accept the increased personal risk associated with policing American society.

The degree of risk that America accepts for its police officers varies. It varies over time, individually and among groups, and with perceived cultural, social, and political realities.

In the end, the accepted risk for police officers must involve balance - the balance of individual rights with the safety of officers.

It is likely that most citizens and police officers would support a reasonable individual-rights and safety-of-officers balance. The challenge is to develop a conception of "reasonable" that would satisfy all, or at least most, of those involved. This challenge is ever present in American society. It is as significant today as it has ever been.

Police officer risk is over-proportionally increased by the comparatively small percentage of persons that hold fanatical, radical, or reactionary views. Of these, some maintain anti-government, anti-police, and anti-authority sentiments. While many such persons voice their opinions lawfully and peacefully, others express themselves through violence.

Those willing to act out violently represent a serious risk to everyone, especially those that do not share their ideology. As dangerous as this is for society at large, it includes an additional danger for police officers: targeted assassination.* Consider recent incidents wherein officers have been killed after being lured into ambush, or killed while sitting in their vehicle, or killed while having lunch inside a local restaurant...and for no other reason than being police officers.

While several occupations may carry a greater statistical risk of being killed on the job, for instance, commercial fishers and underground miners, the cause of such deaths are overwhelmingly accidental. The chances of a fisher or a miner being intentionally killed while performing a necessary part of their job, or being intentionally killed solely because they are a fisher or a miner are nearly non-existent. Yet we see this in policing.

This is the current risk status of policing in America.

* As one of the most visible representations of government and authority, police officers have been singled out as targets for violence by those seeking to address perceived grievances.

Chapter 1

The Transition

I think it's the best job in the world.
-NYPD Commissioner James O Neill, 2019

The transition from civilian to police officer is a complex process, one which requires significant effort and a change in mindset. To make sense of this, you have to think about what it means to learn a new job. When individuals attempt to learn a new job, they must gain knowledge specific to the occupation and acquire relevant skills. This combination of job knowledge and behavioral abilities is sometimes referred to as a skill set. The skill set necessary for a police officer is characterized by the well-known police expression, *serve and protect*.

Serving and protecting in modern society requires a wide range of knowledge and behavioral skill. Police officers must have knowledge of the law, understand discretion, be able to perform life-saving first aid, know how to direct traffic, evaluate child welfare, investigate crimes, assist persons that are mentally ill, operate emergency vehicles, know how and when to protect themselves with appropriate force, make arrests and control violent suspects—well, you get the idea. To begin the process of acquiring the knowledge and skill necessary to become a police officer, police candidates are required to attend training academies (chapter 2).

New officers that have successfully completed their academy training advance to field training. Some officers who have done well in academy training struggle in field training. In fact, not every officer that has successfully completed academy training successfully completes field training. These officers leave field training for a number of reasons. Some leave voluntarily. Other are terminated. Termination occurs when new officers consistently fail to meet minimal acceptable standards of performance in at least one critical area of their field training program.

Policing, Danger, and Accidental/Intentional Injury or Death

New officers must adapt to a work environment where there is danger. Certainly, working in a dangerous environment is not unique to policing. Many occupational environments are dangerous (see Introduction). This is because all work environments produce some risk of accidental injury or death. What makes policing different from most other occupations is that a notable portion of the danger in policing comes from other persons. New officers must adapt to a work environment within which there are persons who, at least at times, *intentionally* seek to injure or kill police officers. This is different from most other occupations, where the primary danger consists of accidental injury or death. For officers, sometimes this person-danger is known. Other times, it is unknown. Confronting an armed bank robber represents a known person-danger. Stopping a vehicle with several occupants represents a possible unknown person-danger. In all cases, officers rely upon their observations and assessment of actual or potential danger to determine the appropriate course of action.

The intention to injure or kill police officers can result in a calculated assassination plan or arise suddenly out of a particular circumstance. For officers, both are equally perilous. But how does a person develop the intention to injure or kill police officers? Where does the intention come from? To fully address these questions would require discussion beyond the current scope, but it is known that there are a multitude of possible rationales. These include personal belief systems, specific delusions that sometimes accompany mental illness, advancement of a political or other agenda, grievances against government, anger at the police, police viewed as an obstacle to achieving a goal, perceived need for revenge, situational fear and panic, and many more. While the intention to injure or kill police officers can have one or several specific origins, all result in potentially deadly outcomes for police officers.

The problem for officers is that most of the time even the deadliest intentions of others remain unknown. In response to this inability to ascertain threat before it is presented, police officers are trained to routinely engage officer safety strategies, such as standing behind the driver's door window during a vehicle stop.

These strategies are designed to increase the margin of safety for police officers. They enhance the probability that officers will be able to mount some defense in the event of an attack. Fortunately, most people respect life and the law, and would not attempt to injure or kill anyone, including police officers.

The exposure to intentional injury or death is not unique to policing. It is also a component of combat military.

Confrontation

Confrontation is an unavoidable stressor of policing. It may directly involve the officer or exist between others. New officers must have or must develop a means of coping with confrontation. Even when the police are requested to assist in particular situations, there is often at least one person who does not want officers present. This increases the probability of direct officer involvement. Some confrontations are mild and consist of verbal discussion or nonverbal posturing. Others are critical and may involve officers fighting for their lives.

Like everyone else, police officers have a right to protect and defend themselves. Unlike everyone else, police officers also have a duty to protect and defend others. This is true even if it means that officers must place themselves in jeopardy. There are consequences for officers that fail to meet this duty including public and private condemnation, departmental discipline, employment termination, and civil lawsuits. The duty to protect and defend others with lethal force if necessary is not present in most other occupations.

Confrontation on a daily basis is one of the unique aspects of policing. Remaining aware of potential confrontation and potential threat is the mindset required of police officers. Officers become complacent and compromise this mindset at their own risk.

Maintaining an awareness of potential confrontation is not the same as viewing and treating everyone as a threat. It means only that it is in officers' best interest to maintain an appropriate level of situational awareness and some readiness to respond to any changes in circumstances.

Beyond Mindset

In addition to the development of the appropriate mindset, new officers must address three other primary challenges: (1) geography, (2) report writing, and (3) the application of authority.

Geography. Some new officers have lived for years in their jurisdiction prior to becoming a police officer. Others moved to the jurisdiction because they were hired. In either case, officers must learn the jurisdiction geography. Officers that have lived in the jurisdiction have some background knowledge of the streets, alleys, businesses, and so forth. Officers new to the jurisdiction must learn it from "scratch."

There are many ways to learn the layout of a jurisdiction. All require effort. If you are a visual person, you can study maps and perhaps mentally retrieve or "see" the map in your imagination when needed. If you are more of an experiential person, there is no substitute for walking or driving the area. Verbal learners will want to be read directions or read about various locations. Most of us can take advantage of all these learning strategies.

For officers that have grown up in the jurisdiction, this fact alone does not guarantee jurisdiction familiarity. Being familiar with the city in which you grew up does not always translate into knowing the city in the way police officers need to know it. Fortunately, the learning of jurisdiction geography is positively correlated with experience and exposure, and most officers soon become adequately skilled in this area.

Report writing. New officers must be able to document their observations and actions. Good writing skills are necessary but insufficient for good report writing. Police report writing must be complete, concise, accurate, and objective. Learning to structure these features into a report can be challenging, even for good writers.

Another difficulty involves how the report is generated. Many agencies require that officers write or dictate their reports. Some officers are good report writers, but poor report dictators. These officers experience *mic fright*, a normally temporary condition characterized by a loss of thought cohesiveness and mind-blank. Mic fright is a type of performance anxiety. It usually subsides or disappears after a period of practice. To manage mic fright, some officers write their reports and read them into the recorder. Unfortunately, this defeats the primary purpose of dictating reports... saving time. Some agencies require that officers type reports, or at the least, have a functional ability to use a computer keyboard. Years ago, officers were not required to have typing or computer skills. Today, these skills are essential. It is another example of how policing has evolved.

Application of authority. New officers must have or must develop a conception of how to best utilize police authority. They must avoid becoming "badge heavy" (exercising police authority in an overly strict manner) while also avoiding a failure to exercise sufficient authority when needed. As part of this balance, new officers must learn *police discretion.* Police discretion is the long-accepted practice of officers exercising individual judgment in specific situations. If you have ever been stopped by a police officer for a traffic violation and released without receiving a citation, you can thank police discretion. Learning how to appropriately apply police authority for the good of the community and to meet the mission of the police agency is a primary challenge for new officers.

Officer Reputation

New officers will earn a reputation. It is inevitable. They will earn a reputation with their trainers, coworkers, supervisors, dispatchers, and citizens. The question becomes, "Being that developing a reputation is inevitable, why not earn a good one?" New officers should make an effort to develop a good reputation. How is this accomplished? A good reputation is best developed through a positive personal attitude and high-level performance. Another way of saying this is, "Don't tell them how good you are, show them how good you are." For new officers, this means working diligently to learn and perform the job, and coming to work with a serve-and-protect attitude.

To succeed, officers must maintain their part of the employment bargain. The officer's side of the bargain is performance. The department's side of the bargain is appropriate training, adequate equipment, competent supervision, and fair compensation. Simply stated, the employment bargain is agency support for officer performance. Officer performance expectations are expressed in the police officer job description, departmental mission and values statements, departmental policies and procedures, supervisory expectations, and the law. When officers fail to meet their part of the bargain, their reputations suffer. The same is true for police agencies. The agency must support its officers and meet its part of the bargain. (Note: the general concept of compensation for performance should not be confused with the various specific pay-for-performance salary systems used by some police departments. Pay-for-performance salary systems tie performance ratings to rate of pay. This is different from the philosophy of compensation for performance outlined here.)

If a poor reputation is developed, it can be changed, but only slowly. To improve a poor work reputation, consistently good work is needed. However, changing a poor work reputation is more difficult than establishing a good one from the beginning. When it comes to reputation, new officers should endeavor to start strong, stay strong, and finish strong. This is easily accomplished by performing conscientiously and maintaining a positive work ethic.

For officers, one of the most clearly seen features of a positive work ethic is responding to calls. New officers should remember throughout their careers: *any call, anytime, anywhere.* Complaining that dispatch is assigning calls too close to the end of shift, out of an assigned district, or beneath some perceived skill level is indicative of a poor work ethic and a sure way to create a poor reputation. Trust your dispatch; take any call without complaint. Keep your part of the bargain. Every call reinforces your work ethic and contributes to your experience. After five years on the job, you want to have five years of experience, not one year of experience five times.

Like new officers, veteran officers can enhance or maintain their work reputation by following the *any call, anytime, anywhere* work ethic.

Police Truthfulness

Always tell the truth. As a new officer it may be tempting to misrepresent an action or observation in an attempt to protect yourself from getting into trouble, to protect another officer from getting into trouble, to accomplish some goal, or to be accepted by a particular group of veteran officers. Don't do it. Lying undermines the very foundation of police professionalism. It will destroy your credibility, tarnish your reputation, and lead to several other major consequences. If you make a mistake, bring it to the attention of supervisors. If a citizen files a complaint about your behavior, be honest when describing your actions during internal inquiry. Many officers have been terminated for being untruthful in circumstances wherein their actual behavior would have resulted in no or lesser consequences. Stay true to this most important of police values: *always tell the truth.*

Police Actions and Recordings

The actions of police officers are now commonly recorded. Police body and vehicle cameras are standard issue in many modern police agencies. However, even in departments not equipped with recording technology, officers should act as if they are being recorded. This idea helps officers to moderate behavior and maintain a high level of professionalism. Acting as if being recorded is an excellent idea. After all, there is a considerable probability that officers *are* being recorded by an unknown camera, voice recording device, or person.

Case in point: a police agency received a complaint about the verbal behavior of an officer during a vehicle contact. After the complaint was filed, the complainant produced a recording of the exchange. Although the complainant was the driver of the vehicle, the recording was made by a back seat passenger using a cell phone. At the time, neither the driver nor the officer knew that they were being recorded. The recording demonstrated the intensity of the officer's communication, as well as the numerous threats, insults, and expletives. Upon internal investigation interview, when confronted with the recording, the officer explained his actions as a simple "chewing out" of the driver and the other young men in the vehicle to help "keep them straight." The department found the recording telling and the officer's explanation lacking. His employment was terminated following completion of the investigation.

This represents one of many times that officers have been undone by recordings made by involved citizens, citizen observers, store surveillance cameras, residential security cameras, and cell phone recorders. Interestingly, the bad behavior of some police officers has been confirmed by their own body or in-car cameras. Evidently, even knowing that one's actions are being recorded is not enough to contain the inappropriate emotion-driven behavior of some officers.

It is worth mentioning that, more times than not, officers have been exonerated by recordings of their behavior. While these cases demonstrate the willingness of some persons to exaggerate or falsify complaints against officers, unlike recordings of alleged officer misconduct, they seldom make the evening news.

The idea of acting as if being recorded is related to the notion of integrity. This is well expressed in U.S. Air Force Doctrine Document 1-1, *Leadership and Force Development*. In this document, integrity is defined as "the willingness to do what is right even when no one is looking" (Dobbins, 2008, 1). This is the other side of the "acting as if being recorded" coin. Whether being recorded or no one is looking, new (and veteran) officers should endeavor to act at all times within the finest traditions of policing. Such a commitment reflects not only the highest level of police professionalism, it is also the best defense for officers falsely accused of wrongdoing.

Psychology of Earning and Psychology of Entitlement

New officers must keep in mind that what can be accomplished is often related to the effort expended. Another way of saying this is, "What you can achieve is often related to how hard you are willing to work for it." This idea is part of the psychology of earning.

The psychology of earning is different from the psychology of entitlement. In the psychology of entitlement, persons believe that good things should happen to them solely because they somehow inherently deserve it (the psychology of entitlement is different from the legal notion of entitlement).

When learning to become a police officer and in other areas of your life, avoid the psychology of entitlement. If you are pursuing a goal, apply effort to increase the probability of success. Make short-term sacrifices for long term gains - like studying for an upcoming exam when you would prefer to go out with friends. Your efforts will almost always be rewarded. In any event, if you work hard and fall short of your goal, you will likely come closer to achieving it. This in itself can increase motivation and provide important information on how to better prepare next time. And if you tried your best, you will know that you gave your best. This is the most that you can ask of yourself.

Life, Work, Luck, and Success

What about life, work, luck, and success? Are some people just luckier and therefore more successful in life than others? Maybe so, but as the saying goes: *the harder you work, the luckier you'll get.* Interesting thought.

There are other sayings about life, work, luck, and success. Nearly everyone has heard the time-honored expressions "If at first you don't succeed, try, try, again" and "Work smarter, not harder." Nice ideas. Certainly, if you do not first succeed, trying again seems reasonable. And working harder in a way that has consistently failed to produce desired results seems to justify trying something different, hopefully something smarter. But how do we make sense of all this? When do we stop trying to succeed at something that, in spite of our best efforts, we fail to achieve? When is it best to alter or abandon certain goals? How do we work smarter?

That's the thing about "sayings." While they can be thought-provoking and sometimes helpful, it is up to each person to interpret them, make them meaningful, and apply them wisely in their lives.

Life balance

Whether trying again, working harder, working smarter, or working harder and smarter, when considering life, work, luck, and success, it is important to maintain a healthy balance among work, home, relationships, and self-care. If this balance is maintained, you can continue to "Put one foot in front of the other" and "Live to carry on another day."

Chapter 2

Field Training and PATROL

Field Training must go beyond just teaching the nuts and bolts of doing a job. We must not only provide the knowledge needed and the opportunity to develop skills to be law enforcement professionals, but we must also develop the entire person wearing the uniform.
-Al Brown, FCPS trainer, The Trainers Edge, 2022

New police officers have always learned the job from veteran police officers. Years ago, the best a new officer could expect was to find a veteran who would "take him under his wing" and "break him in." With this method of training, bad as well as good work habits were passed down from police veteran to police rookie. Too many times this included learning how to pass off undesirable calls, avoid supervisors, take advantage of the system, and where to find free coffee.

If a new officer did not have a veteran willing to assist, the officer had to learn by observation, personal effort, and trial and error. As you might expect, the quality of officers produced by this type of initiation varied. The skills of new officers ranged from acceptable to nearly incompetent. Today, things are much different. There are established minimum standards of officer knowledge and performance. New officers must meet these standards prior to working independently - and accepting free coffee will get police officers fired in many jurisdictions.

New officer training sequence

The modern-day training sequence for most new police officers includes completing (1) a basic police academy, (2) a police department pre-service skills academy, and (3) a field training and evaluation program. In agencies that conduct their own academy, the basic and pre-service academies are combined.

Basic Police Academy and Pre-service Skills Academy

While there are differences among the training academies of various jurisdictions, the core curriculum of most basic police academies is similar. Core curriculum topics normally range from the introduction to the policing mission to the use of deadly force. Core courses typically include classroom instruction (e.g. traffic code, criminal law, search and seizure) as well as skill development (e.g. restraint and handcuffing procedure, CPR, emergency vehicle operation).

As might be expected, basic police academies vary widely in quality, orientation, and structure. Some police academies resemble military boot camps, while others are more casual and have the look of a college campus. In fact, in several states, basic police academy training is conducted through universities and local community colleges. Some states have a single centralized law enforcement academy, while others have several regional academies. Some allow only employed police recruits to attend, while others admit qualified civilians planning to become police officers. Police academies can range in length from less than ten weeks to over twenty-four weeks.

Police agencies that do not conduct their own academies rely on outside basic academy training. Following completion of an external basic academy, most officers enter their department's pre-service skills academy. A pre-service skills academy is necessary to provide new officers with department-specific information and training. This typically includes the completion of any remaining necessary qualifications, familiarization with department policy and procedure, use of department forms, and an introduction to field training. Pre-service skills academies range from little more than a department orientation to weeks of formalized training.

Field Training – OJT and FTO

Modern police field training is different from its predecessor, *on-the-job training* (OJT). Although, like present-day field training,

OJT programs involved new officers working with veteran officers, OJT was somewhat haphazard in its approach. It provided new officers with some supervised instruction and exposure to policing, but did little more. OJT was normally time-limited; an officer would work with various officers for days or weeks, and much of what new officers learned depended upon the willingness of veteran officers to train. This caused the quality of OJT to vary widely among and within police agencies. Still, it was more organized than the "breaking in" method of police training. But similar to "breaking in," just how well-trained new officers were following the completion of OJT was anyone's guess.

In contrast, modern field training is formally structured, has specified goals, processes new officer experiences in a number of ways, and includes standards of performance and evaluation. Field training programs were developed when it was recognized that OJT programs were lacking and academy training was insufficient to best develop the knowledge, skills, and emotional stability necessary to become a competent, independently functioning police officer.

Modern field training programs are designed to build upon the classroom and training exercises of the academy. These programs are known by various names such as Field Training Officer, Field Training and Evaluation, Patrol Training Officer, and Recruit Training and Field Evaluation. All involve the field training of new officers by pairing them with specially trained and qualified field training officers.

Field training has improved significantly over the past decades. There are several formal field training programs in use today. One of the earliest is the Field Training Officer (FTO) program. The FTO program was created in the late 1960s, and for many years served as the gold standard for police officer field training.

The Patrol Training Officer (PTO) program evolved out of the FTO program. The PTO program was developed in the early 2000s. It is the result of U.S. Department of Justice funded research to develop a new and comprehensive police officer field training program. The PTO program differs from the FTO program in philosophical orientation and the manner in which training and evaluation is conducted. Despite their differences, both are in use today, both utilize specific training phases or segments, and both well-prepare new officers for work on the streets.

Field Training Officer

A field training officer is a veteran officer who has received specialized training in how to train and evaluate new officers. A field training officer is called an *FTO* in the FTO program and a *PTO* in the PTO program.

Field Phase or Segment Training

In all formal field training programs, new officers are paired with different training officers within the various program phases. This exposes new officers to the policing and training styles of several training officers. It also mitigates the possibility of new-officer failure within the program due to a "personality conflict" between a new officer and a particular training officer.

As a new officer moves through field training, *car command* responsibilities change. To better understand car command, consider veteran motor-patrol officers working solo. These officers are responsible for patrolling their assigned districts, responding to calls for service, self-initiated activities, and so on. When not on assignment, veteran officers can choose to enforce traffic laws, execute warrants, contact business owners, or perform a myriad of other police related duties. This is possible because, in large part, police officers work autonomously. They have considerable discretion in deciding how to police their district. In other words, they decide what they do within the uncommitted time of their shift. This is what is meant by being in car command.

In the beginning and within the early phases of new-officer field training, training officers retain car command. During this period, training officers function as models for new officers. As the program progresses, and at the discretion of training officers, new officers are permitted to assume greater levels of car command. By the last phases of field training, new officers assume all or nearly all the responsibilities of car command. The general process of transferring car command from training officers to new officers is not only part of field training, it is essential to best prepare new officers for final evaluation and the challenge of working independently. (Note: In reality, training officers are always in car command. This is because new officers are subordinate to their training officers. The transfer of car command to new officers is a feature of field training. This does not prohibit field training officers from directing new officers or resuming car command if circumstances warrant.)

The final evaluation of new officers in field training normally takes place over several work shifts and is sometimes called *checkout*. In some field training programs, the training officer that was first assigned to the new officer returns to complete the new officer's checkout.

To minimize the role of training officers during checkout, most wear civilian clothes. Throughout checkout, new officers are not permitted to use their training officer as a resource. They may use any other normally available resource, including consulting with other officers and supervisors. During checkout, the primary role of the training officer is the evaluation of the new officer's semi-solo performance. While training officers deemphasize their presence during checkout, they will engage in any action deemed necessary in defensive or other emergency situations.

To successfully complete checkout, new officers must consistently meet minimum acceptable standards of performance. If they fail to accomplish this, they are not advanced to independent assignment. Depending upon presenting circumstances, new officers that do not successfully complete final evaluation may be required to undergo remedial training and reevaluation, or may be terminated from the field training program.

Psychologist and Training/Recruit Officer Liaison — the PATROL Program

In an effort to better support new officers entering field training, the *Psychologist and Training/Recruit Officer Liaison* program (PATROL) was developed (Digliani, 1990).

The PATROL program brings the police psychologist and new officers together very early in the training process. PATROL is comprised of a group *orientation and training* presentation within the pre-service skills academy and confidential individual meetings at least once during each of the major field training phases.

The PATROL program is founded upon four principles: (1) that meeting with the department psychologist is a proactive strategy for supporting new officers in training, (2) that inadequate performance and/or problematic behavior while in field training can be targeted for change from a multidimensional perspective, (3) that the learning experiences of new officers are enhanced by meeting with the department psychologist, and (4) that early exposure of new officers to the department psychologist increases the probability that officers will seek support from the psychologist when it is likely to help. Below is a descriptive outline of the PATROL program.

Orientation and Training. During orientation and training many issues are discussed. Topics include career choice, adult learning, stress and anxiety management, family issues, being new to the community, departmental policy, field training program, critical incidents, PATROL and confidentiality, and services of the peer support team and police psychologist.

Meeting during first segment or phase I. Reconciling the reality of police work with expectation is the primary focus of the phase I session. Within this framework, officer observations are processed, officer safety is discussed, stressor and anxiety management strategies are assessed, application of skills is encouraged, and features of reputation and work ethics are explored. Family issues are assessed. Specific work and non-work issues are identified and addressed.

Meeting during second segment or phase II. Issues surrounding the phase II session frequently involve motivation and persistence. Some new officers report that field training is more rigorous or stressful than anticipated. Officers with prior experience sometimes struggle with being in training again. The psychologist works to enhance motivation by pointing out successes, commenting on the growing sense of competence, discussing alternative learning and stressor management strategies, identifying problem areas, and discussing specific interventions. Emphasis is placed upon the assumption of responsibility, officer discretion, and the appropriate application of authority.

Meeting during third segment or phase III. This session centers on rehearsal for final evaluation. In addition to stressor management and job skill enhancement, officers are encouraged to scan their knowledge and skill level for areas in which they may need improvement. They remediate these areas or bring them to the attention of the field training officer for assistance. The training officer then works to provide the new officer with the appropriate review, practice, exposure, or experience. In preparation for final evaluation, new officers implement the three R's: *Review, Rehearse, Repeat.* (If the field training program consists of more than three major segments or phases prior to final evaluation, additional meetings with the psychologist can be arranged.)

Final evaluation. Checkout - Upon successful completion of the third or final segment or phase of field training, the new officer is advanced to final evaluation. As the focus of this phase is independent behavior, a meeting with the psychologist is optional. Appointments with the psychologist in this phase may be requested by the new officer, the field training officer, or recommended by the psychologist. Upon successful completion of this phase, field training is completed.

PATROL Program Features

The PATROL program may be utilized within any field training program. It is flexible and can be modified to meet individual or agency needs. For instance:

1. More than one session per segment or phase may be requested by the new or training officer.
2. The training officer may attend any or all (or portions) of the sessions if requested by the new officer.

3. The psychologist may share information with training officers and supervisors upon request of the new officer (with waiver of confidentiality). This permits a team approach for performance improvement.
4. The training and new officer may arrange joint sessions with the psychologist to address a specific performance issue.
5. Officer spouses or partners may attend meetings at the discretion of the new officer.
6. The new officer may initiate a comprehensive counseling program. Such programs can involve significant others and extend beyond field training.
7. If the new officer is failing to progress as expected, counseling can be integrated into a remedial plan. Such plans may involve family members of new officers.
8. If the new officer is unsuccessful in field training, counseling may assist the officer and/or training officer in processing the outcome.

The PATROL program was new in 1990 and was considered experimental. No one knew how field training officers or new officers would respond to routinely working with the department "shrink" as part of police field training. Consequently, it was with some trepidation that PATROL was first introduced to the field training officers of Fort Collins Police Services.

One of the most controversial aspects of PATROL was the confidential nature of the phase meetings. This feature meant that new officers and the psychologist could safely discuss the department, the behaviors of training officers, training styles, and so on, without any of this information being available to the department or to the training officers.

Following a brief explanation of PATROL, the FCPS training officers enthusiastically endorsed and supported PATROL. They quickly recognized that the training officer, the new officer, and the police psychologist shared the same goal — success of the new officer. The training officers were willing to try something new in the hope that it might enhance their effectiveness and the learning experiences of new officers.

Shortly after PATROL was integrated into the field training program of FCPS, it was presented to the training officers of the

Loveland Police Department, and later to the training officers of the Larimer County Sheriff's Office. The training officers of LPD and LCSO endorsed and supported the PATROL program.

The PATROL program has proven its efficacy and is no longer experimental. Over many years, the feedback received from new officers and trainers alike has been overwhelmingly positive. After decades since its inception, it remains part of FCPS, LPD, and LCSO field training. The PATROL program, in its original or a modified version, has now been adopted by numerous law enforcement agencies.

Due to the success of the PATROL program for patrol police officers, similar programs were developed for jail deputies and corrections officers, emergency services dispatchers (Communications Training Support Program), police administrative and support personnel, firefighters, and emergency medical personnel.

PATROL and Stigma Reduction

One of the most significant ancillary benefits of PATROL has been the reduction of perceived stigma associated with visiting the psychologist. Through PATROL, new officers become acquainted with the psychologist early in their careers. They work with the psychologist through the skills academy and field training. They sit in the psychologist's office and discuss a wide range of topics. They learn first-hand what they can accomplish together. In essence, the mystique of the psychologist's office is diminished. This helps to establish and maintain a positive relationship between new officers and the psychologist. Officers come to realize that meeting with the psychologist is just another venue for addressing relevant issues. Stigma reduction has been a highly desirable secondary benefit of PATROL.

PATROL as a Proactive Program

PATROL was designed as a proactive support program. As such, it is structured to assist new officers *prior* to the development of any stress-related and performance difficulties. However, veteran police officers can also benefit from proactive support. This is especially true for those officers in highly stressful assignments such as SWAT, crisis negotiation, homicide and assault investigation, and the investigation of crimes involving child exploitation.

Some agencies have recognized the wellness benefits of proactive support. They have initiated programs that require or encourage all employees to participate in periodic "wellness check-in" meetings with the department psychologist. Proactive support programs, such as the "Proactive Annual Check-in" (chapter 3) are now considered part of "best-practices" for enhanced employee wellness.

PATROL Information

Information gathered from the officers participating in the PATROL program has led to several relevant insights into police field training. For the most part, new officers speak highly of their trainers and the field training program. This is a testament to the efforts, professionalism, and conscientiousness of the field training officers. Nevertheless, several FTO pitfalls have been identified. FTOs should remain mindful of the pitfalls and work to avoid them.

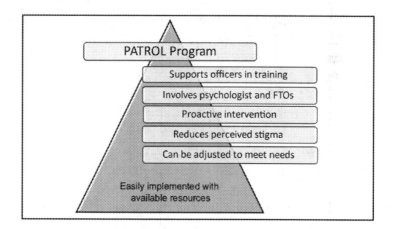

FTO Pitfalls

While the vast majority of new officer PATROL comments have been positive, one of the most common complaints of new officers in field training center around the issue of FTOs not training enough. This is pitfall #1.

Pitfall #1 is assuming that the new officer is learning without an FTO effort to train. This FTO training strategy, or lack thereof, reflects either FTO laziness or an over-reliance upon modeling (recall that "modeling" in field training is the idea that the new officer is learning all that is needed by simply observing the FTO). In the latter case, although modeling is one of the most effective adult learning strategies, high-functioning FTOs engage in active training as well as appropriate modeling. Lacking active training, some new officers have reported that their FTO did not actively train at all. To avoid pitfall #1, *remember to keep the "T" in* FTO.

Pitfall #2 is moving from training to evaluation too soon. New officers in field training need to be trained before they can be fairly evaluated. Assessing the amount of training any new officer requires in specific areas is a primary responsibility of the FTO. Many new officers have reported that they thought their FTOs relied too heavily on prior academy training and did not provide adequate field training in evaluated areas. Moving from training to evaluation too soon is possible in some field training programs because the FTOs have training *and* evaluation responsibilities within the same phase. The Patrol Training Officer program has addressed this issue by separating training and evaluation phases. PTO's either train *or* evaluate. Supporters of the PTO program view this as a significant improvement in police officer field training.

Pitfall #3 is *reverse bias* and is related to pitfalls #1 and #2. Reverse bias involves officers who are new to a department but come with prior policing experience. In some cases, these new officers have more overall law enforcement experience than their FTO. No matter. FTOs must train as they would any new officer. Any advantage held by experienced officers will show itself as they progress through the program. Therefore, pitfall #3 is assuming that new officers with prior experience already know what they need to know. *A word of caution*: having prior policing experience does not always translate into having an advantage in a new police department. Prior knowledge can conflict with new information. Prior skills can interfere with learning new techniques. For example, a new officer that is well-skilled in *arrest and control style A* may have a difficult time learning *arrest and control style B*. This is because the habit-strength of style A must be overcome. This can cause initial confusion and detrimentally influence field performance. In memory theory, when previous information interferes with remembering something new, it is called *proactive interference*. When newer information interferes with remembering something older, it is called *retroactive interference*. FTOs should be able to identify cases of memory interference and address them appropriately. With time, patience, and practice, memory interference will diminish and the desired knowledge or performance will be maintained. In summary, to avoid pitfall #3, actively train all new officers in all areas. Do not get caught in the trap of assuming that new officers with prior policing experience know how to be police officers in their new department.

Pitfall #4 is inconsistent information. In some field training programs, FTOs do not meet on a regular basis. This means that they do not share information. The lack of FTO communication increases the probability of inconsistent FTO performance. It is very confusing for new officers to be told one thing by one FTO and later have that information contradicted by another. This circumstance represents a basic failure in the organization and functioning of the field training program. Although it is recognized that FTOs have varying policing styles, information that *can* be consistent *should* be consistent. This is also true of information or tactics involving non-FTO department instructors. An actual example will help to illustrate this point: several new officers had recently completed the department skills academy. In the skills academy, department instructors taught a specific technique as part of arrest and control. Later, while in the field training program, a new officer applied the technique learned in the skills academy. It was different than that used by the FTO. The FTO "corrected" the new officer. The new officer informed the FTO that "this is the way we were taught to do it in the skills academy." Upon inquiry, the FTO learned that the technique had changed. The new officer knew it; the FTO did not. The technique applied by the FTO had become obsolete and was no longer being used by the department! For FTOs to avoid this pitfall, do not forget that new officers have just completed weeks of academy training. Make certain that your knowledge is consistent with that of academy instructors, updated policy, and other FTOs. In other words, *keep yourself current.*

Pitfall #5 is not enough patience. Many new officers say that in cases where there is no emergency, some FTOs have been too quick to take over for no reason other than lack of patience. Having an FTO take over when it is not absolutely necessary tends to undermine new officer confidence and impede skill development. To avoid pitfall #5, FTOs should be patient in circumstances that permit it.

Pitfall #6 is intentionally adding to stress levels. An actual example will best explain this pitfall. A new officer reported that his FTO would consistently play the police vehicle music radio at a volume that interfered with hearing the police radio. When the new officer informed the FTO that he could not hear the police radio and requested that the music volume be lowered, the FTO responded that the increased volume was intentional to increase stress. Does this make sense? How does keeping a new officer from hearing the police radio contribute to field training? Observing and evaluating a new officer's performance under stressful conditions is part of field training; however, due to the stress inherent in policing, there is little need for an FTO to artificially create stressful situations. And in any event, if the FTO is trying to assess the new officer's ability to manage particular stressors, the new officer's request to lower the music volume is right on. The best way to deal with the stress caused by a music radio that is too loud is to turn down the volume. Better yet, do not play the music radio during field training.

Pitfall #7 is *nit-picking.* FTOs should always remain mindful that there are usually several ways to accomplish any task. As long as the overall manner in which new officers are performing is acceptable, is it necessary that they perform it exactly as you would? In circumstances where it is appropriate, new officers appreciate the latitude to develop their own style. Avoid undermining new officer confidence by becoming overly focused on minutia.

Pitfall #8 is not enough reinforcement. There are two types of reinforcement identified by new officers in PATROL:

1. The first is repetitive reinforcement. As one new officer put it, "I could hear something once and be expected to know it,

no reinforcement." The new officer is actually talking about *encoding*. Encoding is the process whereby information is moved from short-term memory to long-term memory. In the case mentioned, the new officer felt that the FTO did little to assist the encoding process. The original information was not repeated, therefore not reinforced. There are several ways to reinforce encoding. Reviewing, repeating, rehearsing, organizing, visualizing, and categorizing are excellent strategies to enhance the encoding process.

2. The second type of reinforcement is associated with reward for something well done. For new officers, positive FTO comments and nonverbal behaviors are greatly valued. Positive verbal feedback such as "Good job" "I liked what you did" and "That was great" goes a long way to build new officer confidence. Correspondingly, the simple nonverbal reward of a nod, a wink, a thumbs up, and so on from an FTO is highly meaningful to new officers. Most new officers acknowledge that their FTOs provide them with positive verbal and nonverbal feedback. However, many say it is not done often enough. The likely underlying issue here is that many tasks that are seen by the FTO as simple and routine are experienced as a challenge by at least some new officers. When these officers perform well at a task that was for them challenging, they seek the acknowledgement of their FTO. If there is acknowledgement, the new officer feels encouraged and motivated (reinforced). If acknowledgment is lacking, the new officer may come away with feelings of confusion and uncertainty. This can occur even when the FTO is satisfied with the new officer's performance. Communication is the key. One officer summed things up this way, "My FTO barely talks to me. I don't know what he wants. I get no reinforcement. I'm just trying to survive." Keep in mind that when FTOs are non-communicative, it presents a *blank slate* to new officers. They will project some meaning into FTO silence. The meaning projected is almost always negative. FTOs that are naturally introverted must be especially cautious to avoid this pitfall.

FTOs should consistently try to find something that can be reinforced. Even when new officers have a "poor performance" shift, FTOs should think, "Did the officer do *anything* right?" Barring imagined scenarios that are quite unlikely, the answer will always be "yes." This means that following a discussion of performance difficulties, the FTO can close on a positive note. This is *communication for motivation.* Communication for motivation helps the new officer to restore any loss of confidence and increases the probability of continued effort.

Pitfall #9 is inconsistent FTO behavior. When FTOs act significantly different with buddies than with new officers, it leads to very negative perceptions. For FTOs, it is natural to behave somewhat differently with friends and coworkers than with new officers, but to act significantly different is often detrimental. For example, it does little to help new officers when FTOs behave friendly and supportive to friends, only to express *boot camp drill instructor* behavior during field training. Such behavior often appears superficial, intentionally intimidating, and "power tripping" to new officers. None of these perceptions contribute anything positive to field training and the training relationship.

Another form of FTO inconsistency is behaving one way, while instructing new officers to do otherwise. For instance, during a recent PATROL meeting, a new officer reported, "I have a 'do as I say and not as I do' FTO." What message does this FTO behavior send to new officers? The message can range from "I'm an FTO. I don't have to follow the rules" to "This department is sick. I do what I want." Is this a good way to train new officers? It certainly is not a positive model for desired behavior. To avoid confusing new officers and to remain a positive role model, FTOs *must* model desired behavior. When FTOs engage in *do as I say, not as I do* behavior, they undermine themselves and the entire field training program. To avoid pitfall #9, act in accordance with policy and procedure and be consistent.

Pitfall #10 is not being ready to work. Most police departments seek to select FTOs out of those officers who have demonstrated consistently good work performance, a positive attitude, and a willingness to work with new officers. Field training officers are smart, perceptive, intuitive, and have a sense of others. This is one thing that new officers and FTOs instantly have in common. Police agencies look to hire persons who are also smart, perceptive, intuitive, and have a sense of others. These qualities are as sought after in new officers as they are in FTOs. Armed with these qualities, FTOs have little difficulty determining when something is not quite right with a new officer. Is it any surprise that new officers can also easily determine when FTOs are not at their finest? Experienced FTOs know that as they are observing and assessing the new officer, the new officer is observing and assessing them. If the FTO is having a bad day, the new officer knows it. If the FTO is not focused, the new officer knows it. If the FTO is not engaging the new officer, the new officer knows it. In the worst of these scenarios, the FTO is burned out, and the new officer knows it. The latter circumstance was clearly expressed by one new officer in PATROL, "My FTO really does not want to be here." This is unfortunate. It is an example of an officer who either should not have been selected to become an FTO or has become embittered. In any event, he has lost or never had an interest in and commitment to the goals of field training. As a result, he is not an asset to the program. Worse, he is a detriment. Exemplary FTOs strive to stay true to the ethics of field training. They recognize that being an FTO is stressful and they monitor themselves for burnout. They consistently engage stress management strategies and take appropriate breaks from training when needed. In the end, to avoid pitfall #10, FTOs should take care of themselves and come to work, ready to work.

Field Training Officers

What kind of police officer should become a field training officer? There are several attributes that characterize high-functioning field training officers.

Aptitude. Functional FTOs have an aptitude for training. They are competent police officers. They enjoy being with others and enjoy sharing their knowledge. They relate well to others and are positive role models. They are patient.

Interest. It is possible to have an aptitude for training but no interest in training. Functional FTOs have a genuine interest in training and in the philosophy, ethics, and goals of the field training program.

Commitment. Being a FTO requires more effort than not being an FTO. Functional FTOs consistently apply themselves so that the highest levels of FTO performance are consistently achieved. A self-conducted *commitment check* should be performed at least annually. Commitment checks reaffirm a commitment to FTO principles and philosophies. If you became or remain an FTO solely for power and/or to advance your career, you are an FTO for the wrong reasons.

Credibility. FTOs must be credible. Credibility must be part of an FTO's overall reputation. This can only be established by years of honorable service prior to becoming an FTO.

As an FTO, you accept special-unit responsibility. It is appropriate for the department to expect that you will fully meet the responsibilities associated with the special unit. If the duties of being an FTO become too great to manage, talk with your program supervisor. There are several options available for overwhelmed or burned out FTOs. These include learning new coping strategies, taking a training hiatus, and leaving the field training program. No one truly benefits from FTOs who have already given all they can to the field training program.

Field training officers should maintain a goal of becoming better FTOs. To do anything less stalls personal development and freezes the status quo. Field training officers should engage in advanced in-service FTO training and meet regularly to discuss their training experiences. By meeting, FTOs share information and learn from one another.

Exemplary Field Training Officers

Field training officers vary in personality and style. While most FTOs are competent and do an excellent job, there are traits and behaviors that characterize exemplary FTOs.

In a survey some years ago, exemplary FTOs were identified and interviewed. To be considered an exemplary FTO, individual FTOs had to be described as outstanding by field training program supervisors and *all* of the new officers trained by the FTO. Here are some of the more interesting comments collected from exemplary FTOs, no less applicable today:

- "I do not believe that an FTO should ever say, 'I have to find something that you did wrong tonight'."
- No "derogatory language or behaviors."
- No "injection of personal feelings."
- If a trainee and FTO cannot get along, "this is an FTO problem and not a trainee problem."
- "I adjust my personality to give the trainee what he or she needs to succeed."
- "I train the same in each Phase, with respect, however the content changes."
- "I will go back to a prior Phase or Academy and build upon whatever success is there."
- "I will put the trainee into situations where I know they can succeed."
- "Some initial mistakes I do not record on the Daily Observation Report. If the mistake is repeated, then both incidents are documented. This helps to build trust. Then the trainee thinks, maybe he's not here to just hammer me."

Exemplary FTOs consistently remind themselves of their goal, to help develop exemplary police officers. Bruce "Coach Sok" Sokolove, President of Field Training Associates expressed it this way, FTOs "...are entrusted with the future of law enforcement through consistent modeling of excellent service delivery and specific continual feedback resulting in informed self-reliant skilled and ethical street cops. They facilitate the transfer of the probationer's basic police academy instruction to the streets with clarity of instruction, demonstration, redirection, and constant feedback to mold exemplary law enforcement officers" (2022).

Providing Constructive Feedback as an FTO

Field training officers have a complex role. In both of the major components of field training, training and evaluation, there is a need to provide feedback to new officers. Feedback is information that is designed to assist new officers. Feedback can always be constructive. Constructive feedback is characterized by providing at least something upon which the recipient can build.

Performance feedback is communication from others that helps the receiver to alter behavior to achieve an identified performance standard. There are two primary types of performance feedback: (1) feedback for change and (2) feedback for consistency. Feedback for change involves providing information which assists the recipient to achieve some degree of performance competency. Feedback for consistency assists the recipient to maintain performance competency once it is achieved (chapter 7, *Change*).

Summary: FTO Constructive Feedback

In general, FTO feedback should be comprised of items of information. The information that comprises feedback tends to be most useful to recipients when it is characterized by the following:

1. Feedback should be non-threatening. Information that represents a personal attack is more likely to initiate defensive responses. Defensive responses tend to shut down the exchange of information, thereby limiting the effectiveness of feedback. For example, "When you raised your voice, the citizen also raised his voice" is much better than "You're a person who doesn't know how to talk to people."
2. Select and prioritize your feedback.
3. Focus on things that can be changed.
4. Remain aware that your non-verbal communication speaks volumes.
5. Talk about the new officer's behavior. Describe your observations (as in number 1). Present information about what the officer might do differently, followed by what you liked.
6. Restrain from injecting your personal feelings for the new officer into your professional relationship. You may like, dislike, or feel neutral about the new officer. Regardless, keep it friendly and professional.
7. Do not forget the old standby, the use of "I" statements. "I observed that . . ."

8. Know when to "go behind" behavior and talk about reasoning. Some behaviors which seem inappropriate may have reasonable explanations. Avoid making premature inferences to mental states. Most new officers will readily tell you about their observations, motives, thoughts, feelings, and intentions. Appropriately confront unreasonable rationalizations.

9. Specific feedback information is superior to general feedback information.

10. Timing is important. Unless an emergency exists or otherwise duty-bound, provide feedback at appropriate times in appropriate settings. Immediate feedback can be quite effective if you can provide it within this guideline. Non-immediate feedback can be based upon a series of behaviors that were observed over a period of time.

11. To increase the probability that you are understood, summarize your thoughts at various points and at the completion of feedback. In this way, you can check to see if the message you intended to send was accurately received. In essence, *get feedback on your feedback*. Avoid needless or non-productive repetition. Excessive repetition of information will cause the recipient to tune out.

12. Feedback is most effective when the recipient is motivated by your information. ("Let's try that again. The first part looked good.")

13. The addition of humor in feedback can be used effectively if used appropriately. Do not overdo it. The appropriate use of humor does not include making fun of new officers or belittling them for mistakes. Remember, they're still learning the job.

14. Be descriptive in feedback - "I observed... (then describe your observations); be evaluative in evaluations - "Your actions did not meet the performance standard for... (specify the performance standard).

Anxiety

It is normal to experience a degree of anxiety when learning a new job. Anxiety is a feeling of apprehensiveness or fear accompanied by a sense of immediate or anticipated danger. The danger does not have to be physical. Any perceived threat to well-being (such as failing an exam, receiving a poor evaluation, being embarrassed) can trigger anxiety.

Anxiety has physiological components. Everyone is familiar with being so nervous that "I thought my heart was going to jump out of my chest." In addition to a pounding heart (increased heart rate), other physiological components of anxiety include increased blood pressure, a change in blood flow distribution, sweating, rapid breathing, dry mouth, body tremors, and muscle tension or weakness. The physiological components are often accompanied by a degree of mental confusion, diminished ability to make reasonable decisions, impulsive and sometimes uncharacteristic behavior, a sense of panic, and a feeling of fear.

Anxiety and Performance

Anxiety has a long and interesting relationship to performance. Low levels of anxiety do not create significant performance deficits. High levels of anxiety can bring performance to a standstill. On simple tasks, higher levels of anxiety can be experienced without a corresponding degradation of performance. As task complexity increases, there is a decrease in the ability to tolerate anxiety without a decline in performance.

Assisting new officers to manage performance anxiety should be a primary focus of FTOs. Because high anxiety can impede performance, helping new officers to keep anxiety at a manageable level is imperative. If FTOs assist new officers to manage performance anxiety, especially when new officers first attempt a new task, the true capabilities of new officers are more readily observed.

Anxiety and Perception of Competency

With any particular task, one's perception of competency is negatively correlated with anxiety. This means that as a person's perception of competency increases, the experience of anxiety decreases. To fully understand this, think of a man who has a fear of water (water anxiety). He has a fear of water because he cannot swim. Being a non-swimmer, he likely avoids activities associated with water, such as boating, kayaking, and other water sports. If he is on water or in water, he is anxious. His level of anxiousness varies with the actual circumstances. He is less anxious standing in water up to his waist than he is when standing in water up to his chin. In the water, he is *bottom oriented*. He must know where the bottom is to keep from being overwhelmed by anxiety. This is because deep water represents a life-threatening circumstance for him - certainly a reason for anxiety.

One day, he decides to confront his fear by going to the local pool and enrolling in a swimming class. At the first session, his perception of his competency in the water is low, so low that his anxiety is quite high. However, as he begins water training and progresses in the program, he begins to acquire the skills necessary for swimming. His increasing skill is slowly building his confidence and, as a result, his water anxiety is beginning to lessen. It is not a smooth process. He experiences more anxiety in some sessions than others. He thinks about quitting. After all, the experience of anxiety is uncomfortable. But he sticks with it. He consistently confronts his fear of being in water. With perseverance and more practice, he eventually reaches a point where being in deep water, water deep enough so that it is not possible for him to touch the bottom, no longer represents an imminent life-threat. He has become *surface oriented*. As long as he has some idea of where the surface of the water is, he is ok.

There is little doubt that he has increased his competency in the water, and as a result, experiences less water anxiety. As mentioned, the degree to which he experiences less water anxiety depends upon *his* perception of his newly developed proficiency. Consequently, even if others view him as a highly competent swimmer, he will experience anxiety negatively correlated with *his* assessment of his water skills.

So it is for new police officers. As new officers develop a sense of occupational competency in particular areas, their on-duty experience of anxiety in those area will diminish. If new officers fail to develop a sense of competency in an area, they will continue to experience heightened levels of anxiety in that area. This is the reason that new officers will sometimes appear completely relaxed when performing one task (say, interviewing a witness) and quite nervous when performing another (like, conducting a field sobriety protocol).

Many FTOs understand the relationship between anxiety and performance. They use this understanding to enhance their field training artistry and to enhance the learning experience of new officers.

Anxiety and Breathing

For millennia, controlled intentional breathing has been utilized to manage anxiety. *Relaxation breathing* is the best cost-benefit anxiety reduction technique known. Although there are many versions of relaxation breathing, enduring success can be achieved with one of the simplest. It is comprised of the following: (1) inhale deeply through the nose, (2) hold your breath for two seconds, and (3) exhale slowly through the mouth. This simple procedure interrupts the autonomic physiological responses known to accompany the experience of anxiety.

You can increase the effectiveness of this and any other anxiety-reduction breathing technique by simultaneously engaging a verbal or mental coping statement. Examples of coping statements are "I can do this," "Relax," and "I can handle this."

Relaxation breathing can help new officers better perform in situations that naturally produce anxiety, such as emergency response driving. Not only can FTOs teach this anxiety reduction technique to new officers, they can also use it themselves. Regardless of the situation, the next time you feel anxious, try this: take a deep nose breath; hold it for two seconds; exhale slowly through your mouth.

While exhaling, think or say to yourself "I'm ok, I can handle this." You'll be glad you did.

Other anxiety reduction strategies that may be taught and used by FTOs are presented in *Some Things to Remember* (chapter 3).

Field Training Remedial Programs

Police departments have developed various means to assist new officers who fail to progress as expected in field training. A commonly applied remedial intervention involves removing the officer from field training, conducting additional training in the deficit area, and if satisfactorily completed, returning the officer to field training. This remedial sequence is successful in many cases.

To address field training concerns when it is deemed unnecessary to remove the officer from field training, the *Within Phase Observational Period* (WPOP) and the *Within Phase Emphasis Period* (WPEP) can be utilized. While WPEP may include additional classroom training, such training is accomplished within the parameters of on-going field training.

Within Phase Observational Period

The WPOP is best utilized in cases where new officers have previous policing experience. It can help answer questions related to performance anxiety and work consistency. WPOP is designed to provide a respite from the ever-present evaluation of most field training programs. It provides the new officer with a slightly different field training environment. The WPOP is normally engaged in the latter phases of field training and takes place over three work shifts:

First shift: The FTO operates the police vehicle and assumes car command. A daily observation report (if used) is waived. The FTO's primary task is to act as a model. The new officer's primary task is to observe the FTO.

Second shift: The new officer operates the police vehicle and assumes car command. The FTO intervenes only if necessary. The FTO may provide positive feedback to the new officer; however, corrective feedback is withheld unless necessary. The FTO completes a daily observation report, but it is not discussed with the new officer. The primary task of the FTO is observation. The primary task of the new officer is performance.

Third shift: The third shift is the same as the second shift. The FTO completes a daily observation report. At the end of this shift, the FTO and new officer discuss their experiences, observations, and the two completed daily observation reports. The FTO and new officer work together to better utilize the remainder of field training.

The WPOP tends to lower anxiety, increase confidence, and improve the performance of new officers. It has also proved useful to address cases in which new officers feel that the FTO is focusing on insignificant details. In one case that prompted a WPOP, a new officer with previous policing experience complained that his FTO was relentlessly nit picking. The new officer maintained that the FTO was commenting on and correcting things that were really a matter of officer discretion. Following completion of the WPOP, the FTO reported that during the program he had seen the new officer engage several behaviors upon which he wished to comment. But in compliance with the elements of WPOP, he refrained. When the FTO was asked about the behaviors he had observed, he said could not now remember them. Evidently, they were not serious enough to make a lasting impression on the FTO. This appeared to lend credibility to the new officer's complaint.

Within Phase Emphasis Period

The WPEP is best utilized in circumstances where new officers are progressing as expected in all but an isolated area. A WPEP is specifically designed to address the deficit area. The four primary steps of WPEP are:

1. *Issue is identified.* The FTO identifies an area within which the new officer is deficit. The new officer has received remedial field training but the situation has not improved. The deficit does not warrant halting the officer's field training.
2. *Design and duration of the WPEP.* A specific WPEP is designed. It may include specialized field assignments, classroom and scenario training, working with specialist officers, etc. Evaluation may be suspended for all, none, or for a portion of the WPEP.
3. *WPEP is implemented.* The WPEP is implemented for a specified duration.
4. *New officer's performance is evaluated.* If the new officer's performance in the targeted area improves to an acceptable level, customary field training continues - the WPEP has been successful. If performance does not improve, other options must be considered. Additional options include redesigning and implementing a new WPEP, suspension of field training and further remedial instruction, and termination of employment.

Field Training Officer Information

Suggestions and considerations for field training officers:

- In first phase, avoid moving from car command too soon. Allow a reasonable period for the new officer to observe you as a model.
- If not already part of the field training program, in the second and third phases of field training consider an "FTO driving day" - for at least the first day of each of these phases. Traditionally, because different FTOs are assigned to each of the different phases, new officers have the opportunity to observe only the FTO assigned in first phase. FTO driving days allow new officers to observe each of their FTOs as models. FTOs may also consider an FTO driving day *within*

the second and third phases. This provides a break for new officers as well as the FTO. If you plan on doing this, discuss it at the beginning of the phase so that the new officer does not misinterpret its meaning (like FTO dissatisfaction with new officer performance). If used, make certain that an FTO driving day fits within the department's field training policy and philosophy.

- New officers may not respond to strategies that worked well for you when you were in field training. Also, new officers may not respond to strategies that have previously worked well for you as a trainer.
- Be creative. Individualize your field training style and training strategies within the parameters of your department's field training policy and philosophy.
- Avoid over-extending yourself. Long periods of uninterrupted field training will almost certainly exhaust any FTO. Engage in an occasional training hiatus to avoid burnout and to keep yourself healthy.
- Develop appropriate psychological boundaries. Think about your responsibility and limitations as an FTO. Remain mindful of the positive rewards.

Summary: Ten Considerations for Maximizing Field Training Officer Effectiveness

1. *Develop a personal training style.* Develop a personal training style that is consistent with: 1) the training you received to become an FTO, 2) department policy, 3) department field training program philosophy, 4) your previously successful field training interactions, and 5) recommendations from other FTOs.

2. *Use appropriate verbal and nonverbal positive reinforcement.* Many trainers would increase their effectiveness by increasing their use of positive reinforcement. Do not overdo it. Too much positive reinforcement, especially over simple tasks, can diminishes its value. Thoughtful and balanced positive reinforcement is the most effective.

3. *Remember that you are always a model.* It is possible to unintentionally pass on good and bad behaviors. This fact is especially important for FTOs but it is true of all veteran officers. If a new officer observes a veteran officer behaving in a less-than-desirable way, discuss the poor behavior and provide appropriate alternatives.

4. *Encourage encoding.* Encourage encoding by periodically summarizing and reviewing new material. Assist new officer encoding by conceptualizing, categorizing, visualizing, imaging, and emotively processing new information and skills.

5. *Align "content" with "message."* A full discussion of verbal communication *content* (what you say), *message* (what you mean), and *delivery* (how you say it) is included in chapter 7. For now, it is important to remember that *delivery* can alter the *message* of any *content*. Endeavor to avoid *content* with potential multiple meanings. Also, remember that in-person verbal communication takes place within a nonverbal context. Hence, good interpersonal verbal communication requires that you remain mindful of your nonverbal behavior.

6. *Provide feedback.* Provide deliberate and thoughtful feedback on daily observation reports, throughout the shift, and at summary periodic evaluations.

7. *Remember the following*: (1) high anxiety degrades performance and (2) reducing anxiety will allow a more accurate assessment of knowledge and skill. Use and teach relaxation breathing and other anxiety management skills.

8. *Have new officers evaluate their field training experience.* Use this information to improve the field training program. New officers can evaluate their field training immediately after completion of their field training and again at some later time. The later follow-up evaluation asks new officers to reflect upon their field training experiences after they have worked independently for a period of time. This later collection of field training feedback can be gathered up to a year after new officers have completed their field training. There is much to be learned from this evaluation protocol, including what is working well.

9. *Be creative.* You can safely exercise some discretion if you remain within your field training program policy and practices. Share your thoughts with other FTOs. Meet regularly to discuss FTO consistency, FTO skill development, new officers' progress, and field training program features.
10. *Take care of yourself.* You are a better field training officer when you are motivated and feel well.

Chapter 3

Police Stress and Occupational Health

The first wealth is health.
-Ralph Waldo Emerson

There are two primary stress intervention strategies. The first is to change your environment. The second is to change yourself. Changing your environment involves altering or withdrawing from your surroundings. Changing yourself includes learning new coping skills and altering the way in which you conceptualize your environment. The first strategy acknowledges the ability to modify one's circumstances. The second strategy recognizes the transactional nature of human experience.

Stress Equals Demand

Stress equals demand—this simple equation and the confidence we can place in its accuracy comes from decades of study by many talented researchers. The implications of this equation are clear— if you wish to decrease stress, decrease demand; if you wish to increase stress, increase demand.

In terms of historical stress research, a *demand* is anything that places a need for adjustment on an organism. To illustrate this, we return to the swimming pool. Think about what happens when you jump into a swimming pool. At first, you feel the shock of the cool water and become chilled. As you spend some time in the pool, your body adjusts to the water temperature and you feel comfortable. However, if you remain in the pool long enough, you will exhaust your body's ability to cope with the cooler water temperature, and you will again feel chilled.

The demand in this scenario is the temperature of the water. The cool water initiates an *alarm* for adjustment (you feel chilled). The process by which your body adjusted to the water temperature is called *resistance*. When you resist the initial effects of a demand, the demand effects diminish or disappear (you feel comfortable in the water). If the demand continues, *exhaustion* occurs and the effects return (you again feel chilled). If the demand overwhelms resistance, symptoms of distress, sometimes leading to death, may result (if the water is cold enough and you remain in it long enough, you will die from hypothermia). The sequence of alarm, resistance, and exhaustion is called the *general adaptation syndrome* (Selye, 1974). In the general adaptation syndrome, the more intense the demand, the less we are able to resist; resulting in less time needed to produce exhaustion.

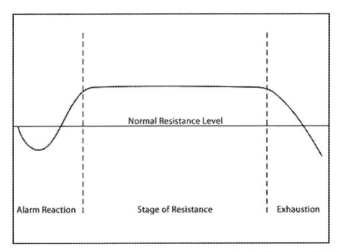

General Adaptation Syndrome (GAS). Factors that influence GAS Include genetics, age, state of health, gender, and socioeconomic status.

Another word for demand is *stressor*. A stressor is anything that causes a need for adjustment. The attempt of your body to adjust to a stressor is called the *stress response*. Therefore, a stressor is anything that initiates the stress response. A common way of expressing this is "a stressor is anything that causes stress." We are never without stress. Even while resting or sleeping, there are the demands for body respiration and circulation. The absence of all stress is death.

On the ends of the social stress continuum lie *overload* stress and *deprivational* stress. Overload stress is characterized by *too much to do, too little time, high expectations,* and *insufficient resources.* This is how most people think about stress. It is likely that everyone has at some time experienced overload stress. The best way to manage overload stress is to decrease stressors.

On the other end of the continuum is deprivational stress. Deprivational stress occurs when there is not enough demand. Nearly every police officer has experienced deprivational stress. Most officers can easily remember slow night shifts that seemed to go on forever. This circumstance is best illustrated by an officer who checks the time and notes that it is 0300. After it feels like an hour has passed, a second time check reveals that it is 0310. In deprivational stress, even the perception of the passage of time is altered.

Persons who experience deprivational stress as a life pattern often report being lonely, bored, and having an unexciting life. Normally, as the sense of deprivation increases, so does the level of discomfort. This makes deprivation and discomfort positively correlated, as one increases or decreases, so does the other. In extreme forms, deprivation can be punishing. This fact is well known to the captors of prisoners of war. If deprivation is extreme for an extended period of time, it is a form of torture.

If you are a parent or have otherwise used *time out* as a child-behavior corrective strategy, you have applied the principle of deprivational stress. By having a child remain in a limited stimulus environment for a period of time following undesirable behavior, the likelihood of similar behavior in the future is reduced. In the penal system, the equivalent of time out is administrative segregation (solitary confinement).

The best way to manage deprivational stress is to increase positive stressors. Think about this for a minute - who ever thought that good stress management might mean increasing stressors?

Is it possible to experience stress overload and stress deprivation simultaneously? Yes and no. Yes, when considering life in general, like stress overload in one area of life (overworked) and stress deprivation in another (lacking a fulfilling social life). No, when contrasting the levels of demands associated with overload and deprivational stress.

While anyone can occasionally find themselves in overload or deprivational stress, the key to healthy stress management is avoiding both as a life pattern. This involves finding a stressor balance that is right for you.

The Stress Response

During the early days of stress research, the terms *stress* and *stress management* seemed like buzzwords. Back then, not much was understood about the physiological and psychological processes underlying the notion of stress. Today, you cannot read a basic psychology textbook without finding at least one chapter dedicated to the topics of stress, stress management, and the stress response.

The stress response is characterized by physiological arousal. It includes increases in blood pressure, increases in heart and respiration rate, increased perspiration, pupil dilation, and changes in blood flow distribution. If this sounds similar to anxiety it is because "there's a fine line between stress and anxiety" (APA, Feb 14, 2022). When under stress, blood flow is altered by the constriction of blood vessels in the extremities, thereby maximizing the blood-borne delivery of oxygen and nutrients to the major organs and primary muscle groups. This is why your hands become cold and clammy when you feel under duress (blood has been constricted away from your extremities thereby lowering hand temperature and there is an increase in perspiration). The stress response is also responsible for the age-old phrase "getting cold feet" to indicate trepidation about engaging in some event. The physiological components of the stress response are so reliable that the stress management technique of biofeedback is based upon them. They also comprise the conceptual foundation of the polygraph, the so-called lie detector.

The process by which the stress response is initiated, maintained, and eventually diminished primarily involves the nervous and endocrine systems. These are the systems activated in response to stressors. They are the systems that improve chances of survival by preparing organisms to do something physical.

Reflections of a Police Psychologist

The acute stress response and fight-or-flight

American physiologist Walter B. Cannon (1871-1945) found that when animals were confronted with a predator or other threatening stimuli their autonomic nervous system became activated and specific hormones were released. He called this dual process the "acute stress response" and reasoned that it served the animal to better fight the threat or run away from it. In recognition of this, he coined the term *fight or flight* (1915). As Cannon viewed it, the fight or flight response prepares organisms, including humans, to do something physical - to fight off an attack or flee from a threat, and thereby increase the chances of survival. The fight or flight response is our inherited natural survival instinct.

In the years since Cannon, research has shown that there are other ways in which humans and other animals react to threat. These include freeze and fawn responses. Both have survival value and both utilize the acute stress response. In freeze responses no action is taken. Fawn responses utilize immediate appeasement behaviors. This has led some to describe the acute stress response as *fight-flight-freeze-fawn* (Frothingham, 2021).

Cannon also discussed and popularized the concept of *homeostasis* (1932). Homeostasis is the process by which the body attempts to keep itself within an operational range necessary for survival. The homeostatic balance is achieved by unconscious body processes and is related to the body's ability to adapt to stressors. Homeostasis is the reason that you sweat when you are hot and shiver when you are cold. Both are attempts to keep body temperature within a functional range.

The stress response is *nonspecific*, meaning that it does not matter if the stressor is viewed as positive or negative. Heart rate, blood pressure, respiration, and so forth will increase whether persons have just learned of the death of a loved one or have been informed that they have won a lottery. The *specific* psychological/emotional response in these instances may differ (sadness in the first case and excitement in the latter), but the physiology remains mostly consistent.

In essence, the body has only one way to cope with stressors—prepare itself for action via the stress response. In earlier times, this response worked well. There were many stressors that were amenable to fight or flight resolutions, such as hunting wild animals, fighting off predators, running from enemies, and so on (Selye, 1974). Today, in "civilized" societies, the number of circumstances in which physical resolutions are appropriate has diminished (but not disappeared). Persons cannot often physically run from or physically fight their problems. Therefore, the stress response has become something to manage. To manage the stress response, one needs to appropriately manage stressors.

The intensity of the stress response varies with the *perceived* intensity of the stressor and the perceived ability to cope with it. Therefore, the intensity of the stress response will be low when confronting a vicious dog if the dog is thought to be friendly. Correspondingly, stress intensity will be high in response to a dog believed to be vicious even though it is friendly.

The intensity of the stress response in both of these "vicious dog" examples is moderated by one's perceived ability to deal with it. This is the influence of "coping ability" on the experience of stress. A person with a high self-assessed ability to deal with vicious dogs will experience no to little stress when confronted by any dog, vicious or otherwise. It is in this way that the stress response is said to be *transactional* - the level of stress experienced being related to one's perceived ability to cope with the stressor.

Occupational Stress

All occupations are characterized by unavoidable stressors. An unavoidable stressor is a demand which is inherent to the occupation. For example, an unavoidable stressor of school bus drivers is interacting with children, an unavoidable stressor of cashiers is handling money, credit cards, and electronic payment, an unavoidable stressor of trial attorneys is contending with judges and juries.

Policing has its constellation of unavoidable stressors. Some of these stressors overlap those of other occupations, such as interacting with people, driving a car, and working in snowstorms. Others are a bit more unique, like the duty to protect others.

Some of the more commonly recognized unavoidable stressors of policing include shift work (policing is a 24/7 occupation), working in a paramilitary-type organization, carrying a firearm, interacting with highly emotional and violent persons, exposure to critical incidents, and role over-identification.

Role over-identification of police officers is the result of a dysfunctional enmeshment of the officer with the job. The identification of some officers with the role of police officer is so complete that they say things like "Policing is not something I do. It's what I am." These officers are treading upon very thin psychological ice. This is because their sense of self, and often sense of self-worth, is intimately tied to their job. If the job is lost, so is their sense of identity and self-value. Realistically, policing is an occupation. Like any occupation, it should be conceptualized as separate from those who engage it. For officers, there is little doubt that the job is important; however, police officers are much more than their job. They are husbands, wives, parents, coaches, and so on. Police officers lose sight of this at their peril.

Police officers must also contend with the unavoidable occupational stressor of being misunderstood by the public. Take the case of Trooper G—Trooper G was talking to Trooper L in the "opposite direction" vehicle position. This position is commonly used by police officers. It involves positioning two police vehicles in opposite directions so that the driver's door of each vehicle is facing the other. In this way, the officers remain in their vehicles, monitor radio traffic, and are able to easily speak to one another. Troopers G and L, parked in this position, were discussing work shift events when they received a broadcast from Dispatch: "Overturned vehicle on the interstate, unknown injuries." They engaged their vehicles' emergency warning lights and siren. They sped toward the reported accident location. Trooper G was the lead car; Trooper L was following close behind. After several miles of running "code 3" (lights and siren) and passing numerous vehicles, Dispatch relayed information that the report was unfounded. Both troopers disengaged their vehicles' emergency lights and siren. They slowed to the posted speed limit. By chance, there was a highway exit close to the location where the emergency response was terminated. There was a restaurant close to the exit. The troopers decided to exit the highway, drive to the restaurant and have lunch. Trooper G parked his police vehicle in front of the restaurant; Trooper L parked nearby. Trooper G exited his vehicle. He noticed a man walking toward him. The man, who had also recently parked near the restaurant, appeared agitated. When the man was within speaking distance of Trooper G, he angrily complained that it was "not right" to use emergency lights and siren to pass others on the highway just to get to a restaurant. To the man, it appeared that the troopers were abusing their authority by using emergency lights and sirens to get to the restaurant. Trooper G explained to the man that he and the other trooper were responding to a report of an overturned vehicle farther up the interstate. He added that when it was determined the report was unfounded, the emergency response was terminated. He further explained that it was just a matter of circumstance that the troopers were at that particular exit and decided to have lunch. Trooper G offered the man the phone number of Dispatch, in the event that he wished to confirm this information. Trooper G added, "If it were you or your family members in an overturned vehicle, would you not want an emergency response from the police?" The man, taken aback by the information, replied, "I'm just sayin'," to which Trooper G responded, "Well, I'm just sayin'." The conversation ended there.

There are many circumstances in which the public has little idea of why police officers do what they do. Many police actions are guided by received and sometimes erroneous information, police procedure, police tactics, and officer safety concerns. Other actions are guided by department policy and directives. All have a rationale and a purpose.

This is not to say that police officers always follow procedure or that procedures always prove adequate. Police officers can and do make mistakes. Additionally, there have been and likely will always be some police officers who betray the "serve and protect" values of policing. These bad cops tarnish the badge and damage the reputation of all police officers. Some are unethical, some are unprofessional, and some engage in criminal activity. The policing profession is on constant alert to identify such officers and to remove them from the ranks of the nation's finest.

Stress Management, Life Management, Life-by-Default, and Life-by-Design

Stress management is the general term used to describe how a person controls, influences, interacts with, and confronts the stressors of life. When thinking of the stressors that comprise the totality of human experience, the term *stress management* seems inadequate. The term *stressor management* can be used to describe efforts to cope with a particular stressor, but beyond that, it also appears lacking. When thinking about the manner in which humans confront the complexities of life, the term *life management* is more satisfactory. The concept of life management is more encompassing and better captures the essence of human efforts to cope with life's complexities.

Life management can be considered from one of two primary life perspectives: *life-by-default* and *life-by-design*. These perspectives are conceptual constructs and describe a theoretical continuum along which a person can engage life.

It is unlikely that anyone lives life totally by default or by design. Most people live sometimes or most times by default, and sometimes or most times by design. Life-by-default differs from life-by-design in that life-by-default is what you get if you do not practice life-by-design. Not much thought or effort goes into life-by-default. Persons who are oriented toward life-by-default often feel powerless. They subscribe to the "This is my life. What can I do about it? It is what it is. What will be, will be" life position. This is very different from the life-by-design philosophy of "taking life by the horns."

Life-by-default does not mean that life experiences are or will be undesirable. Quite the contrary, life experiences can default to very desirable circumstances. It is a matter of probability. The probability that life will default to something great and wonderful is less than the probability of desirable outcomes in life-by-design.

Life-by-design is best described by a single word: *intention*. Persons oriented toward life-by-design act intentionally and accept responsibility for their decisions, behaviors, and outcomes. Life-by-design persons are not passive observers of life. They do not wait for life to simply unfold. They feel empowered and they act in ways to direct their lives. In life-by-design there is no illusion that all things can be directed, controlled, or even influenced. Instead, there is respect for what might be changed and what must be accepted. There is recognition of the influence of personal values, societal values, and cultural influences.

Life-by-design persons do not blindly accept the values of their parents or other significant persons of their childhood. They consider all values, adopt those that are appropriate for them, and live accordingly.

Life-by-design is thoughtful, mindful. To engage life-by-design, persons must accept reasonable risk, endorse the idea that they can decide many things for themselves, and use this knowledge to make a difference in their lives. Making an effort to accomplish this is the first step toward moving from a life-by-default to a life-by-design.

Life by design	• Intentional, mindful, adopts personal values • Accepts responsibility, initiates effort for change • Self aware, self-actualizing, reclaims life
Life by default	• Avoids reasonable risk for desired improvement • Sense of powerlessness to change • Accepts life as "what will be will be"

In summary, life by design involves:

- Increasing your self-awareness
- A reconsideration of "taught" personal values
- Appropriately increasing your assertiveness
- Accepting personal responsibility
- Reducing your anger and frustration
- Improving your time management to include exercise, relaxation, and recreation

- Consistent efforts to recharge your personal and occupational battery
- Ongoing appreciation of functional relationships
- Appropriately confronting dysfunctional relationships
- In general, *reclaiming your life*

Life-by-design, Lifestyle, and The Big Three—Diet, Exercise, and Self-awareness

Life-by-design means being mindful of lifestyle. The big three: diet, exercise, and self-awareness are major components of lifestyle.

Diet

The word *diet* refers to what a person eats and drinks. It represents the totality of what a person consumes. *Dieting* refers to consuming less or different types of foodstuffs in an attempt to lose weight. Based on current knowledge, there are diets that facilitate health and those that are less than healthy.

The diet of most Americans is varied. Not only do Americans consume many types of solid food, they also drink many different liquids. These contribute significantly to daily caloric intake. It is not uncommon for a person to consume 600 to 1000 calories a day in liquids (Johnson, 2015). This finding is interesting due to the fact that some Americans count only solid food calories.

All diets are primarily comprised of three elements: fats, carbohydrates, and proteins. (1) Fat is an ester of glycerol and one, two, or three fatty acids. Triglycerides are the main type of fat in food and in our bodies. (2) Carbohydrates come in simple forms such as sugars and in complex forms such as starches and fiber. (3) Proteins are strings of amino acids, often called polypeptide chains.

Calories

A calorie is a unit of measurement. It is a measurement of energy. A food calorie (kilocalorie) is the amount of energy It takes to raise the temperature of one kilogram (about 2.2 pounds) of water one degree Celsius. Different foods contain different amounts of energy, thus different amounts of calories. A small piece of chocolate contains more energy than a similar size of lettuce; therefore, chocolate contains more calories than lettuce.

When it comes to energy, all calories are the same. A fat calorie has the same amount of energy as a carbohydrate calorie, protein calorie, or alcohol calorie. The energy produced by carbohydrates is four calories per gram. Proteins also provide four calories per gram. Fats are higher in calories. They provide nine calories per gram. Alcohol has seven calories per gram. The number of calories in any diet refers to the amount of energy the diet provides. If a person intakes more calories than are needed each day, the body stores this energy as fat ("Calories," n.d., para.1).

During sleep the human body burns about one calorie per minute. This is approximately the same as sitting on a sofa or inactively watching television. At this level of activity, the body burns about 1440 calories daily.

It takes 3500 excess calories to gain one pound. During any period of time, if you consume 3500 calories more than you burn, you will gain one pound. To lose weight, you must burn more calories than you consume. If you produce a deficit of five hundred calories each day for a week, you will lose one pound. If you stay consistent with this deficit, you will continue to lose a pound each week. The bottom line is that if you want to lose weight, you must burn more calories than you consume (Willet and Skerrett, 2005).

When considering diet, there are three variables that can be manipulated: (1) what you consume, (2) how much you consume, and (3) how frequently you consume. By manipulating these variables, you adjust caloric intake. In conjunction with your activity level and metabolic rate, the calories you consume will determine whether you lose weight, gain weight, or remain at the same weight. Other factors can also influence weight. Genetic make-up, age, metabolism, health status, medications and other drugs, mental illnesses, and whether you use food to manage loneliness or respond to stress (emotional eating) seem to be involved in weight fluctuation.

Weight is different than *mass*. Weight is relative to where you are in the universe. It represents the relationship between mass and gravity. You weigh less on the moon than you do on earth. And, because earth's gravity varies at different locations, you weigh less at the Equator than you do at the North and South Poles. Mass is invariable. Your mass remains the same regardless of where you are (Halliday et al., 2001).

Fat

Fat is stored in *adipocytes*, sometimes called *fat cells*. The average person has about 35 billion fat cells. Some people have as few as 25 billion fat cells, while others may have up to 275 billion. Fat cells accumulate differently for men and women. For men the accumulation is normally around the abdomen (the infamous spare tire), while for women, fat cells accumulate around the hips, buttocks, and thighs. Abdomen fat has a higher correlation with health risk than fat in other body locations.

Fat cells are chemically complex. They expand and contract. Much of weight loss is due to the contraction of fat cells. Cellulite is ordinary fat and is not a function of excess weight. Cellulite is caused by genetic differences in how adipose and connective tissue form. It is less likely to appear in men than women. There is no known specific health risk associated with cellulite. Unfortunately, although there are some differing opinions, physical activity seems to have little effect on reducing or altering the appearance of cellulite (Avram, 2004).

There are several types of dietary fat. Although the consumption of fat is necessary to remain healthy, eating too much can cause problems. A great deal depends on the type of fat consumed. The Harvard School of Public Health summed up the circumstances related to dietary fats: "Bad fats, meaning saturated and trans fats, increase the risk for certain diseases while good fats, meaning monounsaturated and polyunsaturated fats, lower the risk. The key is to substitute good fats for bad fats" (Griffin, 2006, 1).

Health Statistics

The U.S. National Center for Health Statistics estimates that in the United States, 49 percent of women and 59 percent of men are overweight. Nearly one-third of the U.S. population qualifies as obese. For those that were overweight and have lost weight, the statistics are grim. Within three years, about two-thirds of those who have lost weight will regain the weight they lost. Within five years, between 80 and 90 percent of those who lost weight will regain what they lost. These numbers represent those in medically supervised weight loss programs. The numbers worsen in personal programs for weight loss (cdc.gov).

Body Mass Index

Body mass index (BMI) is a way of calculating appropriate weight to height ratios. A person's BMI is weight in kilograms divided by height in meters squared (BMI=kg/m2). For example, a person 1.68 meters tall (5'6"), weighing 68 kilograms (150 pounds) would have a BMI of 24.2. A BMI below 18.5 is considered underweight. Normal weight is represented by a BMI of 18.5 to 24.9. A person is overweight if the BMI is 25 to 29.9, and obese if the BMI is over 30. If the BMI is over 40, the person is considered extremely obese. A BMI of 21 is thought to be ideal (CDC, 2009).

Cardiac Health Risk

Estimates of cardiac health risk associated with waist size and belly fat have been calculated. Research has shown that women with a waist measurement of over 35 inches measured at the belly button have a significantly higher cardiac health risk. For men, similarly measured, it is a waist size of 40 inches.

Glycemic Index and Glycemic Load

Other useful dietary information is provided by the *glycemic index*. The glycemic index is a method of ranking carbohydrate foods by their ability to raise blood sugar. The index ranges from 0 to 100. Foods below 55 are considered low glycemic foods (for example, carrots). Foods that rank in the range of 56 to 69 are midrange (popcorn), while foods that are rated over 70 are ranked high (rice crackers).

Glycemic load is a function of carbohydrate intake and glycemic index (the amount of carbohydrates per serving). Most dieticians recommend that no more than 50-60 percent of the recommended 2000 calories consumed each day come from carbohydrates, and that no more than 30 percent of daily calories should come from fat. Many popular high-protein weight loss diets specify much lower intake levels of carbohydrates and fat.

Further dietary recommendations include the intake of (1) less than 2300 mg of salt daily - with an ideal limit of not more than 1500 mg (American Heart Assn, 2022), (2) less than 300 mg of cholesterol daily, and (3) less than 300 mg of caffeine daily (Willet & Skerrett, 2005).

Water

Water is essential for life – from bacteria to human beings. Without water, living things slowly dehydrate and eventually die. It is the principle chemical component of the human body and comprises 50% to 70% of body weight (Mayo Clinic, 2022).

There is some variability in how much water is needed daily to sustain health. The National Academies of Sciences, Engineering, and Medicine reported that healthy adult men appeared adequately hydrated with a daily intake of about 15.5 cups of water (3.7 liters), compared to about 11.5 cups (2.7 liters) for healthy adult women (2004). Depending upon several variables such as age, activity level, health status, and environment, some persons will require more water per day while others will remain hydrated with less. The vast majority of people stay sufficiently hydrated simply by drinking when thirsty (ibid).

Although there is some variation, most human beings can live without water for 2 to 4 days. This is in contrast with the approximately 3 weeks that most people can go without food (Burch, 2021).

The most common way to intake water is to drink it, straight up or in other beverages. We intake water when we consume milk, coffee, tea, soft drinks, and even alcoholic beverages.

Water is also a component of many foods. For most persons, about 20% of their daily water consumption comes from food. Some foods are over 90% water by weight, like watermelon and lettuce (Mayo Clinic, 2020). All contribute to daily water ingestion.

It is possible to intake too much water. Taking in excessive amounts of water overwhelms the kidneys' ability to remove it. This results in the dilution of the normal sodium (a critical electrolyte) concentration in the blood. The sodium/blood imbalance caused by the intake of too much water is known as *water intoxication*. Early stages of water intoxication include dizziness, headache, nausea, muscle weakness, unstable gait, and mental impairment. If the sodium/blood imbalance becomes severe, *hyponatremia*, a life-threatening condition follows.

Hyponatremia is more common than once thought. It has been identified as a hydration risk factor for elite athletes, the elderly with specific health problems, those on certain medications, and the mentally ill.

One of the most publicized and tragic cases of hyponatremia is that of Jennifer Strange. On January 12, 2007, Jennifer, a healthy 28-year-old California mother of three, entered a radio station water-drinking contest called "Hold your wee for a Wii." As one of eighteen contestants, she drank nearly two gallons of water in about three hours without urinating. She took second place in the contest, winning concert tickets. During and following the contest she complained of headache and abdominal pain. After the contest, Jennifer called her work supervisor and stated that she was not feeling well and was heading home. Jennifer was later found dead in her home by her mother, several hours after the conclusion of the contest. Ed Smith, then an assistant coroner of Sacramento County cited the cause of death as "consistent with a water intoxication" (L.A. Times, 2007).

Another well-known circumstance within which hyponatremia may have been a factor is the 1973 controversial death of actor and martial arts expert Bruce Lee (1940-1973). At the time of his death, and despite various medical opinions to the contrary, some persons claimed that he was assassinated by a criminal syndicate, poisoned by a mistress, killed by a martial arts nerve strike, or killed by supernatural forces. Such claims insisted that Lee was in too great a physical condition to die of natural causes. However, a recent review of his medical history and an examination of the reports following his death led researchers to conclude that he most likely died from complications associated with hyponatremia (Villalvazo et al., 2022).

Vitamins and Minerals

Lastly, for a better understanding of diet, vitamins and minerals must be considered. Vitamins are organic compounds necessary for health. They either cannot be synthesized within the body or cannot be synthesized in sufficient quantities within the body. Therefore, they must be taken in through diet. There are 13 vitamins for humans. Nine are water-soluble (eight B-vitamins and vitamin C) and four are fat-soluble (vitamins A, D, E, and K). One vitamin, vitamin D can be taken in through diet but it is also synthesized in the lower layers of the skin. For this to occur, sunlight, specifically UBV radiation is necessary.

Water soluble vitamins are readily eliminated in urine and need to be replenished daily. Fat soluble vitamins can be stored in the body.

Similar to not consuming a sufficient quantity of vitamins, consuming too great a quantity can lead to health difficulties. Excessive vitamin intake can result in *vitamin toxicity,* with overdose symptoms depending upon the vitamin. For instance, too much vitamin D (hypervitaminosis D) can result in too much calcium in the blood (hypercalcemia), stomach discomfort, and kidney problems.

Vitamin toxicity is usually caused by overdosing on dietary supplements, not food intake or exposure to sunlight. This is especially true of the fat-soluble vitamins.

Minerals, like vitamins, are necessary for good health. Minerals, unlike vitamins, are chemical elements and not organic compounds. Minerals and vitamins work together to perform many of the body's vital functions. Minerals in the human body are sometimes described as *macro, micro,* or *trace,* depending upon the quantity of each found in the body or required for health. Some of the body's macro minerals are calcium, iron, sodium, and potassium. Micro minerals include copper, sulfur, and zinc. Iodine, cobalt, and silicon are among the body's trace minerals (Lieberman & Bruning, 1990).

Dietary Tips for Weight Loss

There are some tips that might help if you are trying to change eating and drinking habits for weight loss:

1. Eat smaller portions more frequently. This way you never become ravenous and overeat before your brain receives the "full" signal from your stomach.
2. Eat slowly. Research indicates that it takes about 20 minutes for your brain to get the full signal.
3. Plate your food and consume only what is on your plate, nothing more.
4. Drink water. For hot drinks, try herbal teas. Stay hydrated. Thirst mimics hunger - you may feel hungry when you're actually thirsty.
5. Brush your teeth after eating. This sends a behavioral signal to your brain that you're done eating. It is especially effective after the evening meal.
6. Do not eat from large containers or snack from big bags. Portion control becomes nearly impossible when eating this way.
7. No eating past a certain time. Set your time, commit to it. Avoid eating at least two hours before bedtime.
8. Take a temporary hiatus from certain foods and drinks. It is difficult to believe, but you can live without pork rinds, soft drinks, and the empty calories of alcoholic beverages.
9. Wait out or distract yourself from unhealthy food or drink cravings.
10. Engage an activity in the place of habitual eating (eating when not hungry), such as walking instead of eating during your work break.
11. Develop new interests or hobbies to occupy yourself so you do not eat out of boredom.
12. Make a contract with yourself or someone else which specifies the changes you are willing to make. Be reasonable. Write the contract so that there is a high likelihood of success. Make it for a specified period of time. Renegotiate after it

Reflections of a Police Psychologist

expires. Each renegotiation will bring you closer to achieving your overall goals. Try new things.

13. Schedule more activity. Any activity is superior to no activity.
14. Keep in mind that change takes time and effort. Do not quit. If you falter, try not to become discouraged. Do not beat yourself up. Instead, resolve to do better. Think of yourself as a work in progress.

Exercise

Metabolism is the process by which the body breaks down food for use as energy. If a person is active, metabolism increases. Conversely, if a person is inactive, metabolism decreases. Muscle is the machine that metabolizes calories and fat. Physical exercise and activity utilize muscles, thereby burning calories and metabolizing fat.

There are two primary types of metabolism: aerobic, in which energy conversion takes place in the presence of oxygen, and anaerobic, where energy is supplied by processes that do not include oxygen. At rest, the body's energy is mostly supplied aerobically. As we increase activity, the demand for energy increases. If the activity is sufficiently strenuous, we soon surpass the level of energy that can be provided aerobically. This is called the *metabolic threshold*. It is the point at which energy production moves from primarily aerobic to primarily anaerobic. In anaerobic metabolism, we build up an oxygen debt. This is why following even brief periods of strenuous anaerobic activity we find ourselves breathing rapidly.

Anaerobic activity also produces by-products which contribute to muscle fatigue. Lactic acid is a well-known by-product of anaerobic activity. It has long been suspected as a cause of muscle fatigue. The role of lactic acid in anaerobic activity is currently the subject of some debate, however it is often cited as one of the reasons that a person can go "all out" for only brief periods of time.

Due to the types of metabolism associated with different activities, some activities or exercises have come to be known as aerobic or anaerobic. Fast walking below the metabolic threshold is an aerobic exercise, while weight lifting is primarily anaerobic. In reference to body conditioning, each type of activity has its benefits. For cardiac conditioning, calorie burning, lessened muscle fatigue, and goals of weight loss, aerobic activity is desirable (more fat burning). For increased muscle mass and rapid performance increases, anaerobic exercises are necessary (more carbohydrate burning). The key for any exercise or activity program is *not too much too soon*. It is also recommended that you warm-up aerobically before engaging in strenuous anaerobic exercises (Maffetone, 2000).

Complexity, Transaction, and Self-transaction

Human beings are complex. We are so complex that we not only transact with others and everything else in our environment, we also transact with ourselves. *Human beings are so self-transactional that we have an ongoing relationship with ourselves.* Talking and thinking to ourselves, about ourselves, is common in human experience. How we talk to ourselves can motivate, energize, and encourage. It can also demean, depress, and generate anxiety. This is why self-talk is important. It is a major factor in how we view ourselves and thereby is intimately connected with self-esteem.

One of the theoretical cornerstones of the cognitive therapies is the idea that negative thoughts drive negative emotions. In cognitive theory, negative thoughts and disparaging self-talk combine to produce depression and other mood disorders. If unabated, they can lead to thoughts of suicide - "I'm nothing" and "I don't deserve to live."

A goal of cognitive therapy is to help persons change unrealistic negative thoughts to more realistic positive thoughts. So, "I'm nothing" and "I don't deserve to live" might become "I am struggling right now" and "I'm not perfect but I can do better."

Cognitive therapies have demonstrated efficacy for many years (Beck et al., 1979). The success of these therapies in the treatment of depression and other disorders demonstrate the importance of the self-relationship and the power of self-talk.

Transaction, Self-awareness, and Self-direction

To be productively self-aware, you must transact with your inner and outer worlds as an active agent. This means that you must engage life-by-design and conceptualize yourself as someone with at least some ability to directly or indirectly influence life. In the quest for increased self-awareness, questions like, "Who am I?" "What is my place in the world?" and "What do I believe, what are my values?" are common. Clarifying beliefs and endorsing particular values are necessary components of enhanced self-awareness. Living in accordance with those beliefs and values are necessary components of enhanced self-direction.

Achieving a higher level of self-awareness and thereby greater self-direction, takes thought and mindfulness. It can take some time. In the search for greater self-awareness, it would serve us well to remember the words of Chinese philosopher Lao-tzu (604-531 BCE), "A journey of a thousand miles begins with a single step." Self-awareness includes being "tuned in" to your body. This involves engaging in self-care. Self-care involves nurturing yourself physically, psychologically, emotionally, spiritually, and socially. Self-care is not selfishness. Selfishness is the pursuit of desires by nearly any means, without concern for personal consequences, personal value violations, or regard for others. Self-care is about personal and social boundaries. Boundaries are limits. When you assume responsibility for things that you cannot control, you are over your boundary. Staying within boundary is recognizing the limits of what you can do for yourself and others. If you exceed these limits for a significant amount of time, you will begin to experience the negative effects of overload stress. The more over your boundary you are, the less time it will take to notice the stressor effects.

In unusual or emergency situations you can exceed healthy boundaries and push yourself to extremes. However, making this a life style will significantly diminish your self-care and result in a degradation of personal well-being. Having appropriate boundaries is necessary for self-care and life-by-design. Utilizing appropriate boundaries is the opposite of "burning the candle at both ends" and being manipulated by others.

Greater self-awareness is empowering. It enhances self-direction. Together, self-awareness and self-direction are the processes by which self-esteem is developed and maintained.

Occupational Burnout

The concept of burnout has been in existence for many years. It was first conceptualized and named by psychologist Herbert Freudenberger in 1974. *Burnout* is used to describe "someone in a state of fatigue or frustration brought about by devotion to a cause, way of life, or relationship that failed to produce the expected reward" (1980, 13). Burnout can occur in all areas of life, including work, marriage, family, sports, avocations, and hobbies.

When police officers burn out, all areas of their lives tend to suffer. This is because being burned out at work often means carrying the fatigue and frustration home. It is an unusual police officer who can feel burned out at work and remain in a positive mental state at home.

There are many indicators that an officer is burning out or is burned out. Lack of interest in work and no concern for the consequences of behavior are two of the most prominent.

As the process of burnout begins, officers work performance gradually deteriorates; they tend to answer calls or meet minimum expectations, but do little more. They slowly withdraw from the behaviors that made them successful.

For patrol officers, as burnout continues, they begin to avoid calls, "milk" calls, and become a nightmare for dispatchers trying to assign calls. This is because burned out officers feel tired and disinterested much of the time. As their performance worsens, they often draw unwanted attention from their supervisors. In some cases, supervisors will initiate performance improvement plans (PIP). Supervisory PIPs normally identify problematic areas and clarify supervisory expectations. Some officers respond well to PIPs and seem to do better. For these officers, the PIPs function as a wake-up call. Other officers, the more completely burned out officers, become more stressed and suspicious. Because they have little to no insight into their behavior, they feel that that they are being unfairly singled out. They often say things like "my supervisor is out to get me."

Due to their lack of insight, burned out officers do not take responsibility for their behavior. They consistently blame others for their problems. They have a difficult time seeing things from any perspective but their own.

Perspective: Can you identify this world-famous landmark?

Burned out officers feel trapped. They feel trapped in a job that they now perceive as no longer desirable or meaningful. To them, everything seems gray, routine, and dreadful. They say things like, "If I could earn this kind of money somewhere else, I'd be outta here in a minute," "I'm sick of people," and "I'm tired of this bullshit department."

Eventually and inevitably, the negative behavior of burned out officers begins to affect their relationships with coworkers. This is because many officers who are not burned out frequently find it difficult to be around officers who are. If nothing is done to address this, even friends of many years will begin to distance themselves. For many burned out officers, life outside of the police department is not much better. This is often due to the officers' lack of tolerance and shortened temper.

Burned out officers often experience increased marital and family discord. They may be drinking more, smoking more, or taking more over-the-counter or prescription drugs (hopefully, not illicit drugs, but this has been known to occur). Physical symptoms increase. These range from gastro-intestinal difficulties to severe headaches. In serious cases of burnout, officers may experience eating disorders, sexual dysfunction, anxiety, low self-esteem, depression, and suicidal thoughts. Overall, due to a lack of concern for consequences, burned out officers behave uncharacteristically poor at work and at home.

Certainly, not all officers that experience burnout will follow the described sequence. Many officers struggling with burnout are able to recover their interest in policing and improve their condition prior the occurrence of any dire consequences.

Perspective: world famous landmark. Eiffel Tower, Paris, France from ground center looking upward.

Avoiding or Managing Burnout - The Occupational Imperative

To avoid or manage burnout, officers need to maintain good personal boundaries and a positive life balance. It is easy to become fatigued and frustrated with work challenges. To buffer against these stressors, officers must continually remind themselves of the Occupational Imperative: *do not forget _why_ you do, _what_ you do.*

The values of policing are noble. History is filled with accounts of police officers' bravery, commitment, and sacrifice. Anyone who has carried or carries a badge inherited this history and has contributed to it. Good police officers believe in service. They believe in safety, the law, and individual freedom. They risk their lives to maintain positive social order. They do this in spite of the knowledge that there are those who would intentionally harm them. Police officers care. This is why they do what they do. When officers lose sight of the values which attracted them to policing, they plunge headlong into burnout. To keep from becoming burned out, *officers need to remain connected to the values that first brought them to policing.*

Many burned out officers need a break. Taking a temporary respite from any stressful work environment is a welcomed relief and can be energizing. While on break, officers can reassess their careers and their desire to continue in policing. If they decide to continue in policing, even if the desire is low, they should try something different once back to work. Occupational withdrawal (trying to stay below the supervisor's radar) should be avoided. This is because continuing to withdraw from the primary elements of the job will almost certainly strengthen the symptoms of burnout. To combat burnout, what is needed is reengagement. Burned out officers must reengage policing and *reclaim their careers*. They need to rediscover their values and engage in policing behaviors which previously provided job satisfaction. They need to reassess and reinstate their personal and professional values and boundaries.

For police officers, a useful way of avoiding burnout and thinking about boundaries is *circles*. Officers need to recognize their *circle of control*. They must think about what can be controlled, what to accept as not controllable, and what to confront in an effort to bring about change. Just thinking in these terms will initiate the self-empowerment process. This is a counterbalance against burnout.

Outside the circle of control is the *circle of influence*. Many things that cannot be controlled can be influenced. The difference between control and influence is that desired outcomes for things that can only be influenced have a lower probability of being achieved. Healthy officers know this distinction and quickly recognize what can be controlled and what can be influenced. Outside the circle of influence lies everything else.

By reclaiming their careers, police officers can look forward to many more years of self-satisfaction, job satisfaction, and service to the community.

Occupational Boreout

In addition to burnout, police officers may also experience *boreout*. Boreout is a term first used by Swiss management consultants, Peter Werder and Philippe Rothlin (2007). They describe it as the opposite of burnout. Although deprivational stress is a part of boreout, being bored out encompasses more than being in deprivation. Boreout involves being "understretched" at work. Being understretched results in feeling unchallenged. This is accompanied by listlessness and a feeling of helplessness arising out of not knowing how to address their condition. Persons who are bored out have lost interest in what they are doing and lack any sense of identification with their job.

For police officers, boreout can occur (1) after the challenge of learning how to be a police officer diminishes, (2) when officers feel underemployed or underutilized, and (3) upon being reassigned, transferred, or promoted. While some officers will be overwhelmed by the demands of reassignment, transfer, or promotion, others will suffer boreout. In one particular case, a sergeant recently promoted to lieutenant found himself in boreout as he found the administrative duties of his new position much less challenging and satisfying than his work as a patrol sergeant.

To address boreout, officers need to reevaluate their position, rewrite job descriptions, initiate new programs, develop new job functions, take on rewarding challenges, contact their supervisors and address assignment parameters, expand job responsibilities, and similar to burnout, *reclaim their careers*. The answer to boreout is creativity.

Life Management Skills

Developing life management skills is empowering and enhances the functionality of person-environment transactions. But what are the skills needed to manage stress, cope with anxiety, and facilitate a positive life balance? To help keep yourself healthy and balanced there are some things that you can do; there are some things that may be helpful to remember.

Some Things to Remember (STR) consists of several strategies and ideas which can help you to maintain a healthy lifestyle. Most are self-explanatory, some are not. This is because some are utilized only as part of specific counseling programs. Other not-so-self-explanatory STR items will be discussed in upcoming chapters.

Some Things to Remember

- Watch how you talk to yourself (relationship with self)
- Relaxation breathing - *breath through stress* - inhale nose/ exhale mouth
- Maintain a high level of self-care, make time for *you*
- Keep yourself physically active, not too much too soon
- Utilize positive and appropriate coping statements

- Add survivorship: "This is difficult but I won't let it defeat me"
- Enhance your internal (self) awareness and external awareness - mindfulness
- Remember the limits of your personal boundary
- Practice stimulus control and response disruption
- Monitor deprivational stress and overload stress
- Use "pocket responses" when needed/consider oblique follow-up to exit uncomfortable situations
- Apply thought stopping/blocking to negative thoughts
- Identify and confront internal and external *false messages*
- Confront negative thinking with positive counter-thoughts
- Break stressors into manageable units; deal with one at a time. Especially useful to avoid feeling overwhelmed
- Change is possible; the *difficult* is not the *impossible*
- A managed experience will lessen the intensity of fear and anxiety. Relax, engage in a graded confrontation of what you fear – reciprocal inhibition/systematic desensitization
- Only experience changes experience, look for the positive
- There are lessons you can learn that no one can teach
- Reclaim your marriage; reclaim your career; *reclaim your life* - life by design vs life by default
- Thinking is not doing. At some point, implement your positive plan - engage behavior. Blueprints do not build a house
- Stressor strategies: confrontation, withdrawal, compromise (can be used sequentially or in combination)
- Match coping strategy with stressor – strategy must address stressor – strategies can be multi-faceted
- Remember: transactions and choice points = different outcomes
- Communication Imperative
- *Work*: do not forget why you do what you do (Occupational Imperative) / *Make it safe*! (Relationship Imperative)
- Utilize your physical and psychological buffers
- Healing involves changes in intensity, frequency, and duration
- Use your shield when appropriate (psychological shield against negativity)
- Things do not have to be perfect to be ok

- Create positive micro-environments within stressful macro environments
- Think of strong emotion as an *ocean wave*- let it in, let it fade. You will soon return to a more normal state
- Trigger anxiety— *I know what this is; I know what to do about it* - anxiety management - discomfort is not danger
- Goal to become *stronger and smarter* (with the above = the 2 and 2) - survivorship vs victimization
- *Walk* off and *talk* out your anxiety, fears, and problems (walk and talk). Activity helps dissipate the stress response
- Being vulnerable does not equal being helpless
- Enhance resiliency - develop and focus your innate coping abilities. Resiliency is common, not exceptional
- Develop and practice relapse prevention strategies
- Develop and utilize a sense of humor, learn how to smile
- Time perspective: past, present, future (positive- negative)
- Things are never so bad that they can't get worse*
- Do not forget that life often involves selecting from imperfect options. Available options often include a down side
- Access your power: the power of confidence, coping, and management. You are more capable than you think
- Stay grounded in what you know to be true
- Keep things in perspective: keep little things little, manage the big things

Practice *Some Things to Remember* as part of life-by-design

*The notion that "things are never so bad that they can't get worse" is intended as an aid to help keep things in perspective. It is not intended to minimize the difficulty of any stressful circumstance. At its best, this idea encourages toleration, increases motivation for change, and enhances positive life management.

Stress Management and the Proactive Annual Check-in

The Proactive Annual Check-In (PAC) is a preemptive stress management program consisting of an annual meeting between police employees and the police psychologist, a member of the peer support team, or another police department support person. The PAC offers a positive exchange of thoughts and information within a confidential setting. The Proactive Annual Check-in is comprised of six primary elements:

(1) Annual visit with the department psychologist, member of the Peer Support Team, or other police department support person
(2) Confidential meeting that does not initiate any record
(3) No evaluation – it's a check-in, not a check-up
(4) There does not need to be a problem
(5) It's a discussion of what's happening in your life
(6) Participation is voluntary and encouraged*

The goal of the PAC is to provide a safe, non-threatening, proactive forum for police employees to talk about their lives. It is an opportunity to exchange information with a trained support person before any significant stress-related issues arise.

Following a PAC meeting, additional meetings or the initiation of a more comprehensive support program are available if requested.

*In their pursuit of enhanced police employee-wellness some police agencies offer incentives (like time off) to attend PAC meetings or have made annual meetings with the psychologist or other support personnel mandatory.

Strategy for Comprehensive Officer Wellness - COMPASS

The Comprehensive Model for Police Advanced Strategic Support (COMPASS) is a career-long inclusive strategy for officer wellness. It begins with appropriate pre-hire psychological assessment and extends beyond retirement.

Comprehensive Model for Police Advanced Strategic Support - COMPASS

The four COMPASS points are (1) officer and family, (2) health and wellness, (3) police officer career, and (4) professional and peer support.

For more information about the Comprehensive Model for Police Advanced Strategic Support and a graphic illustration of COMPASS visit www.jackdigliani.com.

Chapter 4

Critical Incidents

It is strange to think how to this very day I cannot sleep a night without great terrors of the fire; and this very night could not sleep to almost two in the morning through thoughts of the fire.
-Samuel Pepys (1633-1703), after the London fire of 1666

Critical Incidents, Psychological Injury, and Trauma

Critical incidents are characteristically different from the stressors of everyday life. While the circumstances of everyday life can be stressful, critical incidents are those events that lie outside the range of normal everyday experiences.

Incidents deemed "critical" differ from everyday stressors in that they are often unexpected, high in intensity, and have the potential to overwhelm normal coping mechanisms. They almost always represent a threat to the health, safety, and welfare of self or others, and may involve bodily injury, death, or near death.

In addition to possible physical injury, involvement in a critical incident can cause varying degrees of psychological injury, often referred to as *traumatization*. The experienced degree of traumatization is determined by a complex transaction between incident circumstances and personal variables. This is why two persons involved in the "same" critical incident in similar ways can experience different degrees of traumatization. It also means that no matter how similar the circumstances, a critical incident is never really the same for any two participants.

Some of the variables known to influence the degree of traumatization are: personal beliefs; perceived sense of control; prior training; personal assessment of possible options; assessment of personal performance; action after planning; action on impulse;

suddenness of the incident; age of others involved; degree of blood, gore, and body destruction; and specific incident circumstances.

Some incidents that appear critical when viewed from the outside may cause no or little trauma. Conversely, some incidents that appear common or non-critical may traumatize significantly. Another way of thinking about this is that "critical" is a description or feature of the incident - it appears to be outside the norm of everyday experience; while "psychological injury" and "traumatization" are concepts associated with human experience. Simply stated, any incident, whether or not it appears "critical" to an outside observer, may traumatize or psychologically injure one or all of those involved.

The degree of traumatization following a critical incident can range from no or minimal distress to a constellation of physiological, psychological, and sociological symptoms and impairment collectively known today as *posttraumatic stress disorder* (PTSD).

Brief History of Posttraumatic Stress Disorder

Human responses to critical incidents have been observed since ancient times. Various societies conceptualized and explained these responses in a variety of ways. Much of how they were explained depended upon cultural beliefs, the state of medical knowledge, and observations of soldiers exposed to the extreme stressors of warfare (Cosmopoulos, 2007).

In America, as elsewhere, it was recognized that many soldiers exposed to stressful battlefield conditions complained of a racing heart, sweating, chest pain, and fatigue long after leaving the field of battle. This syndrome was not uncommon and eventually came to be known as *soldier's heart*. In 1871, this condition was described in detail by American Civil War physician and surgeon, Jacob M. DaCosta (1833-1900). DaCosta called the condition *irritable heart*. It later came to be known *DaCosta syndrome*. Today, DaCosta syndrome is viewed by most psychologists as the physiological components of stressor traumatization - traumatization caused by the exposure to the extreme stressors of war.

The Great War, World War I (1914-1918), produced the notion of *shell shock*. Shell shock was thought to be caused by neurological damage resulting from the percussion of exploding artillery shells.

Those suffering from shell shock experienced uncontrollable tremors, developed an inability to engage their environment, and were observed to exhibit the "thousand-yard stare." Many soldiers exposed to artillery bombardment developed shell shock. The shell-shocked condition of some soldiers improved once they were removed from the front. Others were not so fortunate. They continued to experience symptoms long after their service at the front ended.

It was soon noticed that some soldiers who were not exposed to exploding artillery shells also developed shell shock. While it took some time to sort out, clinicians eventually came to realize that although artillery bombardment was implicated as a causal factor of shell shock, other circumstances could also produce the condition. This challenged the idea that neurological damage due to exploding shells was the sole cause for the symptoms of shell shock. However, within the science of the time, not much more was made of this observation.

It was during World War II (1941-1945 for America) and under the theoretical influence of Sigmund Freud (1856-1939) that the concept of *combat neurosis* was developed. This condition was also known by a variety of other names such as combat fatigue, battle fatigue, and war neurosis. The observation that some soldiers developed combat neurosis while others did not, led to the idea that personality factors were involved. Within the conceptions of Freud's psychoanalytical development theory, such personality factors were thought to have their origin in childhood. It was hypothesized that soldiers who developed combat neurosis had done so due to poorly resolved childhood conflicts resulting in the personality factors that led to the development of combat neurosis.

Consider the following: "...a 25-year-old gunner on a B-24 with 25 combat missions presented symptoms of depression, tiredness, paleness, anxiety, suicidal thoughts, homicidal ideation, and intense intolerance of his circumstances. He had been in the Army Air Corps for 27 months, experiencing two crashes in the United States and 2 combat related crashes in Europe. In addition, he was once fired upon by a German battleship shells screamed past his plane. On another occasion, while he was flying at 27,000 feet, the engines of his bomber failed, and the plane fell some 25,000 feet before they restarted. On his 23rd mission, his plane was hit and he was knocked out of his turret by the explosion; the copilot, bombardier, and radio man were all killed.

Despite his traumatic military history, it was finally resolved that this veteran's presenting symptoms were primarily due to a problematic childhood and some severe feelings of hostility he had harbored for his mother, brother, and others representing authority. Ultimately, the veteran was forcibly discharged from the service with a diagnosis of psychopathic personality" (Goodwin,1987, 2). Such was the influence of psychoanalytic theory. Very little thought was given to the gunner's war experiences as a factor in his symptomology and diagnosis.

The Vienna, Austria home of Sigmund Freud, Berggasse 19.
Freud moved to London in 1938 to escape Nazi persecution.
Berggasse 19 is now a museum. Photo circa 2006.

Following the *brainwashing* and *zombie reaction* observed in captured American soldiers during the Korean War, came Vietnam. The American military in Vietnam utilized the DEROS system of deployment. DEROS was the acronym for *Date of Expected Return from Overseas*. It provided a return date for all military personnel assigned to serve in Vietnam. From the deployment date, DEROS was thirteen months for marines and one year for all other services.

In the vernacular of the day, military personnel, volunteers and drafted, would arrive *in country* on one date and return to *the world* a year or so later. Thanks to DEROS, everyone who went to Vietnam (except general officers) knew before they departed, the date upon which they would return. The theoretical benefit of DEROS was that military personnel did not have to be wounded or decompensate psychologically to leave the combat environment. To leave the war behind, all that was needed was to survive until the assigned DEROS date (ibid).

Initial DEROS results were promising. In Vietnam, there were far fewer evacuations for psychological symptoms than in World War II or the Korean War. Based on this early finding, military psychiatrists proudly announced that they had discovered the secret to avoiding combat fatigue and mental decompensation in combat. However, this optimism soon faded. Although many Vietnam veterans managed to endure their war experiences for their tour of duty, once home, they developed serious psychological problems. The psychological difficulties experienced by these Vietnam veterans upon their return to the United States are now nearly legend (ibid). Similar circumstances were observed in some Vietnam veterans of other countries.

In light of these observations and the growing understanding of the psychological effects of exposure to critical incidents for all persons, whether or not war veterans, the American Psychiatric Association developed and approved a new stressor-related diagnosis. In 1980, the third revision of the Diagnostic and Statistical Manual of Mental Disorders (DSM-III) included for the first time ever, the diagnosis of posttraumatic stress disorder. As then conceptualized, PTSD was placed within the category classification of anxiety disorders.

The diagnostic criteria for posttraumatic stress disorder have changed several times since its inception, although critical exposure has remained a constant. In DSM-III, the critical exposure was defined as "Existence of a recognizable stressor that would evoke significant symptoms of distress in almost everyone" (238). Over the years, this has evolved into the current day "Exposure to actual or threatened death, serious injury, or sexual violence in one (or more) of the following ways." Of the four "following ways" specified, criterion A4 is especially interesting, "Experiencing repeated or extreme exposure to aversive details of the traumatic event(s) (e.g. first responders collecting human remains; police officers repeatedly exposed to details of child abuse). Note: Criterion A4 does not apply to exposure through electronic media, television, movies, or pictures, unless this exposure is work related" (DSM-5-TR, 2022, 301).

In 2013, the diagnosis of PTSD was removed from the list of anxiety disorders and placed within the newly created category, *trauma and stressor-related disorders* (APA, DSM-5). This change acknowledged that PTSD is characterized not only by anxiety but by multiple emotions. All of the disorders within this new category, including acute stress disorder and adjustment disorder, require exposure to stressful events.

There has been some discussion about a formal name change for PTSD. Several organizations, including the U.S. military, have advocated that *disorder* be changed to *injury*. It is argued that *posttraumatic stress injury* (PTSI) is (1) more descriptive of the condition, (2) better reflects the true nature of traumatization, (3) reduces stigma associated with the term "disorder," and (4) makes it more likely that a person would seek treatment. Those opposed to the change argue that the word "injury" is too imprecise for a medical diagnosis (APA, 2013b). As it stands in 2023, posttraumatic stress disorder remains the formal diagnosis. Time will tell if the PTSI advocates win out.

Although anyone can develop PTSD under circumstances that meet diagnostic criteria, for veterans, the National Center for PTSD estimates that about 30% of American Vietnam veterans have had PTSD in their lifetime, compared to about 12% of Gulf War veterans and 11% to 20% of veterans of the Iraq wars (2022).

PTSD can be conceptualized as a spectrum disorder, depending upon the number and intensity of symptoms. Mild PTSD is thought to exist when minimum criteria are present to make the diagnosis. Severe PTSD is indicated when all or nearly all of the diagnostic criteria are present in extreme form.

Involvement in a critical exposure necessary for the diagnosis of posttraumatic stress disorder can include experiences of various and unusual perceptual phenomena.

Critical Incidents: In-progress Perceptual Phenomena

Out-of-the-ordinary perceptual experiences can occur during a critical incident. One of the most common is *slow motion*. During this phenomenon, events seem to slow down, much like in some Hollywood movies. Many police officers have experienced slow motion during critical incidents. They reported seeing bullets fired from their guns travel slowly through the air, watching objects fall at a slow rate of speed, and seeing persons running as if in water.

The opposite of slow motion, fast motion, is another perceptual distortion that sometimes occurs during a critical incident. The experience of seeing things move faster than normal during critical incidents is less common than seeing things in slow motion.

Other in-progress perceptual phenomena reported during critical events include time distortions, heightened visual clarity, sound distortions, automatic pilot (behavior without conscious thought), tunnel vision, and temporary paralysis (Artwohl & Christensen, 1997).

The Aftermath of Critical Incidents

There are many possible responses following involvement in a critical incident. Some are more typical than others. One of the most common is a *heightened awareness of danger*. Heightened awareness of danger following a critical incident can be experienced generally but is often experienced most intensely when a person is in the environment within which the critical incident occurred. To better understand this, consider a person shopping in a grocery store. He has shopped in this store for years. He has had many pleasant experiences in this store and has always felt safe while shopping there. On one particular day, a gunman enters the store while our shopper is perusing the aisles. The gunman shoots a number of patrons (unfortunately, an all too real scenario). Some are killed, some are wounded. Our shopper is lucky. He finds a place to hide. And while he witnessed the entire incident prior to the police subduing the gunman, he is uninjured, at least physically. Now the question – do you think he will ever feel as safe in this grocery store as he did prior to this experience? In *any* grocery store? Likely not.

In fact, it is possible that he will not feel safe anywhere in public, at least for a while.

Although the probability of a gunman entering a grocery store and targeting workers and patrons is extremely low, it is not zero. Such incidents do occur. For our shopper, the potential of such a scenario occurring, became reality - the *potential* has become *real*. The previously "safe" feeling once common while shopping is lost. Shopping at the grocery store, once considered a safe and maybe even enjoyable activity, has become a task fraught with potential peril. His "assumption of safety" has been shattered, replaced with the anxiety-provoking "assumption of possible threat." This is the heightened awareness of danger. Environments that previously felt safe now feel dangerous.

Like our grocery store shopper, anyone can experience a heightened awareness of danger. Victims of robbery, assault, burglary, gang violence, and so forth often talk about not feeling safe anymore. The same is true of persons involved in motor vehicle accidents. Following an accident, some persons that have been driving for years without fear can become anxious when in or operating a motor vehicle. In these cases, the dangers which were always present when in a motor vehicle have gone from the potential to the real.

Police Officers, Psychological Defense Mechanisms, and Heightened Sense of Danger

Police officers start every shift with the knowledge that they could be called upon to confront violent persons, respond to life threatening situations, and otherwise be placed in harm's way. They also realize that during their tour of duty they may be injured or killed. The emotional responses that accompany such knowledge are suppressed by psychological defense mechanisms.

Psychological defense mechanisms are thought to be unconscious. We are not aware of them or their influence on our thoughts and behavior. Psychological defense mechanisms make working in potentially dangerous environments tolerable.

Repression, *denial*, and *rationalization* are three of several psychological defense mechanisms. Repression is the process by which stressful or disturbing thoughts are blocked from consciousness. Denial is a defense mechanism in which an individual refuses to recognize or acknowledge objective facts or experiences that appear obvious to others. Rationalization involves justifying difficult or unacceptable feelings or behavior with self-constructed and seemingly logical reasons and explanations (psychologytoday. com, n.d.). All work to protect us from discomfort and anxiety. All are frequently seen in police officers.

Officers repress fears of being injured or killed on duty by simply avoiding such thoughts (I don't think about getting hurt, I just go out and do my job); they frequently deny the danger of policing (I have done this for years and I'm still here); and they mitigate any feelings of trepidation, fear, and anxiety by rationalizing (I can handle anything that comes my way).

When officers are exposed to critical incidents, these defense mechanisms can be overwhelmed. To the degree this happens, the protective power of defense mechanisms is diminished. In severe cases, critical incidents strip officers of their defense mechanisms, leaving them emotionally raw and psychologically unprotected. The end result of this is increased discomfort, anxiety, and a heightened sense of danger. The weakening or stripping of defense mechanisms brought about by the reality of a critical incident, coupled with the corresponding increase of discomfort, anxiety, and heightened sense of danger, creates an emotional challenge for officers - especially when returning to work. They must now confront the environment within which the critical incident occurred. Further, they must do this without the full-strength defense mechanisms that once served them so well.

For officers, it is important to remember that in most cases the environment within which the critical incident occurred was likely as dangerous the day before the incident as it was the day after. This is the first step in managing a heightened sense of danger. It also means that the danger level of the environment does not need to change to bring about a heightened sense of danger. It is the *sense* of danger *in* the environment that changes when the sense of danger increases. Of course, if the danger level of any policing environment actually increases, a heightened sense of danger, even in the absence of a critical incident, is completely adaptive.

In addition to a heightened sense of danger, other after-the-fact responses to critical incidents may include anger, blaming, sleep difficulties, second guessing, emotional numbing, guilt, isolation, grief, depression, anxiety, loss of interest in sex and other activities, family difficulties, and pretty much any other experience possible for human beings.

Realtown, U.S.A.

Case study: There is no telling what might emerge as the primary issue following a critical incident. The case of Realtown, U.S.A. provides an illustration.

One of the last places a critical incident might have been expected was in the small community of Realtown (fictional name for an actual community). Realtown is comprised of less than five hundred residents. Realtown had one police officer. Several years ago, during the summer months, the police officer, who also had responsibilities to turn on the town park's irrigation system, began his work shift. As was his practice, he would leave his home, go to the park, turn on the sprinklers, and return home for a coffee break. After coffee, he would return to the park, turn off the watering system, and continue his duties.

One afternoon, he followed his normal routine. He left his home, went to the park, and turned on the irrigation. He headed home. When he arrived in the driveway, he heard high-pitch screaming coming his house. He thought that his wife might have fallen. He entered his home through the back door. Once in the house he observed his wife, a woman in her 50s, face down on the floor. A man was crouched over her, straddling her. He was holding her head with his left hand. In his right hand was a knife that he had just pulled across her throat, cutting her throat as he drew the knife from left to right. She was bleeding profusely but still conscious. The officer, also in his 50s, drew his weapon and fired three times. The man was hit and fell away from the officer's wife. She managed to get up, make her way to the bathroom, and wrap a towel around her throat.

The officer called for emergency medical assistance. First responders were dispatched. First responders are community residents trained to provide first aid. In small communities, where more sophisticated emergency responses may take some time to arrive, they are the only nearby available medical assistance. This was the case in Realtown.

As the wife held the towel around her neck, a first responder arrived. To the shock of the officer, the first responder began to treat the perpetrator. It was not until the arrival of other medical personnel that the wounds of his wife were addressed. The first arriving ambulance transported the perpetrator to the hospital. About fifteen minutes later, the officer's wife was transported.

Upon her arrival at the hospital, the officer's wife was rushed into surgery. During a two-hour procedure, she received eleven pints of blood. Her right and left carotid arteries had been injured. Fortunately, the surgery was successful and she survived her wounds. Emergency physicians later stated that had she arrived at the hospital about three minutes later than she did, her wounds would have been fatal. She would have bled to death.

The perpetrator died. Investigation revealed that he lived in a nearby town. The officer and his wife reported that he was a total stranger to them. There was never a motive established for the assault.

A few weeks after the wife was released from the hospital, she and her husband came to my office. Although I had been advised of the incident, I was not quite certain what to expect. When they sat down, I could clearly see the results of her neck wound. By its appearance, I remember feeling surprised that she survived. As I listened to their account of the incident, I was struck by how well adjusted the couple appeared. They had come to terms with the home invasion, the random violence, her near death, the death of the perpetrator, and the defense of the wife by the husband. There was only one obstacle on the path of their continuing psychological recovery. The husband, pointing to his wife, expressed it this way, "She was dying, and the medics ignored her and were helping the bad guy!"

Shock, Impact, and Recovery

Various researchers have identified several predictable responses to critical incidents. These can be reduced to three principal phases: Shock, Impact, and Recovery. This general response pattern is frequently observed in persons exposed to critical incidents.

Shock—psychological shock is often the initial response to a critical incident (the physical symptoms of shock may also be present). Shock is comprised of a host of discernible reactions including denial, disbelief, numbness, giddiness, bravado, anger, depression, and isolation. Shock reactions, although common following trauma, are not limited to trauma. Shock can occur in response to any significant event. Football players who have just won the Super Bowl frequently respond to questions from sports interviewers by saying, "I can't believe it" (disbelief) or "It hasn't sunk in yet" (no impact).

Impact—after the passage of some time, the amount of time differs for different people, there is impact. Impact normally involves the realization that "I could have been killed" or "This was a grave tragedy." These thoughts and the feelings that accompany them can be overwhelming. Officers should not be returned to full duty while they are working through the impact of a critical incident. Police agencies would do well to have policy directives which provide for administrative or other appropriate leave until an experienced police psychologist evaluates and clears the officer for return to duty.

Recovery—recovery does not follow impact as a discreet event. Instead, with proper support and individual processing, impact slowly diminishes. As impact diminishes, recovery begins. A person can experience any degree of recovery. No or little recovery can result in lifetime disability. Full recovery involves becoming stronger and smarter, disconnecting the memory of the incident from disabling emotional responses, and placing the incident into psychological history. Without recovery, persons remain victims of trauma. With recovery, they become survivors.

Posttraumatic Stress Disorder

We have seen that the diagnosis of posttraumatic stress disorder has an interesting history and since its 1980 inception has undergone several re-conceptualizations. Perhaps the most significant feature of PTSD as first developed, and as it remains today, is the emphasis on an "outside" event as the causal agent. This represents a major departure from the historic, long-standing belief that psychological difficulties must be generated from "inside" a person.

The following is a categorical summary of the contemporary diagnostic criteria for posttraumatic stress disorder (APA, 2022):

- Exposure to qualifying stressor(s)
- Intrusive memories, dreams, and other reactions
- Avoidance of stimuli associated with the incident
- Negative alterations in cognitions and mood
- Alterations in arousal and reactivity
- Duration: symptoms for more than one month
- Clinically significant distress or impairment
- Not caused by a chemical substance or medical condition

PTSD diagnostic specifiers: (1) *with dissociative symptoms*- depersonalization/derealization (2) *with delayed expression* – at least 6 months after event

While it was always theorized that a person of any age could develop PTSD, explicit diagnostic criteria for *Posttraumatic Stress Disorder in Children 6 Years and Younger* was first developed in 2013 (APA).

In addition to PTSD, the International Classification of Diseases, 11th edition (ICD-11) includes the diagnosis *Complex Posttraumatic Stress Disorder* (CPTSD). CPTSD includes the criteria of PTSD and is further characterized by "severe and persistent 1) problems in affect regulation; 2) beliefs about oneself as diminished, defeated or worthless, accompanied by feelings of shame, guilt or failure related to the traumatic event; and 3) difficulties in sustaining relationships and in feeling close to others." CPTSD is most likely to be developed following exposure to "prolonged or repetitive events from which escape is difficult or impossible (e.g. torture, slavery, genocide campaigns, prolonged domestic violence, repeated childhood sexual or physical abuse" (2018, 1). The current DSM, DSM-5-TR does not include the CPTSD diagnosis.

Posttraumatic stress disorder as a diagnosis and clinical disorder is not without its detractors. Some clinicians have criticized the PTSD diagnosis on grounds that (1) it includes a clear over-simplistic cause - critical event(s), (2) several normal reactions to less than desirable events are specified as symptoms, (3) many of the criteria of the diagnosis are seen in those who have not experienced a critical event, (4) any symptoms observed following a critical event are better accounted for by existing anxiety and depression diagnoses, and (5) because the diagnosis seems to be applicable following almost any stressful life event, it has become somewhat meaningless (Rosen et al., 2008).

While changes in the diagnostic criteria have attempted to address these concerns, and despite these issues, posttraumatic stress disorder remains an independent psychiatric diagnosis. It is likely that the diagnostic criteria for posttraumatic stress disorder will continue to evolve.

Posttraumatic Stress, Posttraumatic Stress Disorder, and Acute Stress Disorder

Posttraumatic stress (PTS) is common following a critical incident. PTS is comprised of the predictable and often observed responses to a critical event. This is because by their very nature, critical incidents derail a person's normal coping mechanisms. PTS often involves some degree of intrusive thoughts, second guessing, heightened awareness of danger, appetite/sex/sleep disturbances, and physiological arousal.

The primary difference between PTS and PTSD is that the reactions comprising PTS do not cause clinically significant distress or impairment. With positive social support and personal resilience, PTS often resolves within several weeks.

In between PTS and PTSD is *Acute Stress Disorder* (ASD). In ASD, clinically significant distress or impairment is present, as are symptoms similar to PTSD. However, by definition, ASD cannot be diagnosed until at least 3 days after the relevant incident and the symptoms of ASD do not last longer than one month. If the symptoms of ASD are present for more than one month and are sufficient to meet the criteria for PTSD, the diagnosis is changed from ASD to PTSD.

In otherwise psychologically healthy persons, PTSD can initiate other mental disorders. The most common is depression. This is because the symptoms of PTSD are in themselves depressing. The symptoms of PTSD may also lead to higher levels of anxiety, suspiciousness, alcohol abuse, and marriage and family problems. Officers who suspect that they are suffering from ASD or PTSD should seek professional assistance without delay.

Treatments for ASD and PTSD have improved significantly over the past decades. While certain medications may prove helpful, several evidence-based therapies have also demonstrated efficacy. These include cognitive-behavioral therapy, cognitive processing therapy, eye-movement desensitization and reprocessing, prolonged exposure, and accelerated resolution therapy. In many cases, a combination of medication and therapy yields the best results. For more information about available treatments for ASD and PTSD visit www.ptsd.va.gov.

Traumatic Exposure, Visual Hallucination, and Vivid Images

Visual hallucinations in the absence of a psychotic disorder (chapter 9) or a history of mental illness can also be part of a traumatic experience. When present, the visual hallucinations associated with the aftermath of traumatic exposure can be surprising and even frightening.

Hallucination following traumatic exposure

Case study: Mrs. X was the front-seat passenger in a vehicle being driven by her daughter. While traveling down a busy city street, a small child, a girl about five years old, suddenly ran into the street. The child was struck. When the vehicle struck the child, the force of the contact flipped her onto the hood of the car and across the passenger side of the windshield. The image of the child as she rolled from the windshield to the ground was impressed into the memory of Mrs. X. The child died at the scene. Although shaken following the accident, Mrs. X was eventually able to gather herself and return home.

The next morning at her home, Mrs. X was standing at the top of the second-floor staircase. As she moved to descend the stairs, she glanced downward. At the bottom of the stairs, she saw the deceased child, standing and staring upward. She screamed and looked away. When she looked back, the image had disappeared. After dressing for work, and still a bit unnerved, she left her home and got into her car. In the rearview mirror, she could see a man sitting on the back seat of her vehicle. She screamed and instantly turned to check the back seat area. The image had disappeared. Although she had never met the father of the deceased child, she sensed that the man she saw was the child's father. She realized that the images she perceived were not real. They were hallucinations related to her experiences during the tragic loss of the child.

Following brief psychological support, Mrs. X did not report any further hallucinations.

Incidentally, investigation revealed that the driver, the daughter of Mrs. X, was not careless and could not have avoided the accident. She was not charged with any traffic or criminal offense.

Vivid images

It is also possible to experience *vivid images* during a traumatic event. Vivid images, while a visual perceptual phenomenon, are different from hallucinations. Unlike hallucinations, vivid images involve actual visual environmental stimuli.

Case study: Officer M responded to a call of a disturbance and found himself in a backyard, face to face with a seventeen-year-old male armed with a butcher's knife. Officer M drew his weapon and ordered the young man to drop the knife. The man did not comply and began walking toward Officer M. As he was walking, the young man began shouting "shoot me, shoot me!" Officer M, hoping to bring about a non-lethal resolution, began backing away. By backing away, he could keep himself safe without having to shoot. As the young man continued his advance, he unexpectedly drew the knife across his forehead. This caused profuse bleeding. Officer M could barely see the man's face.

Officer M retreated until he was backed into a corner, between a fence and a wood pile. He continued trying to reason with the young man. When he could not withdraw any further, he advised the man that if his advance continued, he would have to shoot. The man was now approximately seven feet from the officer, still holding the knife. Officer M began to pull the trigger of his weapon. It was pointed directly at the man's chest. Officer M recounted, "My thoughts were at Mach I, but everything else was moving super slow." He remembered seeing the hammer of his handgun cocking back in preparation for firing. At this instant, several things happened. (1) Officer M saw the man bare-chested, with two bullet holes in his chest. This was despite the fact that the man was still wearing a shirt and Officer M had not fired his weapon. (2) Thoughts began to run through Officer M's mind. The first thought was "Why is this weapon not firing?" (3) Officer M thought of his children. They were close to the age of this person. What would they think of their father killing someone so close to their age?

About this time the man unexpectedly stopped and dropped the knife. He surrendered. To this day it remains unclear why. Maybe his anger and frustration had run its course. Maybe he realized that he did not want to die. Whatever the reason, this young man had come very close to being killed by an officer who had literally run out of options (see *Option Funnel versus Threat Funnel*). Once the man surrendered, Officer M reported that everything snapped back to present reality. His thoughts and perceptions returned to normal. The man was taken into custody, not shot and still wearing his shirt.

The next day, Officer M was at home and in the shower. He was thinking about the incident and his strange experiences of the day before. Suddenly and to his surprise, he again saw the bare-chested young man standing in his bathroom. Again, there were two bullet holes in the young man's chest. The image was so clear that it was "like a photograph." He was instantly overcome by a "deep sadness." He remembered, "Feelings flooded my body like I killed him, like I had done a horrible, horrible thing." He thought "I'm a cop. I shouldn't be feeling this way." He wondered where this image and these feelings were coming from. How were they even possible? He could not get the image out of his mind. He recalled that he thought he was going crazy. He considered quitting policing.

In this case, Officer M had experienced vivid images as the incident was unfolding and an identical visual hallucination the following day. For Officer M, these images and associated feelings ceased soon after receiving professional support. Officer M returned to policing.

In traumatic situations, vivid images and visual hallucinations are more common than most people realize. Although the exact cause of such experiences is unknown, there is some speculation that it is related to increased levels of the stress hormone cortisol, as well as other physiological alterations that take place when under high stress.

Many persons are reluctant to report hallucinations and vivid images for fear of being perceived as mentally ill or psychotic. If fact, they are neither. Visual hallucinations and vivid images are part of the brain's reaction to high-stress events. In most cases, they are short lived.

Psychotic and Other Stressor-related Reactions to Critical Events

True psychotic symptoms can be caused by traumatic exposure. In *brief psychotic disorder with marked stressor(s)* (previously known as *brief reactive psychosis*) several symptoms including visual and other kinds of hallucinations may be present. By definition, the symptoms of brief psychotic disorder last at least one day but persist for no longer than one month. If the symptoms continue for a longer than a month, the diagnosis must be changed.

Other mental disorders that can occur as a result of traumatic exposure include adjustment disorder, functional neurological symptom disorder (conversion disorder), and a variety of mood disorders.

It was once thought that for police officers the severity of posttraumatic responses followed the *rule of thirds*. In this conceptualization, it was hypothesized that about one-third of all officers exposed to critical incidents would experience mild posttraumatic responses; another third would experience moderate posttraumatic responses; while the remaining third would experience significant to severe posttraumatic responses, including PTSD and other mental disorders. Although more research is needed to fully understand officer posttraumatic responses, police researchers Audrey Honig and Steve Sultan found only a 4 percent chronic PTSD rate in police officers involved in shootings. This is in contrast to 30 percent for combat veterans (2004). This suggests that the rule of thirds may be accurate for some populations and not for others. It is likely that the chronic PTSD rate varies not only among populations, but also within the same population over time. There are many variables, some constant and some changing, which might account for population chronic PTSD rate differences.

While there is little doubt that some officers experience severe reactions following critical events, others seem to manage very well. It is not unusual following a critical event for officers to ask if it is "abnormal to feel ok." The answer is "No, it is not abnormal to feel ok." Many officers manage the aftermath of critical incidents, including having to defend themselves with lethal force, quite well and suffer no long-lasting ill effects.

Second-best Option and Time Machine

Treating the psychological aftermath of critical incidents is the second-best option. The best option would be a time machine. With this, we would be able to move backward in time and change, better prepare for, or prevent the incident. As this is not possible, the best we can do is to support those experiencing posttraumatic stress and appropriately treat those diagnosed with incident related disorders.

Although it may sound frivolous, talking about a time machine and the second-best option with those that have been involved in a critical incident often helps them move past the normal phase of "wishing it did not happen." It is the discussion of a fictional device and the knowledge that it is not possible to move back in time that helps diminish the wish fantasy. Such discussion is especially helpful when persons become stuck in wishful thinking. The seemingly simple process of gently talking about a time machine and the impossibility of undoing the incident helps persons to accept the reality of the incident. This is the first step toward psychological recovery. From here, the person can begin to move forward.

In addition to the time machine, there are many other considerations involved in the support and treatment of those that have been involved in critical incidents. Several of these are discussed below, beginning with *second guessing*.

Second Guessing

Second guessing is common in human experience and it is nearly always a feature of posttraumatic responses. Second guessing is the thought that your behavior might have been or should have been something other than what it was. It involves thoughts such as "Did I do the right thing?" "Why did I do that?" "I should (should not) have done X" and "Why didn't I do X."

Variations of the "why" and "should" second guessing include the "what if" and "if only." Officers sometimes refer to this as playing the "what if" or "if only" game. These "games" are not intentionally played and they are not really games. They are interactive thought processes which seem to take on a life of their own. They replay over and over, intruding on other thoughts, disrupting activities, and disturbing sleep. The thoughts of these variations are usually something like "What if I turned right instead of left" "If only I departed a few minutes later" "What if I didn't go to the store" "If only I had stopped for coffee." This form of second guessing is possible because of the manner in which most persons conceptualize reality - we commonly think that we could have done something other than what we actually did.

Considerations that are sometimes helpful with this type of second guessing is the understanding that in reality, even if "what if" and "if only" alternatives were possible, the outcome might not have been better. Maybe if you turned right instead of left, something more tragic would have occurred. This is possible because we live in a world of contingency (chapter 12). Also, we are always doing something. There is no way to do nothing, even if you are "doing nothing." Doing nothing *is* doing something. This may sound confusing but it is a fact of life. So because we are always doing something, it is impossible to avoid outcomes, even if they are at times undesirable.

Second guessing often involves evaluating a decision or action with information that was obtained after the decision had to be made or the action had to be taken. Officers can never know all of the factors involved in particular situations. This is because human behavior is ultimately unpredictable and some circumstances are so unusual, so unlikely, that officers cannot anticipate them. This means that persons can behave in ways which have no foundation in officer training or experience. Holding oneself accountable for failure to know, guess, predict, or otherwise anticipate the improbable behavior of others extends officers beyond the limit of human capability. The truth of the matter is that *every officer, every day*, makes decisions and takes action based on limited and sometimes flawed information. In spite of this, police officers consistently perform well. It is remarkable that in the police world of limited and often inaccurate information, officers perform as well as they do.

When confronting second guessing, officers should talk to themselves in the same manner that they would talk to another officer confronting the same circumstances. Many officers are much kinder to other officers than they are to themselves. To other officers, many officers are understanding, compassionate, and supportive. To themselves, they are rigidly unforgiving, perfectionistic, and overly critical. Learning to talk to yourself in the manner that you would talk to others is a functional, realistic, and productive way to address the complications of second guessing. Give it a try.

For police officers, second guessing is a force to be reckoned with because of the gravity of some police actions. Officers can "do everything right" and outcomes can still be tragic. Second guessing in such situations can be psychologically punishing and career ending.

Single-exposure (One-shot) Learning

Single-exposure or "one-shot" learning has nothing to do with firearms or bullets. One-shot learning is a type of the classical conditioning paradigm made famous by Ivan Pavlov (1927). Simply stated, Pavlov demonstrated that an *unconditioned stimulus* could produce an *unconditioned response*. He showed this by administering meat powder to the mouth of dogs and measuring their salivation. Theoretically, the salivation upon the introduction of the meat powder did not represent learning. Salivation occurred as a natural response to the meat powder. In classical conditioning terms, the meat powder was the unconditioned stimulus, the salivation the unconditioned response. When Pavlov paired the introduction of meat powder with the sound of a metronome, the meat powder continued to produce salivation in the dogs. After a series of meat powder/metronome pairings, the sound of the metronome alone produced salivation. The sound of the metronome had become a *conditioned stimulus*, and the following salivation the *conditioned response*. The dogs had learned to salivate upon the sound of the metronome. Notice that the unconditioned response and the conditioned response are identical - salivation. The difference between the two responses is the stimulus that produced it.

One-shot learning is similar to the conditioning process observed in Pavlov's dogs with one significant difference, a series of parings is not necessary to produce learning. Instead, a single exposure to a particularly intense unconditioned stimulus can bring about a lifetime conditioned response. Often, the response is dysfunctional and unwanted. For example, consider the case of Mary G, a woman who was assaulted by a man with a beard. During the assault she experienced an overwhelming fear that she would be killed. She survived the assault and recovered from her injuries. The perpetrator was arrested, convicted, and imprisoned. However, from the night of the assault onward, Mary experienced intense fear whenever she saw a man with a beard. Mary's fear response (unconditioned at the time of the assault) had become conditioned to the previously neutral stimulus, *man-with-a-beard*. Beards had become a conditioned stimulus. Men wearing facial hair that approximated a beard produced varying intensities of fear for Mary; the actual response being dependent upon the degree of approximation. This is a process known as *generalization of conditioned stimuli*.

For police officers, one-shot learning works much the same. Following survival of a critical incident, officers can become conditioned to nearly anything, including the sight of police uniforms, police vehicles, certain odors, and the sound of police radio traffic. Conditioned fear or anxiety responses must be neutralized prior to an officer being returned to duty.

Unfortunately, historically, officers that suffered from undesirable conditioned responses managed them with alcohol, false bravado, or by simply gutting it out. Today, enlightened police agencies engage psychologists, other mental health professionals, and peer support teams to assist officers to disconnect dysfunctional conditioned responses from the conditioned stimuli resulting from critical incidents.

Surface Lesson-Deep Lesson

Related to conditioning and one-shot learning is *surface lesson - deep lesson*. Surface lessons are comprised of specific knowledge gained from a critical incident. To illustrate a surface lesson, consider a woman who decides to walk in front of a stationary, running, unoccupied motor vehicle. She does not think twice about her crossing, as she has safely done this several times before. However, on this day, as she is walking across the front of the car, something unusual occurs and the car lurches forward. She is run over and pinned beneath the vehicle. She can barely breath. It is difficult to call for help. Eventually, a passerby hears her weakened cries for help. He calls emergency services. She is rescued but seriously injured. After several days in the hospital, she returns home. She suffers from a minor permanent disability but overall is feeling well. With the passage of some time, her life returns to near normal, with one significant exception. She now feels uneasy around automobiles. In fact, she feels uneasy most of the time. She understands feeling uneasy around automobiles. After all she was run over and nearly killed. She is aware that being around autos triggers thoughts and emotions associated with her near-death experience. But she has no idea why she feels uneasy almost all the time, even when sitting quietly at home.

Surface lesson: for certain she has learned that it is not always safe to walk around the front of a running, especially if unoccupied, automobile. This is a well learned lesson and similar behavior is not likely to be repeated.

Deep lesson: while surface lessons readily reveal themselves, deep lessons can be somewhat more difficult to discern. Deep lessons are often unconscious, affecting us in ways that lie outside of our awareness. But while deep lessons may be unconscious, they can be discovered and expressed. In the above case, the deep lesson might be something like "I thought that I was safe when I crossed in front of the car, I was wrong. I think I'm safe now, I could be wrong." This unconscious deep lesson will create and sustain a high level of stress - in preparation for some unanticipated event. It will drive feelings of uneasiness, fear, anxiety, and discomfort across many environments, even sitting quietly at home. But why does this happen? Likely because it is part of an ancient evolutionary brain process, deeply ingrained, that increases the readiness of response and thereby, increases the probability of survival. In other words, it is the brain's way to safeguard you against once again becoming a victim of unforeseen circumstances.

Depending upon the intensity, frequency, and duration of the discomfort associated with deep lessons, persons may find it difficult to ever feel safe.

Like one-shot learning and conditioned responses, troublesome deep lessons, like the one described above, must be disengaged from surface lessons in order to minimize their impact and influence. This is what needs to be accomplished for the woman in our scenario to once again feel safe.

The Walk and Talk

The physiology of the stress response prepares us to do something physical. Critical incidents involve stressors which initiate and maintain the stress response. This means that during a critical incident your body is in a perpetual physiological state of heightened stress arousal. The increased arousal inherent within the stress response helps us deal with the demands of the incident (the well-known "fight or flight").

Once the incident is over, the need for heightened arousal ends. Your body will eventually "reset" itself to more normal levels of functioning (now known to be assisted by endocannabinoids that influence cannabinoid receptors in the brain and throughout the body). Until this process is complete, you will continue to experience the effects of the stress response. You can help your body to restore system balance by engaging in the *walk and talk*. Walking and talking will reliably dissipate the physiological arousal associated with the stress response.

The walk and talk is an important peer support team member skill. Peer support team members are trained to walk and talk with officers experiencing heightened stress arousal.

Based upon what we know about the stress response, police officers should not be locked in the backseat of a patrol car or be left alone in small confined building spaces following involvement in a critical incident. Officers should be placed in a secure area, large enough to walk while they talk to persons with appropriate confidentiality protections.

The 2 and 2 – Stronger and Smarter, and Controlling One Part of the Brain with Another Part of the Brain

Accomplishing the *2 and 2* is a primary goal for recovery following a critical incident. The first 2 is "stronger and smarter." Stronger and smarter is a guiding principle. It serves as the most desirable outcome following a traumatic experience. After all, following traumatic exposure, would "weaker and traumatized" suffice? Stronger and smarter endorses the idea that surviving a traumatic experience should contribute to personal growth and wisdom. It is a conceptualization that helps to integrate the experience into our life and in some way profit from it.

To avoid lifetime traumatization and to become stronger and smarter, something positive must be found in every traumatic exposure. If you are traumatized by exposure a critical incident and something positive is not readily apparent, you must search the experience until something positive is found. This does not mean that you ever have to view the incident as positive, but only that you must find something positive within it. To assist in your search, you must open the experience. You must look at the big picture. To focus on the worst of the experience is to provide it with power. Looking at the entire incident provides balance. It provides a more accurate and realistic view so that positive recovery becomes possible. When searching for the positive, remember, at the very least, it is positive that you survived. But keep looking. You will find more.

The second 2 is "I know what this is. I know what to do about it." It is knowledge and skill that will help manage the nearly inevitable anxiety and strong emotion that follows most traumatic events. To manage anxiety, it works like this: (1) officers identify the items or circumstances that trigger anxiety when there is no actual danger (these are the conditioned stimuli responsible for triggering conditioned responses), (2) when anxiety is experienced in the absence of actual danger, officers engage previously learned coping and anxiety-reduction strategies, (3) the anxiety of the conditioned responses is thereby reduced.

Understanding the source of the anxiety and knowing how to reduce it is empowering and provides a degree of psychological security. Officers can now interpret such anxiety as discomfort, not danger, because they now realize that their experience of anxiety is not in response to a real threat. Instead, it is little more than a conditioned response originating from the historical traumatic incident. This knowledge helps to remove any sense of mystery and uncontrollability, sometimes expressed as "I don't understand it, I can't control it, it comes out of nowhere."

"Knowing what this is and knowing what to do about it" involves *controlling one part of the brain (emotional) with another part of the brain (thinking)*. The more the officer succeeds in reducing anxiety over time, the more effective the intervention becomes. "I know what this is. I know what to do about it" is a component of becoming "stronger and smarter." Together these features are the cornerstones of the 2 and 2.

Chronological History and Psychological History

Officers who have experienced critical events want to place the incident behind them and move on. The difficulty for many officers is that the incident continues to impact their lives in undesirable ways. This is because the incident, while in chronological history, is not yet in psychological history. The incident is in chronological history the instant that it is over. However, when thoughts and other stimuli associated with the incident evoke powerful traumatic and disabling responses following the incident, the incident is not in psychological history.

Placing the incident into psychological history involves disconnecting the memory of the incident from the undesirable and sometimes gut-wrenching emotional responses experienced during or immediately after the incident. When an incident is in psychological history, conditioned responses are minimized or eliminated entirely. And while thoughts of the incident may produce emotional responses, they will not be disabling. This allows the officer to move forward, no longer psychologically stuck in the incident.

A major component of critical incident recovery is placing the event into psychological history.

According to psychologist Albert Ellis, PhD (1913-2007), author of Rational-Emotive Behavioral Therapy (REBT) there are 12 primary irrational ideas that cause and sustain psychological difficulty. Irrational idea number 9 is presented here because of its relevance to "placing the event into psychological history" and as a reminder of what can be accomplished. *REBT Irrational Idea Number 9*: The idea that because something once strongly affected our life, it should indefinitely affect it - Instead of the idea that we can learn from our past experiences but not be overly-attached to or prejudiced by them.

Having the Right versus Is It Right

An issue that is especially relevant for police officers is *having the right* versus *is it right*. Police officers may find themselves in situations where they need to defend themselves with lethal force. In this defense, someone may die. Police officers know that they have the right to defend themselves and a duty to protect others. This is a legal matter and not overly difficult to sort out. But is it right to defend oneself or others if it means killing someone? This is a moral issue that should be considered by every police officer. It is best to think and feel through this issue before it is ever confronted in reality.

Option Funnel versus Threat Funnel

The idea of *option funnel versus threat funnel* helps officers to place critical events into perspective. When there are several options available for interacting with others, the threat to officers is usually low. As the number of options decreases, the threat to officers generally increases. Therefore, "options versus threat" is negatively correlated. At the bottom of the option funnel is self-defense. When self-defense is the only remaining option for officers, the threat level becomes incredibly high.

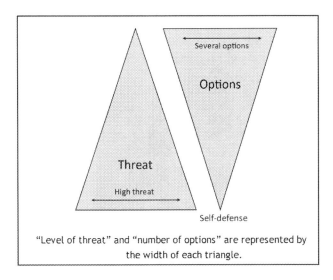

"Level of threat" and "number of options" are represented by the width of each triangle.

Police officers can be brought to the bottom of the option funnel very quickly. The case of Officer R provides an example of a situation wherein an officer was rapidly brought to the bottom of the option funnel and was left with no other option but self-defense: Officer R was one of several police officers dispatched to a reported incident of possible domestic violence. The informant, Julia, contacted police and reported that she was concerned for the safety of her daughter, Lisa. Lisa and Lisa's husband Roy, both in their 20s, had driven to Julia's location and left their child with her. They departed shortly thereafter. As this was unusual, Julia became worried about Roy's intentions. Julia provided police with a description and the license plate number of Lisa's car. Officers did not have many details, only that Roy had a violent history and that he had access to firearms.

In calls like this (*possible* domestic violence), the goal of police officers is to contact those involved, ascertain their welfare, and make certain that there have been no criminal violations. This was the intention of Officer R.

Officer R obtained the address associated with Lisa's vehicle license plate. He drove to the vicinity of the address in an attempt to locate the couple. After a short period of area surveillance, Officer R saw Lisa's vehicle approaching the couple's residence. He used the police radio to communicate his observation and coordinate the response of other police units. His plan was to wait until back-up units arrived, then stop the vehicle to ascertain Lisa's safety.

Although Officer R did not engage his vehicle's emergency lights, Lisa's vehicle suddenly stopped. Having little choice, and with back-up yet to arrive, Officer R maneuvered his police car behind Lisa's vehicle. The windows of Lisa's car were darkly tinted and Officer R could not see inside. He used the public address system of his police radio to advise Lisa to exit the vehicle. Her exit would help ensure her safety. The passenger door of the vehicle opened and a person stepped out. It was not Lisa. It was Roy. Roy turned clockwise and began walking toward Officer R.

By this time, Officer R had positioned himself in the "V" of his police vehicle. The V is the position behind the opened driver's door, looking across the hood of the vehicle. Due to the nature of the call and standard officer safety practices, Officer R had drawn his handgun. He began to shout commands to Roy. Because of the placement of the vehicles, Officer R did not immediately see the pistol-grip shotgun that Roy was carrying. As Roy continued walking toward Officer R, he raised the shotgun, pointed it at Officer R, and fired. Officer R returned fire. The first of Roy's shots imbedded buckshot into the grill area of Officer R's police car. Roy fired a second round which missed Officer R, partially due to Officer R's evasive movements.

During the seconds-long shootout, Officer R fired seven rounds. Roy was struck by two of them. Roy was stopped only five feet in front of Officer R's position. He died from his wounds. Officer R was uninjured. Sometime after the incident, Lisa's aunt, representing the whole of the family, wrote this letter to Officer R (reproduced as written, names changed to protect identity):

> Dear Officer R. First let me apologize for being so long writting this to you. I was out of town for awhile after it happened. I know you want to try to put all of this behind you & get on with your life. I am Lisa's aunt, her Mother is my Sister. Thank you for saving Lisa's life. We are sad that Roy (Rick as we knew him) had to die at such an early age & in this manner. But I am glad he is out of our lifes. We tried to help him by accepting him into the family. He really made Julia & her families life pretty much "hell" in the 2 years he & Lisa were married. He was a time bomb waiting to explode & He did. Justice was served & I praise & thank God that no one else was hurt or killed. I pray you can put all of this behind you. Please don't feel guilty in any way. You did what you had to do. Thank you. God bless you in your job & in your life as you serve your community in this way. Sincerely, Catherine Parker (reprinted with permission)

Lisa also wrote to Officer R. She wrote three pages of hand written text. Below are some excerpts. It began:

> Dear Officer R, sorry its taken me so long to get this to you but I haven't had much spare time . . . I really wanted you to know how sorry I am for everything you have been through . . . I have absolutely no hard feelings towards you . . . I'm so relieved you were not hurt or killed . . . I hope you will continue to be a police officer . . . The force needs all the good men & women it can get . . . Finally, I would like to thank you for saving my life & the life of the baby inside me. If Roy would have taken you out, he would have probably taken me next. Because of you I'm alive & the baby's holding on . . . There's no way I could ever really thank you enough. I guess this sums up what I needed you to know ... You ... will be in my thoughts & prayers for a long time to come. Sincerely, Lisa

Note: Persons unfamiliar with police tactical defense might ask, "How is it that Officer R fired seven rounds and only two struck the suspect?" A moving suspect with the intention to kill, advancing and firing a weapon represents one of the most difficult and deadly situations faced by police officers. Seconds or fractions of a second are all that is available for officers to defend themselves. In this case, there was no time for Officer R to acquire a "sight" target. Therefore, Officer R is point shooting. He is attempting to stop an advancing, moving threat by pointing and firing his weapon. This is different than sight shooting, where an officer has time to acquire a sight picture over the target sights of a weapon. Point shooting is often the only option available to police officers. It tends to become more accurate as the distance between the shooter and the target is reduced. Point shooting, a moving target, and physiological arousal due to the exigencies of the situation explain the results of officer R's shooting. The suspect was also point shooting.

Second Injury and Secondary (Vicarious) Trauma

The concept of second injury acknowledges the fact that persons can be traumatized or further traumatized by the way in which they are treated following a critical incident. In policing, treating an officer like a suspect, especially after an officer-involved shooting, will almost certainly create a second injury. Unless there are specific reasons to interact with an officer in this way, the last thing officers need following a fight for their lives is to be treated like a suspect. Police officer second injury can also be caused by insensitive press stories, undeserved criticism from city leaders and police department staff, political activists with an agenda, comments by spouses and family, statements of relatives of the suspect, and many other sources.

For police agencies, buffering their officers against second injury is best started long before officers "hit the streets." It should start with orientation training in the police department pre-service skills academy. It should continue through the careful design of protocols and policies which guide the actions of department members following critical events.

Second injury is different from secondary trauma. Secondary or *vicarious* trauma is the term used to describe the traumatization of those who are exposed to persons who have been traumatized. This includes those attempting to help traumatized persons by listening to their account of their experiences. Mental health professionals, peer support team members, police officers, and police family members are at risk for secondary trauma. The concept of secondary trauma recognizes the fact that interacting with traumatized persons can itself be traumatizing. Those exposed to traumatized persons must seek support and assistance for themselves in order to avoid or manage secondary trauma.

Pocket Responses

Following a critical incident, involved officers will almost certainly be approached by others who wish to know details about the incident. Providing an account of the incident over and over to curious acquaintances can in itself traumatize or at minimum, contribute to retraumatization. To avoid this without appearing discourteous, officers should consider using pocket responses. A pocket response is a previously thought-out reply (kept in your psychological pocket) to undesired or repeated inquiries. For instance, the response, "I'm ok. Thank you for asking. Good to see you" is a pocket response to a question about your welfare. A pocket response to the question, "What happened?" is "It was something. I'm fine. Thanks for asking." With pocket responses, officers do not have to think about what to say. They have a response ready to go. When a pocket response is used, stress and perhaps retraumatization (or simple annoyance) is avoided.

Any reply can be used as a pocket response. Officers should construct pocket responses that best fit their personalities and best meet their needs in various anticipated circumstances.

Officers can add an *oblique follow-up* to the pocket response. A useful oblique follow-up is saying something like "Got to go, take care" and walking away. By using a pocket response and an oblique follow-up, officers can readily address inquisitive persons and remove themselves from situations wherein they can be asked further undesired questions.

Administrative and Criminal Investigations

There are many circumstances that can cause a police agency to initiate an investigation of its police officers. Some have to do with suspected wrongdoing while others involve a matter of protocol. In officer-involved shootings and some other critical incidents, two investigations will be conducted: administrative and criminal.

An administrative investigation is conducted to determine if there has been a violation of agency policy. A criminal investigation is conducted to determine if there is probable cause to believe a crime has been committed.

Police officers are aware of these types of investigations. They also know that if they are involved in a use of force incident, these investigations will be initiated. This is a fact of police life. However, knowing this does not make these investigations stress free. It is always stressful to be the subject of investigation, even when officers know that there was no violation of either policy or law.

There are particular civil rights that accompany criminal investigations. Hollywood has made famous the U.S. Supreme Court ruling in *Miranda v. Arizona* (1966), which mandates that police read suspects their constitutional rights prior to a custodial interview: "You have the right to remain silent. Anything you say can and will be used against you in a court of law. You have the right to talk to an attorney and have an attorney present with you while you are being questioned. If you cannot afford to hire an attorney, one will be appointed to represent you before any questioning if you wish. You can decide at any time to exercise these rights and not answer any questions or make any statements."

Police officers, like others, have the full protection of the Constitution in criminal investigations; they have the right to remain silent, and so forth. This applies even when officers are being investigated by their own departments.

Administrative investigations are somewhat different. Under the U.S. Supreme Court ruling which arose out of *Garrity v. New Jersey* (1967), police employees do not have the right to remain silent. In fact, they must cooperate with an administrative investigation or face discipline, including termination. The following paragraph is part of an actual employee advisement (sometimes called a Garrity

Advisement) of a police agency. The advisement is read aloud and communicated in writing prior to interviewing an employee involved in an administrative investigation:

> You must cooperate with this investigation. Failure to cooperate will result in termination. Anything you say in this investigation cannot be used in any subsequent criminal investigation.

This paragraph highlights the relationship that exists between the two types of investigations. Information from a criminal investigation may be utilized in an administrative investigation, but information developed in an administrative investigation cannot be used in a criminal investigation. This is because in the administrative investigation, cooperation is mandatory (at risk of employment termination), while in a criminal investigation, police employees have the constitutional protections set forth in the Miranda advisement.

Trauma Intervention Program

The Trauma Intervention Program (TIP) is a critical incident protocol guide for police agencies. It consists of several recommended components and strategies designed to assist officers and their families with the physical, emotional, and psychological aftermath of a critical incident.

The Trauma Intervention Program works best for officers when certain precursors have been completed. These are: (1) comprehensive pre-hire psychological assessment, (2) stress inoculation and trauma management training in the pre-service skills academy, (3) participation in the PATROL program during field training, and (4) involvement of spouse/family in agency familiarization and specialized education.

The Trauma Intervention Program: (1) has some elements that are implemented simultaneously and some elements that are implemented sequentially, (2) is flexible and may be modified to meet the needs of any agency, (3) may be modified to fit within available resources, (4) incorporates a police psychologist and a properly supervised peer support team, and (5) may be adjusted to accommodate circumstances wherein the involved officer was injured.

The Trauma Intervention Program is presented in outline form with elaborative information in italics.

Trauma Intervention Program

Precursor Programs—Pre-hire psychological assessment, pre-service skills academy training, PATROL, and spouse/family education.

1. *On-scene support*—provided by the police psychologist and the peer support team. *On-scene support begins with the police psychologist and/or selected members of the peer support team. The officer becomes the client of the police psychologist so that confidentiality privileges are established. A psychologist/officer counseling support program is initiated.*

2. *Critical incident debriefing or small group/individual intervention*—as needed, provided by the police psychologist and peer support team. *Group debriefings are best utilized for critical incidents where a need for a group debriefing has been identified. Often, individual or small group interventions are adequate. The appropriate interventions are decided upon by the police psychologist with input from the peer support team. Members of the peer support team play a significant role in this part of the TIP. Officer participation in any group intervention is voluntary.*

3. *Considerations for intervention*—police psychologist. *The police psychologist initiates a counseling support program and continues to work with the officer and family. The following represent some of the issues which are considered. (Adjusted if the officer has been injured or is hospitalized):*
   - incident specifics and officer's contact information
   - criminal and administrative investigation issues
   - officer and officer's family security

- spouse/children/family considerations
- history—background and current status (bio-psycho-social)
- medical, medications, psychological, social-support
- support interventions: assessment and implementation
- supportive therapy (cognitive/emotional/EMDR, etc)
- memory—stress response and frequent outcome
- photographs, recordings (body, car, other sources) and reports—as appropriate
- legal considerations - involvement of attorneys
- resiliency and mindfulness
- educational and informative material—as appropriate

4. _Current work status: administrative leave or other_—modified work status in accordance with policy. _The police psychologist works with agency administrators to ensure that an agency contact person is appointed, that agency support continues, that any obligations that existed prior to the incident are managed in a satisfactory manner, and that the officer is not further traumatized._
   - department contact person
   - _ongoing_ department support
   - administrators, supervisors, and peers
   - officer and family security
   - court, training, meetings, and so on
   - police vehicle and equipment
   - modified-duty considerations

5. _Equipment and other stimulus reintroduction if necessary_— anxiety triggers (uniform, patrol vehicle, radio traffic, etc). _This component of the TIP is unnecessary in some cases and absolutely necessary in others. Much depends upon whether there has been an acquired undesirable conditioned response to a previously neutral stimulus._

6. _Incident site visit_—visit to location of incident from a psychological perspective. _Although the officer may have returned to the location of the incident for investigative_

purposes, this is insufficient to accomplish what is intended in the TIP site visit. TIP site visits are informative, experiential, sometimes emotional, and are used to help the officer further process the incident. They are also used to rule out the presence of anxiety triggers and other conditioned responses.

7. Firing range—shooting exposure for shooting incidents (non-qualification, qualification). If the critical incident involved the use of an officer's firearm, prior to returning to work, the officer shoots a non-qualifying course of fire for exposure (can be a loaner weapon). This is to ascertain whether the officer has any difficulties handling a firearm post-incident. The timing of this exposure is critical to the officer's recovery and is to be determined by the police psychologist. Later, prior to returning to duty, the officer shoots a qualifying course of fire. If the actual firearm used in the incident was taken for evidence, the officer shoots a qualifying course with the weapon once it is returned. The psychologist or a peer support team member may accompany the officer if requested or otherwise assessed appropriate.

8. Officer Wellness Assessment (OWA)—as a component of the psychologist's support intervention (clinical interview, mental status examination, symptom assessment, rule out clinically significant incident-related distress or impairment). The OWA is utilized to: (1) determine if the incident generated a stress disorder that would prevent the officer from safely returning to duty, (2) determine if the incident exacerbated a pre-existing condition that would prevent the officer from safely returning to duty, and (3) help determine optimal timing for the initiation of graded reentry.

9. Graded reentry—return-to-duty protocol. Graded reentry allows the involved officer to work with a selected partner and gradually resume the responsibilities of solo duty. See "Return-to-duty Protocol" below.

10. *Additional involvement of peer support team*—as needed. *The need for continued support from the peer support team is assessed and provided as requested or deemed appropriate. See #12.*

11. *Other considerations*—specific to the officer and incident. *This component of the TIP assesses, acknowledges, and addresses issues specific to the officer. Other persons or agencies may become involved if needed to address specific issues.*

12. *Follow through for the year of firsts*—first birthday, Christmas, and other meaningful dates, since the incident. *A member of the peer support team is chosen by the officer to provide support throughout the first year. This PST member helps the officer process any issues that might arise on holidays, the anniversary date of the incident, or any other date significant to the officer. Psychologist meetings as needed.*

Return-to-duty Protocol

Return-to-duty (RTD) protocols specify the graded reentry for police officers. They have varying lengths and components, depending upon the assessed circumstances. RTD protocols that consist of less than thirty-five hours are not recommended. In most cases, a thirty-five-hour RTD will accomplish the goals of the protocol. These include allowing a supported return to duty, re-exposure to the environment within which the incident occurred, anxiety management skills application, and checking for the presence of conditioned anxiety stimuli and responses.

Return-to-duty protocols make use of "buddy officers." It is recommended that agencies make every effort to allow officers undergoing a RTD to select their buddy officer(s) and to permit the buddy officer to participate even if it means a temporary transfer from another shift or division. This is because officers in a RTD must have a partner with whom they trust and work well together.

Buddy officers function solely as a working partner during the RTD. They have no training, supervisory, or evaluation responsibilities. Officers and buddy officers are briefed prior to the RTD being initiated. Buddy officers understand their role in the RTD and are part of the *safety net* of the protocol. The safety net also includes contact with the psychologist. The psychologist and returning officer arrange for several strategically placed telephone calls during the RTD. In this way, the officer's return to duty process can be monitored, assessed, and adjusted if needed.

When the RTD is completed, a follow up meeting with the psychologist is scheduled. The follow-up meeting allows for a brief assessment after the returning officer has worked solo for a period of time. Meetings beyond the scheduled follow up are arranged only if requested or deemed necessary. To view an actual Return-to-Duty protocol visit www.jackdigliani.com.

RTD options: If required, in-person meetings can replace some or all of the telephone calls between the returning officer and psychologist. During in-person meetings, the officer and psychologist discuss the return process and work together to overcome any difficulties experienced by the officer. Buddy officers may attend these meetings at the discretion of the returning officer.

In cases where officers cannot continue in the protocol due to overwhelming anxiety or other circumstances, the returning officer may be withdrawn from the RTD. The officer then receives additional counseling and preparation before re-entering a second RTD. If all attempts to return to duty are unsuccessful, officers and agencies must consider the likelihood of a total or occupational disability.

Critical Incident Information: Officers and Spouses

Officers sometimes wonder about how much incident information should be provided to their spouses. There is no single answer. Of the several factors that might be considered, two of the most important are (1) is the officer retraumatized by recounting the incident and (2) how much information is desired by the spouse.

For some officers, talking about their involvement in a critical incident is not problematic. They can recount the event and their experiences without much difficulty. For others, this is not possible. For them, each retelling of the incident is retraumatizing. In the latter cases, responding to a spouse's repeated request for more information may be detrimental to the officer's recovery.

Following a critical incident, some spouses want to know every detail. They want to see photographs, read case reports, listen to dispatch tapes, and so on. Other spouses desire or can tolerate only a broad description of the incident. For these spouses, providing more than general information may result in vicarious traumatization. This is especially true if the incident details involve blood and body damage.

To keep officers from being retraumatized and spouses from being vicariously traumatized, a healthy balance must be struck between how much information officers can provide without detriment to themselves, and how much information is desired by spouses.

A particularly difficult circumstance arises when the officer's need to talk about the incident exceeds the capacity of the spouse to listen. Capacity may be overwhelmed by the nature of the incident or the sheer number of times that the spouse has heard the story. Even if the officer is still struggling with the incident and feels better after talking about it, at some point most spouses will become *incident-info saturated*. They want to move past the event and get back to normal. For these spouses, like the spouses that cannot tolerate much incident detail, further exposure may result in vicarious traumatization.

Following a critical incident, things generally improve with time, but there may be no getting back to what was previously normal. Some traumatic events will change persons and relationships forever. The officer and spouse (the entire family) must find a new normal and live on from there. The new normal may be better than the old, but the opposite is also possible.

Some police officer relationships do not survive critical incidents. The incident either creates new and unbearable difficulties or intensifies previously existing problems. Some relationships collapse under the strain, and the couple separates. Other relationships appear to be strengthened by the pulling together of officer and spouse following the officer's involvement in a critical incident.

Suggestions for Supporting Officers Involved in Shootings and Other Trauma – Colorado and Other Jurisdictions

The following "Suggestions for Supporting Officers Involved in Shootings and Other Trauma" were written by Alexis Artwohl and published in her book, *DEADLY FORCE ENCOUNTERS,* co-authored by Loren Christensen (1997). My comments are represented in italics (added with permission). This information can be easily adapted to all jurisdictions.

1. Do initiate contact in the form of a phone call or note to let a traumatized officer know you are concerned and available for support or help (don't forget to acknowledge their significant others). In the case of a shooting, remember that the non-shooters who were at the scene are just as likely to be affected by the incident as the shooters. Remember that there are many other events besides shootings that traumatize cops. When in doubt, call. *Do not fall into the trap that "others will do it, so I don't have to." Your expression of support will be appreciated.*

2. Offer to stay with a traumatized officer/friend for the first day or two after the event if you know they live alone (or help find a mutual friend who can). Alternatively, you could offer for the officer to stay with you and your family. *This type of support for an officer living alone can be quite beneficial for the first few days following a critical incident.*

3. Let the traumatized officer decide how much contact he/she wants to have with you. They may be overwhelmed with phone calls and it may take a while for them to return your call. Also, they and their family may want some "down time" with minimal interruptions. *The police psychologist or Peer Support Team (PST) may advise through email or other appropriate means when involved officers need a communication hiatus.*

4. Don't ask for an account of the shooting, but let the traumatized officer know you are willing to listen to whatever they want to talk about. Officers may get tired of repeating the story and find "curiosity seekers" distasteful. Be mindful

that there is usually no legally privileged confidentiality for peer discussions. *Legal confidentiality privileges exist for particular relationships. These include licensed mental health professionals, attorneys, licensed or ordained clergy members, spouses, physicians, and some others. In Colorado and several other states, legislatures have passed laws that provide a privilege of confidentiality for specified peer support teams that meet statutory requirements. However, this state-based protection is limited and does not apply in criminal cases. Because of these limitations, peer support team members should avoid talking about the incident with involved officers. Peer support team members are ethically responsible to specify the limits of their confidentiality protections prior to engaging in any peer support interaction.*

5. Ask questions that show support and acceptance such as, "Is there anything I can do to help you or your family?" *In some cases where the pre-existing relationship will support it, just doing instead of asking is appropriate.*

6. Accept their reaction as normal for them and avoid suggesting how they "should" be feeling. Officers have a wide range of reactions to traumatic events. *If part of their reaction is thoughts or feelings of homicide or suicide, or should they appear to be experiencing a psychological crisis of any kind, contact the police psychologist, a member of the PST, or other appropriate resource immediately. Do not leave the officer alone.*

7. Remember that the key to helping a traumatized officer is nonjudgmental listening. *Just listening without trying to solve a problem or imposing your views can go a long way to support traumatized officers.*

8. Don't say, "I understand how you feel" unless you have been through the same experience. Do feel free to offer a BRIEF sharing of a similar experience you might have had to help them know they are not alone in how they feel. However, this is not the time to work on your own trauma issues with this person. If your friend's event triggers some of your own emotions, find someone else to talk to who can offer support to you. *It's worthwhile to keep in mind that*

individual officers will frequently perceive a critical incident in a somewhat unique way. However, there is enough overlap in our experiences to allow us to relate to the experience of involved officers. A good rule to follow: If the involved officer asks you a question about your experience or how you handled a past incident, respond fully to the question, then re-focus on the officer. If additional questions are asked, respond in a similar fashion . . . the officer is requesting more information from you. Your responses are likely to normalize the feelings, thoughts, and behaviors which may be new or strange to the officer. Keep your responses concise and talk in plain language. Do not get stuck in your own unresolved issues. The last thing an officer who has experienced a critical incident needs from you is to become your therapist.

9. Don't encourage the use of alcohol. It is best for officers to avoid all use of alcohol for a few weeks so they can process what has happened to them with a clear head and true feelings uncontaminated by drug use. *Remember, alcohol is a behavioral disinhibitor in small dosages and a central nervous system depressant in larger quantities. It is best not to be affected in either of these ways when attempting to process a critical event. Additionally, in order to avoid over stimulation and symptoms of withdrawal, caffeine intake should remain close to normal. Caffeine is a diuretic and vasoconstrictor. Its stimulant properties increase autonomic arousal and can cause a jittery feeling. Even small amounts of caffeine can interfere with sleep onset and maintenance in those not accustomed to it. Officers should stay within their normal range of caffeine consumption.*

10. Don't "congratulate" officers after shootings or call them names like "terminator" or otherwise joke around about the incident. Officers often have mixed feelings about deadly force encounters and find such comments offensive. *Mixed emotional responses can include feelings of elation that the officer survived the incident and performed well, while at the same time realizing that he or she had to injure or kill another person in order to survive. Mixed feelings, along*

with a heightened sense of danger, are two of the most common after-effects of shooting incidents.

11. Offer positive statements about the officers themselves, such as, "I'm glad you're O.K." *Critical incidents frequently bring forward emotions and thoughts not present in everyday living. Making positive statements demonstrates support and caring. This frequently helps officers deal with the issues inherent in critical and traumatic experiences.*

12. You are likely to find yourself second-guessing the shooting, but keep your comments to yourself. Critical comments have a way of coming back to the involved officer and it only does harm to the officer who is probably second-guessing him/herself and struggling to recover. Besides, most of the second-guessing is wrong anyway. *Keep in mind that the best anyone can do is to make reasonable decisions based upon perceptions and the information available at the time. No one really knows what it was like for a particular officer to be involved in a particular incident. Saying things such as "I would have done . . ." or "He (or she) should have . . ." is never helpful and almost always damaging.*

13. Encourage the officers to take care of themselves. Show support for such things as taking as much time off as they need to recover. Also encourage the officer to participate in debriefings and counseling. *Officers involved in shootings and other serious critical incidents are engaged in peer support, debriefings, and counseling as appropriate. Remember, employees may, at any time, seek confidential assistance from the police psychologist, the PST, or the Employee Assistance Program for any event or ongoing stressor. To access the names of PST members, contact appropriate agency sources.*

14. Gently confront them about negative behavioral and emotional changes you notice that persist for longer than one month. Encourage them to seek professional help. *A general rule of confrontation: confront to the degree that the underlying relationship will support. In other words, if done in a caring way, the closer your relationship with*

the person, the more you can confront them without jeopardizing the relationship or creating harm. If this rule is followed, the likelihood of the officer responding positively to any confrontation is maximized.

15. Don't refer to officers who are having emotional problems as "mentals" or other derogatory terms. Stigmatizing each other encourages officers to deny their psychological injuries and not to get the help they need. *Getting through critical incidents is difficult enough. We do not need to make it more difficult by derogatory labeling. This includes general attitudes communicated in everyday speech as well as specific comments following a particular event.*

16. Educate yourself about trauma reactions by reviewing written materials or consulting with someone who has familiarity with this topic. *The police psychologist and PST have informational materials that can assist you in learning more about trauma and traumatic responses. Contact any member of the PST to obtain this information.*

17. Officers want to return to normality as soon as possible. Don't pretend like the event didn't happen but do treat the traumatized officers like you always have. Don't avoid them, treat them as fragile, or otherwise drastically change your behavior with them. *It is normal for officers who have been through a critical incident to become a bit more sensitive to how others act toward them. This increased sensitivity is usually temporary. You can help the involved officer work through this sensitivity as well as larger aspects of the incident aftermath by just being yourself.*

18. Remember that in this case, your mother was right: If you don't have anything nice to say, don't say anything at all. *In the final analysis, we cannot know which side of a critical incident we will find ourselves: an officer looking to others for support or an officer attempting to provide support. Our strength and defense lie in how we treat each other.*

Police Shootings, Officer Safety, and Normalcy Bias

Many officers respond to the news of an officer-involved shooting by better utilizing well-known officer safety strategies. This is true even for officers who have become somewhat complacent. Unfortunately, this renewed effort for officer safety does not seem to last long. After some time without additional similar incidents, some officers again fall into unsafe "routine" police practices. These unsafe practices can be seen in lackadaisical responses to business alarms, the manner in which vehicle stops are conducted, positioning when talking to suspects, and so on.

Unsafe police practices may be influenced by the *normalcy bias*. While the normalcy bias is thought to be a major factor in why people do not heed warnings about impending danger, like approaching hurricanes, it can also play a role in police officer behavior. If business alarms are "normally" false, vehicle stops are "normally" without incident, and suspects are "normally" cooperative, officers may miss or not respond to signs of danger or impending aggression.

Like many things in policing, officers become "biased toward the normal" and/or complacent at their own risk.

Recovering from Traumatic Stress

Recovering from traumatic exposure takes time. Trauma causes a "mental injury" which requires time and support to heal (Zimbardo et al., 2012). The most difficult challenge for action-oriented officers is to be patient in recovery. If you are traumatized during a critical incident, accept your feelings even if they surprise you. Many officers have reported "crying like a baby" following shootings and other critical incidents. They describe this experience of strong emotion as *having lost it*. In fact, they have not lost anything. Instead, they have found something. They have found the emotion that underlies their traumatic experience.

When strong feelings surface, let them in, let them fade. Experience and explore the emotion. It is a natural part of being human and a natural part of emotional recovery. Imagine intense emotion as an ocean wave. It will come and it will go. Although it may feel overwhelming, you can manage it. You know what it is: it is the healthy expression of strong emotion. You know what to do about it: you breathe through it and implement self-care.

Keep in mind that physical symptoms sometime accompany strong emotion. These will normally subside as recovery continues. Additionally, remember that family members may not fully understand your experiences. Try not to become angry. They cannot know what it is like for you. Be kind to yourself. Be kind to those you care about. Assume an active role in your recovery. Seek assistance if you feel stuck. You do not have to go it alone.

PTSD and Total or Occupational Disability

The nature of policing places officers at greater risk for exposure to work-related critical incidents. If an officer develops PTSD following a critical incident, and the symptoms are severe and enduring, the officer may become *totally* or *occupationally* disabled.

Total disability occurs when the severity of the symptoms renders an officer incapable of engaging in any employment.

Occupational disability is different. When officers become occupationally disabled due to PTSD, they experience significant symptoms in the policing environment but remain relatively symptom free in other work environments. This prevents officers from returning to policework but able to work elsewhere.

Occupational disability sometimes occurs because traumatic experiences have the ability to "split" environments. That is, whereas officers were previously PTSD symptom free in the policing environment prior to the critical incident, following the incident, the policing environment triggers disabling PTSD symptoms. In this way, work environments have been split – split into those that produce symptoms and those that do not. However, these environments are not marked by distinct boundaries. They shade into one another. Therefore, the more similar any work environment is to the policing environment, the more likely it is that occupationally disabled officers will experience some degree of PTSD symptoms.

Positive Side of Critical Incidents

There is a positive side to critical incidents, a side that is seldom discussed. This aspect of critical incident survivorship was well-expressed by a British police officer that was involved in an incident several years ago. He was compelled to shoot a suspect that had taken a hostage. The suspect was killed. He knew he did was what necessary to protect the hostage but like many police officers, it took him some time to psychologically and emotionally process the event. He described part of his experience this way:

> "...I am also aware how having come through both the incident and the aftermath, that I changed in a positive way too. I believe that dealing with the incident made me more resilient, able to cope better with problems and difficulties (based on a mind-set that goes something like "If I can deal with all of that, I can deal with anything that life throws at me"). The incident also reinforced my personal levels of professionalism (and my expectations of it in others). Over time these positives have, I believe, come to the fore, whilst the negative reactions have faded." (personal email, May 19, 2015).

Resiliency

"Resilience is the process of adapting well in the face of adversity, trauma, tragedy, threats or significant sources of stress — such as family and relationship problems, serious health problems or workplace and financial stressors. It means "bouncing back" from difficult experiences. Research has shown that resilience is ordinary, not extraordinary. People commonly demonstrate resilience.

Being resilient does not mean that a person doesn't experience difficulty or distress. Emotional pain and sadness are common in people who have suffered major adversity or trauma in their lives. In fact, the road to resilience is likely to involve considerable emotional distress. Resilience is not a trait that people either have or do not have. It involves behaviors, thoughts and actions that can be learned and developed in anyone" (APA, n.d., 1).

Law Enforcement Critical Incident Handbook

The *Law Enforcement Critical Incident Handbook* is designed to provide concise and practical information to officers that have recently or historically experienced a critical incident. It includes much of the critical incident information discussed in this chapter. It can be kept as quick reference or sent to officers known to have experienced a critical incident. Handbook topics include:

- Critical and Traumatic Incidents
- Critical Incident Information
- Posttraumatic Stress, PTSD, and Acute Stress Disorder
- Traumatic Stress: Shock, Impact, and Recovery – Stronger and Smarter
- Option Funnel verses Threat Funnel
- Critical Incident Issues, Strategies, and Concepts
- Incident Debriefing Information
- Danger, Unavoidable Stressors, and Confrontation
- Suicide by Cop
- Witness to Suicide
- Police Spouse Anxiety and Critical Incidents
- 25 Suggestions and Considerations for Officers Involved in Critical Incidents
- Officers and Spouses: Critical Incident Information

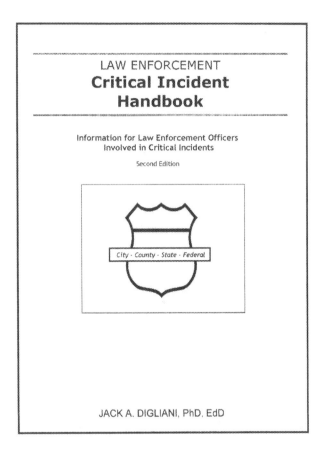

LAW ENFORCEMENT
Critical Incident Handbook

Information for Law Enforcement Officers
Involved in Critical Incidents

Second Edition

City - County - State - Federal

JACK A. DIGLIANI, PhD, EdD

To download a copy of the Law Enforcement Critical Incident Handbook at no cost visit www.jackdigliani.com.

Chapter 5

Critical Incident Group Debriefings

Critical Incident Group Debriefing is a short-term group intervention process that focuses on an immediate event.
-Crisis & Trauma Resource Institute

The efficacy of critical incident group debriefings has been the topic of much debate. For several years, conducting group debriefings after a critical incident has been the standard of intervention for emergency service personnel. However, recent research has provided some evidence that formal group debriefing may not always be helpful, and in some cases may be harmful.

The National Center for Posttraumatic Stress Disorder (NCPTSD) identified several types of incident debriefings. It further described the possible negative outcomes of formal critical incident stress debriefing (CISD). The NCPTSD makes the following distinctions:

- *"Operational debriefing* is a routine and formal part of an organizational response to a disaster. Mental-health workers acknowledge it as an appropriate practice that may help survivors acquire an overall sense of meaning and a degree of closure.
- *Psychological or stress debriefing* refers to a variety of practices for which there is little supportive empirical evidence. It is strongly suggested that psychological debriefing is not an appropriate mental-health intervention.
- *Critical Incident Stress Debriefing* (CISD) is a formalized, structured method whereby a group of rescue and response workers reviews the stressful experience of a disaster. CISD was developed to assist first responders such as fire and police personnel; it was not meant for the survivors of a disaster or their relatives. CISD was never intended as a substitute for therapy. It was designed to be delivered

in a group format and meant to be incorporated into a larger, multi-component crisis intervention system labeled Critical Incident Stress Management (CISM). CISM includes the following components: pre-crisis intervention; disaster or large-scale demobilization and informational briefings (town meetings); staff advisement; defusing; CISD; one-on-one crisis counseling or support; family crisis intervention and organizational consultation; follow-up and referral mechanisms for assessment and treatment, if necessary.

Currently, many mental-health workers consider some form of stress debriefing the standard of care following both natural (earthquakes) and human-caused (workplace shootings, bombings) stressful events. Indeed, the National Center for PTSD's Disaster Mental Health Guidebook (which is currently being revised) contains information on how to conduct debriefings. However, recent research indicates that psychological debriefing is not always an appropriate mental health intervention. Available evidence shows that, in some instances, it may increase traumatic stress or complicate recovery. Psychological debriefing is also inappropriate for acutely bereaved individuals. While operational debriefing is nearly always helpful (it involves clarifying events and providing education about normal responses and coping mechanisms), care must be taken before delivering more emotionally focused interventions.

A recent review of eight debriefing studies, all of which met rigorous criteria for being well-controlled, revealed no evidence that debriefing reduces the risk of PTSD, depression, or anxiety; nor were there any reductions in psychiatric symptoms across studies. Additionally, in two studies, one of which included long- term follow-up, some negative effects of CISD-type debriefings were reported relating to PTSD and other trauma-related symptoms. Therefore, debriefings as currently employed may be useful for low magnitude stress exposure and symptoms or for emergency care providers. However, the best studies suggest that for individuals with more severe exposure to trauma, and for those who are experiencing more severe reactions such as PTSD, debriefing is ineffective and possibly harmful" (2022).

Concerns with Critical Incident Stress Debriefing

The formal CISD process is comprised of several phases: introductory phase, fact phase, feeling phase, information phase, and reorganization phase (Mitchell, 1983). Some of the concerns that have evolved from outcome research of the CISD process as it is currently employed include:

1. Lack of choice—Many agencies mandate participation in debriefings.
2. Poor timing—CISD recommends the debriefing take place between forty-eight and seventy-two hours of the incident. This may be too soon for some persons.
3. Retraumatization—Persons may be retraumatized by the intensity of particular CISD phases, especially the fact and feeling phases.
4. Vicarious traumatization—Others in the debriefing that are not significantly traumatized may become traumatized by listening to the account of the incident.
5. Interference - CISD debriefing may interfere with the normal processing of a traumatic event.
6. Superficiality—CISD may not adequately address the more serious issues of those participating in the debriefing (Carr, 2003).

The Case for Critical Incident Stress Debriefing

Jeffrey Mitchell, president emeritus of the International Critical Incident Stress Foundation Inc., responded to reports that CISD may be ineffective or even harmful in an article entitled "Crisis Intervention and Critical Incident Stress Management: A defense of the field." Mitchell reported that thousands of clinicians have chosen to ignore the negative outcome research on CISD and continue to conduct debriefings. He identified numerous research studies that support the efficacy of CISD. In part IV of the article, he criticized the negative outcome research, indicating that: "A) No evidence has been found that any of the *negative outcome* researchers have been trained in the field of CISM or the CISD small group crisis intervention tool, B) Inappropriate target populations have been chosen by the researchers, C) Inappropriate interventions were provided under circumstances for which the CISD group process was never intended, D) The negative outcome researchers have engaged in a mixing and blending of terms to a point that it is difficult to tell what was done to who and by whom, E) Major flaws exist in all of the negative outcome studies, F) Randomized controlled trials are *not* the only way to measure outcomes, G) Inappropriate outcome measures were often applied, H) The "Type III" error was present in every case." (Type III error involves faulty model implementation). Mitchell summarized, "More research is clearly needed. But instead of trying to prove that something does or does not work, efforts should be made to more clearly understand what interventions should be implemented for which populations and at what times and by whom" (2004, 52).

There are efforts underway to determine just this. In the meantime, there has been a move toward a resiliency-based group intervention following critical events. One such approach has been described by Slawinski and Blythe (2004). It involves a service offering meeting, group resiliency briefing, individual resiliency briefing, follow up, and additional resources information. The service offering meeting (SOM) takes place within twenty-four to seventy-two hours after the incident. During the SOM, involved personnel are provided information and options for support. Although done in a group setting, the SOM is not a psychological debriefing. Following the SOM, for those that are interested, there is a *group resiliency briefing* (GRB). The GRB allows for group discussion of the incident, but the focus is on support and health. Graphic reenactments of the incident are avoided. People may share their reactions, but without reprocessing distressing facts. Crisis professionals facilitate the GRB and offer individual assistance to those wishing more support. *Individual resiliency briefings* (IRB) are provided as needed. The IRB is a personal meeting that takes place in a therapeutic setting. This allows for individual treatment without concerns of traumatizing others. *Follow up* is conducted at various intervals for up to one year. Information about *additional resources* is provided to assist involved persons to use and develop resiliency techniques.

Freezeframe Model for Group Support

The freezeframe facilitation model for group support (Digliani, 1992) was originally developed to provide an alternative to the prescribed phases of CISD. It was developed out of necessity. Its conception originated from a debriefing situation wherein the phases of CISD appeared difficult to utilize. Although freezeframe can be used to process facts and feelings, it is easily adaptable to a resiliency or strength-oriented group process. The freezeframe model for operational debriefing has proven its value on many occasions.

The freezeframe model utilizes an exploration within various "frames" of an incident. To use the freezeframe method, the primary facilitator requests information from the group. When the information indicates a point of significance, the facilitator freezes that frame and initiates processing. This sequence continues until all pertinent elements are processed. Freezeframe facilitation is especially useful when processing large groups, complex events, and incidents where several persons were involved.

Actual freezeframe processing: Freezeframe processing can be easily started by asking a question similar to "How did this call come in?" If through dispatch, the events in the dispatch center become the first frame to process. Once this frame is frozen, group information can be processed. The facilitator continues until all issues within the frame are processed. If discussion begins to drift out of the current frame, the facilitator refocuses the group on the frame being processed. Frames range from "narrow" to "wide" and will vary during the processing. When processing within a frame is completed, the facilitator offers a *brief* summary. The frame is now cleared, and the facilitator can engage the group to discover the next frame. The facilitator can make mental or discreetly written notes about significant issues that have surfaced. These are addressed when appropriate. This might be within a frame, between frames, or following the processing of all frames.

Timing is important when using the freezeframe. If the facilitator moves too fast through the frame, or from one frame to another, some group members may not have the opportunity to process appropriately. If the facilitator moves unnecessarily slow, the group will feel that the process is heavy and cumbersome.

Following a critical incident, if a group intervention is deemed appropriate, a skilled group facilitator can utilize freezeframe to disseminate information, normalize responses, and strengthen resiliency.

Group Debriefings and Police Agencies

Should police agencies continue to group-debrief following a critical incident? A good working hypothesis is *yes, with consideration.* Based on current research, police agencies should continue to engage in operational debriefings. These debriefings have anecdotal efficacy and lack any clear research-established negative outcomes. More formal psychological debriefings, such as CISD, in the manner traditionally practiced, should at least for now be used only with great caution. It is irresponsible to ignore the research indicating that CISD may cause harm to some persons. Resiliency and strength-based group interventions following a traumatic event represent a viable alternative to the criticisms and possible negative outcomes of traditional CISD. Until additional research helps to clarify the conflicting and confusing current state of affairs, police agencies should err on the side of safety.

Mandated or Voluntary Participation for Group Debriefings

In the early days of police psychology, mandating officers to attend a group debriefing was thought to remove any stigma associated with voluntary participation. In those days, there was much concern over the issue that officers would not be able to overcome their desire to appear tough, and thereby would not attend group debriefings. This concern is not near as great as it once was. Most police officers and other emergency services workers now see group debriefing as part of a positive supportive process. Many officers look forward to operational debriefings. They have heard or know from experience that such debriefings can be helpful.

With this perceptual change and the fact that several other types of support interventions are available for officers who might opt out of group debriefings, the mandatory provision for debriefing attendance has outlived its usefulness. In the final analysis, there is little to recommend mandated group debriefing attendance. Unless and until some notable efficacy is demonstrated, attendance for group debriefing should be voluntary.

Voluntary group-debriefing attendance does not conflict with the components of the Trauma Intervention Program (chapter 4). Officers directly involved in critical incidents and initiated into the TIP may attend or opt out of the incident group debriefing at their discretion.

Group Debriefing Confidentiality—Licensed Clinicians

Prior to the beginning of a critical incident group debriefing, clinicians must specify the confidentiality limitations of group discussion and clarify the responsibilities of group members. This is necessary because debriefings are a group therapy process. Defining group debriefings as therapy is contrary to the position of Mitchell and Everly (1995). However, without this, group debriefings would not be protected under many state confidentiality statutes.

The argument that clinician-facilitated critical incident debriefings are therapy and thereby protected by state confidentiality laws is supported in developing case law. The Iowa Supreme Court, in *City of Cedar Falls v. Cedar Falls Community School District* (2000) considered a motion for discovery filed by the school district. In its opinion the court stated, "The City resisted discovery and the (police) officers refused to answer questions concerning the sessions on grounds the information discussed at these 'critical incident stress debriefings' was protected by the mental health professional/patient privilege." The court held that "We agree with the City that the matters discussed at the debriefing sessions are privileged. The record indicates the sessions were conducted by a licensed mental health professional for purposes of assisting the officers to deal with the stress of the traumatic incident they had just experienced."

Group Debriefing Confidentiality and Peer Support Team Members

Appropriately trained peer support team members can facilitate group debriefings. Many emergency services personnel have been helped in operational debriefings facilitated by specifically trained and experienced members of a peer support team.

The situations in which peer support team members can effectively conduct group debriefings are those in which a critical incident does not generate a concern for the appropriateness of the actions of emergency services responders, for example, a particularly distressing suicide. Investigating such a tragic event may traumatize investigating officers and others, but there is little question as to the officers' actions relative to the incident itself. This is very different from an officer-involved shooting, where the issue of appropriate officer behavior might arise. In the latter category of cases, group debriefings, if appropriate, should be facilitated by licensed mental health professionals.

Various states have provided some confidentiality protections for peer support team members functioning within group settings. To view the *Peer Support Team Limits of Confidentiality - Debriefing Statement,* a document designed to be read by peer support team members prior to facilitation of a group debriefing, see the Law Enforcement Peer Support Team Manual (chapter 6). Although the Debriefing Statement is written in terms of Colorado law, it can be readily adapted to comply with the provisions of any state/federal statutes.

Chapter 6

Peer Support and Police Peer Support Teams

A police officer should never not have a place to go.
-FCPS peer support team motto,1986

Brief History of Peer Support

Peer support has a lengthy history. Eons before the arrival of the modern-day conception of peer support, members of various groups relied upon one another for support. It is easy to imagine ancient peoples sharing their thoughts and comforting one another when confronting challenges. Ancient writings and historical documents are filled with such accounts.

More recent times saw the development of organized peer support. Most of these peer groups were created to help those struggling with alcohol addiction. In America, the earliest of these groups included the Drunkards Club, established in the 1870s, and the United Order of Ex-Boozers, established in 1914. Several other "sobriety groups" were created during the late 1800s and early 1900s, but they soon vanished. A notable exception was Alcoholics Anonymous (AA), established in Boston in 1935. AA outlasted all of its predecessors and remains a force in the treatment of alcoholism and addiction to this day. While there were differences, such groups had two things in common. They recognized the supportive power of the peer group to facilitate desired change and they endorsed the *helper principle.*

The helper principle is the idea that one is helped by helping others. The helper principle has long been a part of the foundation of AA and has become an essential component of all similar support groups.

Peers and the Power of the Peer

Peers are persons that have something in common. They may have similar past experiences, similar current circumstances, or have a similar background or history. Just about any commonality will suffice to consider one person a peer of another. As individuals, such peers may be quite diverse, sharing only a single commonality.

Modern peer support groups operate under a mutually agreed upon set of rules. These rules are designed to make group meetings "safe." They often include requirements for anonymity, confidentiality, equality (no one is better than anyone else), non-judgmental listening, respectful verbal and nonverbal communication, and being open to feedback.

Being part of a support group and listening to successes and setbacks of others that have "walked a mile in your shoes" has proved to be inherently supportive. Being allowed to present personal experiences in a safe environment contributes to the benefit. At the least, being part of a support group encourages an understanding that one is not alone. This is the true "power" of peer support - this is the *power of the peer.*

Peer Support, Counseling, and Psychotherapy

Peer support differs from counseling and psychotherapy. Peer support is a non-professional interaction wherein one person attempts to support another person with whom they have something in common. Counseling and psychotherapy involve a professional relationship wherein licensed or otherwise qualified clinicians endeavor to help clients achieve identified goals through the application of psychological theory and therapeutic intervention.

Peer Support Interactions - Level I and Level II

When thinking about peer support, it is useful to differentiate two levels. Level I peer support can be thought of as traditional support. It is found in the everyday interactions of families, friends, co-workers, and others. Level I peer support is characterized by "family and friends talking" and often "giving advice." It can consist of a one-time discussion or long-term ongoing interactions, like those often seen in families. This level of peer support includes the *booze and buddies* (the *B and B*) strategy for support. In the police world, the B and B was popularized by former cop Joseph Wambaugh in his 1975 novel, *The Choirboys*. As you might guess, the B and B strategy of peer support has been known to produce less than desirable results. Clearly, the outcomes associated with any Level I peer support can vary widely, ranging from very effective to quite dysfunctional.

Level II peer support has much in common with Level I, but there are some important differences. Level II peer support:

(1) is provided by members of an agency-recognized peer support team functioning within applicable state statutes and/or department policy

(2) is provided by persons trained in the fundamentals of peer support

(3) interactions are characterized by elements of functional relationships which encourage exploration, empowerment, and positive change

(4) encourages independent decision making – advice giving is avoided

(5) is guided by ethical and conceptual parameters – this makes it different than just "family and friends talking,"

(6) has positive outcomes as its goal – this is not always the case in Level I peer support

(7) team members are clinically supervised by a licensed mental health professional – this provides a "ladder of escalation" if consultation or referral is needed

(8) while non-judgmental, includes a safety assessment – it has an evaluative component. The evaluative component of Level II peer support includes assessing for suicidality and issues that exceed the boundaries of peer support. If either are present, peer support team members are trained to act by providing information about available resources, making appropriate referrals, moving up the ladder of escalation, or initiating emergency interventions.

Peer support team members capable of providing Level II peer support may continue to engage in Level I peer support. However, the confidentiality privileges afforded to peer support team members during Level II peer support do not apply to Level I interactions.

Level II Peer Support

Like Level I peer support, Level II interactions can consist of a one-time contact or an ongoing supportive relationship. Often, persons will initiate contact with a peer support team member only to ask a question or to obtain some information. Other times, peer support is engaged regularly or intermittently over a period of time.

Level II peer support is frequently the only support service engaged by police officers, although it can be utilized in conjunction with a comprehensive professional counseling program.

The Early Days of Police Peer Support

In the early days of police peer support, informal support groups were the order of the day. These groups were comprised largely of officers who had been involved in shootings. The officers and the Level I peer support they provided, were not officially sanctioned by their departments. Instead, they came together and supported one another on their own, sometimes to the dismay of department administrators. It was group peer support in its most rudimentary form. Officers became members of these early support groups by default. That is, in order to become a member of this group, an officer had to have been involved in a shooting.

As time passed, and more became known about what was then called *trauma syndrome, post-shooting syndrome,* and *post-killing syndrome,* some police agencies came to rely upon officers who had survived armed confrontations to help other officers involved in similar incidents. Unfortunately, during this period, no one gave much thought to whether the officers being asked to help others had successfully processed their personal shooting experience.

Officers with a shooting incident in their history answered their department's call and did everything they could to support other officers involved in shootings. They did this without formal training, without regard to their recovery, and without a department structure to support them. These officers gave all they had to support other officers – sometimes at the expense of their psychological health. Many were traumatized or retraumatized by their efforts to help. This created the unfortunate situation wherein both officers, the supporter and the supported, became susceptible to psychological and emotional decompensation. It was not long after this realization that enlightened police agencies began to reach out to psychologists and other mental health professionals for assistance. Formal psychological support programs were designed. These programs often included the development of specially trained, clinically supervised agency peer support teams.

Peer Support Team Members

Police peer support team members may be sworn or civilian, employees or volunteers. Regardless of their status, peer support team members, like FTOs (chapter 2), should possess an aptitude for helping and three primary characteristics: interest, commitment, and credibility (ICC):

(1) A peer support team member must have an interest in helping others and in the fundamental principles of peer support. Without interest, even the most skilled peer support team members eventually fail. Team members lacking interest are perceived by peer support recipients as distant, inattentive, and uninvolved in the peer support process. Interest is a vital component of functional peer support.

(2) With interest, a peer support team member must have commitment; commitment to the ideals of peer support, commitment to the peer support team, and commitment to the recipients of peer support. This is expressed in their willingness to complete training, respond to requests for assistance at all hours, and to function in compliance with peer support team policies and guidelines.

(3) Peer support team members must be credible. Credibility is established by ethical personal and professional behavior over time. The perception of credibility has a great deal to do with reputation. For example, it is not likely that an officer with a reputation for gossiping would also be seen as a person who can keep confidences. Therefore, officers with such a reputation lack the credibility necessary to become members of a peer support

team. New employees should have at least two years of service before being considered for a peer support team. They will need at least this amount of time to become known in the department and to establish credibility.

Peer Support Team Structure

Police (and other) peer support teams can be organized in several ways. The *Team Coordinator* (TC) model utilizes an appointed peer support team coordinator. The team coordinator can assume any of the responsibilities specified within agency policy and the team's operational guidelines. The TC model is best applied in agencies where there is no or little funding. While not recommended, the team coordinator model is preferable to not having a peer support team. The most significant shortcoming of the TC model is that there is no program-endorsed licensed mental health professional providing clinical support for the members of the peer support team. Without such support, peer support team members are left to make decisions best made with professional consultation.

The *Clinical Advisor* (CA) peer support team model utilizes a licensed mental health professional to advise peer support team members. The clinical advisor contracts with the agency not only to provide consultation for peer support team members, but also to meet monthly with the team. Monthly meetings enhance team cohesion, provides for ongoing training, and a degree of clinical supervision. The CA model includes the appointment of a team coordinator and can be established with modest agency funding.

The preferred, albeit the most expensive peer support team model is the *Clinical Supervisor* (CS). The clinical supervisor of the agency's peer support team is a licensed mental health professional who is either an employee of the agency or a contracted professional. The clinical supervisor assumes all of the responsibilities of a clinical advisor and additionally provides direct counseling services to agency employees and their families. The actual services provided by the clinical supervisor are determined by either a job description or elements of a contract. In a fully developed CS model, the clinical supervisor assumes the position of agency psychologist (if licensed as a psychologist*). As with the CA model, the CS model utilizes a team coordinator. All models may include peer support team assistant coordinators.

*Colorado, like many other states, has four mental health therapist licenses: psychologist, social worker, professional counselor, and marriage and family therapist. All are title protected. A doctorate is required to be licensed as a psychologist. The other licenses require a master degree.

Peer Support Team Confidentiality - Colorado

In 2005, the Colorado legislature considered a bill to add a paragraph (m) to C.R.S. 13-90-107, *Who may not testify without consent*. This bill proposed the inclusion of "law enforcement or firefighter" peer support team members to those protected under the statute. The bill became law the same year (2005) and established Colorado as the fourth state to provide some confidentiality protection for specified peer support team members. It was amended in 2013 to include "emergency medical service provider or rescue unit peer support team member." In 2017, it was again amended to remove the restrictive "individual interactions" provision. In 2022, district attorney and public defender peer support teams were added. Specified peer support teams must meet several criteria to be afforded the privileges of C.R.S. 13-90-107(m) (2022).

Since the passage of Colorado's peer support team confidentiality statute, several additional states and the federal government have enacted similar legislation. The number of states providing confidentiality protections for specified peer support teams continues to increase.

Confidentiality Complexities - State and Federal

The confidentiality protections provided to peer support team members by state statute is limited. While peer support team confidentiality statutes differ from state to state, all have one similar provision – all exempt information pertaining to criminal acts from protection. This is the reason that peer support team members should support officers involved in use-of-force incidents *without discussing the incident*. Although the vast majority of such incidents do not result in officers being charged, if this were to happen, information discussed in peer support interactions is subject to disclosure (see "Frequently Asked Questions" #5).

While it is often helpful for involved officers to discuss their actions and experiences during and following a critical incident, such discussion is best left to state and federally protected confidential resources such as spouses, attorneys, psychologists, and clergy. Peer support team members must remain aware of their confidentiality limitations and not be lulled into a false sense of security by their peer support confidentiality statute.

State statute provisions for peer support team confidentiality do not commonly apply to the federal court system. In states with a peer support team confidentiality statute, the confidentiality privilege established by state statute may or may not apply in *civil* cases within the federal court system. Whether the state confidentiality privilege applies in a federal civil case depends upon the "rule of decision" as specified in the Federal Rules of Evidence - "The common law — as interpreted by United States courts in the light of reason and experience — governs a claim of privilege unless any of the following provides otherwise: the United States Constitution; a federal statute; or rules prescribed by the Supreme Court. But in a civil case, state law governs privilege regarding a claim or defense for which state law supplies the rule of decision" (Federal Rules of Evidence, 2017, Rule 501, *Privilege in General*). Currently, there is no U.S. Constitutional provision, federal statute, or U.S. Supreme Court ruling that provides confidentiality privileges within the federal court system for *non-federal* peer support teams.

In November 2021, Congress granted qualified *federal* law enforcement peer support teams specified confidentiality privileges within the federal court system with the enactment of the U.S. *Confidentiality Opportunities for Peer Support Counseling Act*, also referred to as the *COPS Counseling Act* (U.S. Public Law 117-60). Similar to existing state statutes, "an admission of criminal conduct" is exempt from the confidentiality privilege.

In a federal *criminal* court proceeding, the information exchanged in peer support interactions is subject to disclosure. This is important to remember because incidents involving municipal, county, and state law enforcement officers move to the federal court system when there is a federal criminal allegation of civil rights violation. These claims are normally pursued in federal court under Section 1983, Title 42, The Public Health and Welfare, United States Code. In such and similar actions, city, county, state, and federal peer support team members can be compelled to testify.

Peer Support Team Policy

Regardless of the peer support team model, agency peer support teams must be formalized in policy. Most policies establish the team and specify its parameters. If the agency also develops peer support team operational guidelines, it best serves if the policy adopts them. A model policy for law enforcement agencies is presented at www.jackdigliani.com. The model policy is written for the clinical supervisor model but it may be readily adapted to accommodate the clinical advisor or coordinator structure. Any agency wishing to establish a peer support team can readily edit the model policy to meet its needs.

Peer Support Team Operational Guidelines

While some agencies rely solely upon their peer support team policy to define team organization and responsibilities, team functioning can be enhanced by the addition of operational guidelines. Peer support team operational guidelines can: (1) include information not normally incorporated into policy, (2) include information thought too lengthy for policy, and (3) normally be edited much easier than policy. This allows swift adjustment to new or previously unseen team issues.

A model for peer support team operational guidelines is presented at www.jackdigliani.com. The model operational guidelines are considered a companion document to the model policy. Some information included in the model policy is intentionally duplicated in the model operational guidelines. This repetition is necessary because the peer support team policy and the peer support team operational guidelines must address several critical areas independently.

Peer Support Team Considerations

(1) Peer support teams may serve a single agency or multiple agencies. They may be comprised of personnel from one or several agencies, and include some members qualified to facilitate group critical incident debriefing.

(2) Peer support teams do not work in opposition to administrative staff. There is no "us versus them" mentality in agencies with high-functioning peer support teams. When properly initiated and maintained, peer support teams soon become an integral part of the agency. Once established, peer support teams become nearly indispensable. As one high-ranking officer of a sheriff's department put it, "What did we do before we had a peer support team?"

(3) Many police administrators do not recognize the need for peer support teams. This is because most agency employees have access to a jurisdiction-wide employee assistance program (EAP). Most EAPs are comprised of a number of mental health professionals who contract with the jurisdiction to provide counseling services. Usually, the number of employee visits to the EAP is limited, anywhere from six to twelve visits per year or issue. There are many excellent EAPs.

The availability of EAP counseling represents a significant advancement in the delivery of counseling services. However, for police officers, EAPs, although helpful, appear insufficient. They are helpful in that they are utilized by some officers who might not otherwise seek assistance. They are insufficient in that despite their availability, they do not and cannot meet the needs of many police officers.

(4) Peer support teams occupy a niche that cannot be readily filled by either an EAP or agency psychologist. If the agency wants to do the best it can to support its employees, a peer support team is necessary.

(5) High-functioning peer support teams do not rely upon the initiative of others to engage members of the peer support team. History has demonstrated that many employees who are open to and would benefit from peer support do not initiate peer support contacts. There are several reasons for this, ranging from lack of knowledge about the peer support team to an exaggerated sense

of self-reliance ("I don't ask for help from anybody"). Recognizing this, most peer support teams include a *reach-out* provision in their operational guidelines. This permits peer support team members to take the initiative in cases where it is thought that proactive peer support would be beneficial. Reach-outs must not be intrusive, embarrassing, or be conducted in such a manner that they create a problem.

(6) A peer support team is one of the most valued resources for a police psychologist. Many police psychologist counseling programs are designed to incorporate the efficacy of peer support.

Frequently Asked Questions

Being a member of a peer support team can be challenging. There are many questions that arise for peer support team members. The responses to the following frequently asked questions are applicable to members of peer support teams that have adopted the supervisor model and the basic tenants of the model policy and model operational guidelines.

As a peer support team member . . .

1. *Do I need to check with my clinical supervisor or team coordinator before I engage in a peer support interaction?* No. As a trained peer support team member, you may initiate or respond to a request for peer support. Independent peer support team member interactions, which are in compliance with law, the peer support team policy, and operational guidelines are appropriate and encouraged.

2. *How do I respond to a person who asks if peer support interactions are confidential?* When asked if peer support interactions are confidential, you should fully explain the limits of peer support team member confidentiality. Remember to include that PST information must be provided to your clinical supervisor. An unacceptable reply to this question would be some cursory remark such as "Yeah, they're confidential. There's a law . . ."

3. *What happens when the person I have been providing peer support waives the privilege of confidentiality?* When a person to whom you have been providing peer support waives confidentiality, you may communicate freely with those identified in the waiver. A person waives confidentiality for some reason, usually so that you can communicate with department staff, family members, and lawyers. Regardless of the person(s) or reason, under the waiver, information relating to the recipient of peer support as well as the peer support team member becomes available. A peer support team member should always remain aware that the information discussed and the actions taken within peer support interactions, including what the PST member said and did, may at some point become available to others. Additionally, keep in mind that the prohibition against revealing peer support information without consent (within confidentiality limits) restricts only the peer support team member. The person with whom you are involved in a peer support interaction is free to discuss any or all of your peer support interactions. The recipient of peer support does not need your permission to reveal any information you provided. This includes anything that you said and anything that you did, and this information can go *anywhere.* Bottom line, remain professional.

4. *Do confidentiality waivers have to be in writing?* Although there is a common practice that allows verbal confidentiality waivers in certain circumstances, it is best to have a written waiver before disclosing any protected information.

5. *What do I do if a person confesses to a crime or talks about criminal behavior during a peer support interaction?* To answer this question fully would involve addressing all possible combinations of several variables. For our purposes, suffice it to say that in this situation, peer support team members should contact their clinical supervisor immediately. Together, the appropriate action will be decided upon and implemented. Some of the variables that must be considered are: (1) whether you advised the person of the limits of peer support team member confidentiality (if yes, this likely means that the

information was communicated because the person wants to confront the consequences of behavior with your support), (2) you failed to advise the person of the confidentiality limitations (it may be that the person communicated this information with an expectation of confidentiality, which does not make it confidential), (3) the type of information presented, (4) whether you are a mandatory reporter of any information, including actual or suspected child abuse or neglect, danger for at-risk elders, or others, (5) whether you are a police officer, and (6) whether the information involves a crime within a domestic relationship. Regardless of the circumstances, you should (1) stop the conversation in this area immediately, (2) continue peer support, (3) advise the person (again if done previously) that information indicative of criminal conduct is not protected, (4) tell the person that it would be better if a confidential resource was contacted to discuss this information, (5) inform the person that you must contact your clinical supervisor, (6) contact your clinical supervisor, and (7) assist the person to contact a confidential resource (all referral resources have the responsibility to advise the person of any limitations of their confidentiality). _Discussion_: Stopping the conversation when a person begins to discuss information indicative of criminal conduct is not a peer support effort to assist the person to conceal or cover-up a crime. Quite the contrary, peer support interactions encourage honesty and the assumption of personal responsibility. Instead, stopping the conversation and following up as indicated recognizes the fact that you can better assist the person if you are not placed in a position where you might become a witness in a possible prosecution. As it is, you may be required to take action and/or testify based upon the information already presented. No matter what the specifics are in any case, if persons reveal information indicative of any criminal conduct, _do not leave them alone_, especially if the person is a police officer. Stay with the person until otherwise directed by your clinical supervisor. Peer support team members are committed to helping others; however, _peer support team members are not required to and do not jeopardize themselves professionally or ethically by concealing ongoing or past criminal activity._

6. *What do I say to an internal affairs investigator who asks me about my peer support conversations with an employee being investigated?* Most peer support team confidentiality statutes and the model policy prohibit a peer support team member from disclosing information in an administrative investigation without consent. Such protection is necessary for the proper functioning of a peer support team. If you are contacted by an administrative investigator and asked about your peer support interactions with an employee, you should politely remind the investigator that to respond to the inquiry would amount to a violation of statute or department policy. If the recipient of peer support wishes to waive confidentiality for the investigator, you may communicate freely. Administrative, and for that matter, criminal investigators should not be permitted to "fish" the peer support team in an effort to determine whether an employee has sought peer support and if so, what was discussed.

7. *What do I say to a criminal investigator who asks me about my peer support conversations with an employee being investigated?* Information indicative of criminal conduct revealed during peer support interactions is not protected. If you are approached by criminal investigators, advise them that you must contact your clinical supervisor. When contacted, together you will determine whether there was information indicative of criminal conduct. If it is determined that the recipient of peer support provided you with information indicative of criminal conduct, you must respond to the investigator as you would if you received this information in a non-peer support interaction. In order to avoid complications and undermining the credibility of the peer support team, you must remember to specify the confidentiality limits of peer support team members *prior* to beginning your peer support interactions.

8. *Am I covered by my agency's policy and operational guidelines if I am providing peer support to personnel from other agencies?* Yes, within the parameters of your agency policy. Under mutual aid policies and the model operational guidelines there are provisions for assisting other agencies. Your coverage is

dependent upon meeting and remaining within the criteria specified in your policy and operational guidelines.

9. *Should I keep records or notes in reference to my peer support interactions?* No. As long as you remember to bring your PST interactions under clinical supervision, there is no requirement or need to keep a record. Many persons would be reluctant to utilize peer support if they thought that peer support team members were maintaining a record of their interactions. It is acceptable to record the number of your peer support contacts and the amount of time that you spend in your peer support role. This is for statistical purposes only and it can be used to determine the activity and utilization of the peer support team. Some agencies require that this information be recorded and you can do so without concern.

10. *Why is clinical supervision necessary? It is not required by state statute.* Simply stated, clinical supervision is necessary to meet the "best practice" standard of peer support. Of the three discussed models for peer support team structure, the most professionally developed is the clinical supervisor. The clinical supervisor model provides for ongoing PST in-service training, immediate PST member consultation, professional support for PST members (*support for the supporters*), and creates a resource for PST referral. This best-practice model includes clinical supervision. Clinical supervision provides clinical oversight of PST interactions and thereby enhances the delivery of peer support services. When clinical supervision is required by an agency, it is because the agency has endorsed the value of clinical oversight. The model policy and guidelines establish peer support clinical supervision so that there is a ladder of escalation (PST members may move up a rung in the "ladder" and involve the psychologist in issues deemed beyond peer support). A peer support team member that has lost connection with the value of clinical supervision cannot continue with the PST. To do so would damage the team and worse, may harm those that the team is committed to supporting. Some states, including Colorado, require that eligible agencies develop written PST guidelines and

that PST members function within them in order for the statute to apply. Any PST interaction outside of the guidelines renders the statutory protections null and void. Therefore, if clinical supervision is specified in the PST guidelines, PST members must bring their PST interactions under supervision for statutory confidentiality protection. Bottom line: stay in compliance with your guidelines. Keep in mind that one PST member has the ability to defeat years of successful PST performance. *The reputation of a PST is truly this fragile.*

11. *What if I fail to bring a peer support interaction under clinical supervision?* This question pertains to peer support team members structured under a clinical supervisor, but it may also apply to peer support teams organized with a clinical advisor. An intentional violation of any of the primary obligations of team members as specified in the model operational guidelines is a serious matter. It is not difficult to keep your PST interactions under supervision. Failing to bring your peer support interactions under clinical supervision represents a serious breach of PST member ethical standards of conduct. In the event that such behavior is discovered, peer support team administrative censure, up to and including removal from the PST, is likely.

12. *What happens if I fail to act in compliance with the peer support team policy or operational guidelines?* An intentional act of non-compliance with the peer support team policy or operational guidelines is a serious breach of trust, ethics, and commitment. It is justification for removal from the peer support team. Unintentional non-compliance or well-intentioned errors can be evaluated on an individual basis. Remaining in compliance with your PST policy and guidelines is not difficult but it requires periodic review. You cannot act in compliance with them if you do not remember what they are. The PST policy and guidelines exist to protect peer support team members, the recipients of peer support, and to consistently provide the highest possible quality of peer support. Stay familiar with these documents.

Peer Support: Does it Work? Survey Project 2018

Peer support teams within law enforcement agencies have existed for decades. Although many law enforcement officers and police psychologists have advocated for peer support programs, there has been surprisingly little research demonstrating the efficacy of police peer support.

In 2018, to gather information about the use and outcome of agency peer support, employee experiences of the Larimer County Sheriff's Office (LCSO), Loveland Police Department (LPD), and Fort Collins Police Services (FCPS) (Colorado) were assessed utilizing the *Peer Support Team Utilization and Outcome Survey* (Digliani, 2017).

The LCSO, LPD, and FCPS Peer Support Teams

The peer support teams of LCSO, LPD, and FCPS are well established, similarly structured, and function under the oversight of a licensed mental health professional. Each member of the peer support teams was initially trained within the Police Peer Support Team Training program (Digliani, 1986-present).

Methodology: In-person distribution and collection

The applied in-person methodology for survey distribution and collection produced a combined-agency return of 644 surveys. This represented approximately 78% of the survey-eligible population. Of the 644 surveys collected, 631 were returned completed. The number of completed surveys represented close to 98% of surveys distributed and slightly over 76% of the survey-eligible population.

The rate of return and the resulting data is sufficiently robust to reasonably conclude that had all survey-eligible employees completed the survey, there would not be meaningful differences in outcome proportional values.

The extrapolation of survey results to law enforcement agencies with similarly trained and organized peer support teams can be made with some confidence. The extension of survey results to law enforcement agencies that maintain peer support teams with alternative training and structure, and to non-law enforcement first responder and other agencies, can only be done with confidence limitations.

Use of peer support

Nearly one-half of surveyed employees reported participation in peer support interactions. Of the 631 employees that completed the survey, 305 (48.3%) reported having used peer support.

Reasons for non-use of peer support

The most frequently identified reason for the non-use of peer support was "I have not had a need for peer support" (77.1%). This was followed by "I'm not the kind of person that asks for peer support from peer support team members" (13.7%). Several respondents cited both. A small percentage, 3.5%, reported "I don't know how to initiate peer support."

No meaningful associations were found between non-use of peer support and years of service. This suggests that years of service is less a factor in the utilization of peer support than the perceived need for it, and that personality and personal perceptions are a factor for some employees that choose not to engage peer support.

Survey findings

(1) Peer support is helpful for a remarkable majority of those that have used it. Nearly 9 out of 10 employees that reported peer support interactions stated that peer support was helpful to very helpful in addressing the issues discussed or managing the stress associated with the issues. Close to 8 out of 10 employees reported that they would seek peer support again in the event of future stressful circumstances. Nearly 9 out of 10 employees reported that they would recommend peer support to co-workers known to be dealing with stressful circumstances. Over one-half of those that participated in peer support reported that it had directly or indirectly helped them to better perform their job and/or improve their home life.

(2) Nearly 6 out of 10 employees that reported not having participated in peer support interactions stated that they would be likely to very likely to seek peer support should future stressful circumstances arise. This finding reflects the positive standing of the peer support teams within their agencies, even among those that reported not having used peer support.

(3) There is significant employee confidence in the confidentiality of peer support team interactions. This is likely the result of three factors: (I) agency peer support policy, peer support team operational guidelines, and statutory provisions for peer support team member confidentiality, (II) the consistent exemplary behavior of peer support team members and their adherence to the peer support team code of ethical conduct (Appendix A), and (III) the steadfast support of agency administrators and supervisors.

(4) Greater consistency is needed in the area of advising or reminding peer support recipients of the limits of peer support confidentiality before engaging in peer support. For their most recent peer support interaction, 23.8% of respondents reported that the peer support team member did not disclose or remind them of the limits of peer support confidentiality; 12.9% reported being uncertain if this information was provided...a total of over 36%. Disclosing or reviewing the limits of peer support confidentiality is an ethical obligation of all peer support team members wishing to do the best they can for recipients of peer support.

(5) The peer support teams have done well with reaching out to employees and offering peer support when appropriate. However, survey results revealed that about 2 in 10 employees reported that they had experienced work-related circumstances where they felt they should have been contacted by the peer support team and were not contacted. This information suggests that peer support teams may need to reexamine their "threshold" for peer support outreach. It is possible that some employees are more stressed by their involvement in particular events wherein neither the event nor their involvement would normally generate a peer support contact. It is also possible that the event never came to the attention of the peer support team or that individual employees, especially if on the "periphery" of an incident, were simply missed and not included in peer support efforts. Special attention in any threshold

and outreach reexamination should be given to civilian employees, particularly agency dispatchers, evidence and lab technicians, and records personnel.

Conclusions

This study supports the use and efficacy of police agency peer support. Peer support provided by trained and clinically supervised members of peer support teams has been shown to be a significant resource for those that use it. It has also been shown to be a significant potential resource for those that have not used it. Law enforcement agencies without a peer support team would be well advised to consider developing one.

Agency peer support programs have become an integral part of "best practices" for sustaining employee wellness. To help employees better manage the unavoidable stressors of policing, the cumulative effects of work-related stress, and the trauma frequently associated with law enforcement critical incidents, there is simply no substitute for a well-trained, appropriately structured, clinically supervised peer support team.

To view and download the complete 2018 Peer Support Team Utilization and Outcome Survey report visit www.jackdigliani.com.

Peer Support: Does it Work? Survey Project 2022

A follow up study using the *Peer Support Team Utilization and Outcome Survey* was initiated in late June and concluded mid-July 2022. The same three northern Colorado law enforcement agencies were surveyed using an electronic version of the survey.

Survey methodology 2018/2022

The 2018 survey utilized in-person distribution and collection. An inherent shortcoming of this methodology was that not all survey-eligible employees received a survey. This was because a number of employees were not readily available during the survey project.

In 2022, the survey was distributed to all survey-eligible employees. Each was sent a digital copy via their agency email.

Completion of the survey required that recipients open the email, click on the "begin survey" button, respond to survey questions, and click on the "done" button. This last action sent survey responses to data collection. Without it, survey responses were not recorded. Like the 2018 survey, completing the 2022 survey was anonymous and voluntary. Both projects relied upon the willingness of employees to complete the survey.

Survey completion and response rates

The 2022 project distributed 910 surveys to the three participating agencies; 265 were returned. Of these, 255 were returned completed. This represents an overall completed-survey return rate of 28.0%, a far cry from the almost 98% completed-survey return rate of the 2018 project. Why such a difference? Foremost, the methodology. It seems that employees were much more willing to return the survey when it was distributed and collected in-person. As to return rates, these projects clearly demonstrate the superiority of in-person survey distribution and collection over an electronic mail survey.

Historically, the return rates of electronically distributed surveys are notoriously low. They average about 33% (Lindemann, 2021). This makes the 2022 combined agency return rate close to but less than average.

While the combined-agency completed-survey return rate represented 28.0% of those that received the survey, the individual-agency completed-survey return rates varied from a high of 34.7% (148 respondents/426 recipients LCSO), a middle of 28.9% (46/159 LPD), and a low of 18.8% (61/325 FCPS). The reasons for these differences are unclear. Any attempt to specify them without further research is little more than speculation. Regardless, one thing is certain – a significant majority of employees that received the 2022 survey did not return it.

Of the 910 survey recipients, 263 did not open the survey email. Of the 647 recipients that opened the email, 279 (43.1%) clicked the "begin survey" button. Of these, 255 completed the survey, 39.4% of those that opened the email. Was it something about the survey that discouraged over 60% of those that opened the email from completing it? Not likely. The 2022 survey is the same survey that produced a near 98% completed-return rate in 2018. Was a program glitch responsible? Not likely, 255 surveys were successfully completed and returned. The reasons for the *opened-versus-completed* disparity remain unknown. What is known is that well over half of the recipients that opened the survey email did not complete the survey.

Completed-survey population composition

The 255 combined-agency employees that returned completed surveys were comprised of 172 (67.5%) sworn and 83 (32.5%) civilian personnel. Of the 83 civilian personnel, 23 (27.7%) were dispatchers/call takers. Years of service: 110 (43.1%) employees reported having over 10 years of service with their agency; 58 (22.7%) reported being employed for under 3 years.

Survey findings

Of the 255 combined-agency employees that completed the survey, 164 (64.3%) reported utilizing their peer support team. [48.3][1] Of these 164:

- 139 (84.8%) found peer support to be helpful to very helpful. [88.7]
- 109 (66.5%) were advised of peer support confidentiality limitations. [63.2]
- 132 (80.5%) would seek peer support in the future if needed. [76.4]
- 149 (90.9%) would recommend the peer support team to others. [89.8]
- 107 (65.2%) reported it helped them to better perform their job. [59.2]
- 83 (50.6%) reported it helped them improve home life.[2] [50.2]

Of the 255 combined-agency employees that completed the survey, 88 (34.5%) reported not having utilized their peer support team [51.7]; 3 were uncertain. Of the 91 (88+3) that reported not having utilized their peer support team or uncertain:

- 68 (74.7%) reported they had not had a need for peer support. [77.1]
- 29 (31.9%) reported that they are not the kind of person that asks for peer support from the peer support team. [13.7]
- 7 (7.7%) reported not knowing how to initiate peer support.[3] [3.5]
- 3 (3.3%) reported contacts with peer support team members but were uncertain if their contacts were peer support. [not assessed in 2018]
- 45 (49.5%) reported likely to very likely to seek peer support should stressful circumstances arise. [59.7%]

Of the 255 combined-agency employees that completed the survey:

- 174 (68.2%) reported being contacted and offered peer support by their peer support team. [60.7]
- 55 (21.6%) reported experiencing a work-related incident where they felt they should have been contacted by the peer support team and were not contacted. [20.3]
- 192 (75.3%) reported being confident to very confident in peer support team confidentiality. [76.8]
- 15 (5.9%) indicated they did not know enough about peer support team confidentiality to rate their confidence. [7.7]

1 Numbers in brackets are percentages of those responding to same item in the 2018 survey.
2 26 respondents cited both: "better perform the job" and "improve home life."
3 Total number of responses to first 3 items are greater than 91 due to several recipients selecting multiple options.

Conclusions

The combined and individual-agency completion rates were insufficient to confidently extrapolate survey results. Although the 2022 survey project provided reliable information about the experiences of those that completed surveys, there is no way to know or reasonably conclude that their responses reflect the sentiments of their agency.

A notable difference between the 2018 and 2022 survey projects was observed in the percentage of those that reported using peer support, 48.3% in 2018 compared to 64.3% in 2022. There is no way to know whether this result represents a true increase in the use of peer support or if it means that those who have used peer support were more likely to complete the 2022 survey. Nonetheless, several proportional values of the 2018 and 2022 survey were remarkably similar.

Law Enforcement Peer Support Team Manual

The Law Enforcement Peer Support Team Manual is available without cost at www.jackdigliani.com.

LAW ENFORCEMENT
Peer Support Team
MANUAL

Reference and Resource Manual
Edition 8.4

Law Enforcement Peer Support

Serve – Protect – Support – Surpass

JACK A. DIGLIANI, PhD, EdD

"One thing that is clear is that all discussion and research into improving and protecting the mental well-being of law enforcement officers constantly circles back to the importance of peer support and behavioral health partnerships" (Spence & Drake, 2021, 2).

Chapter 7

Police Marriage and Family

The secret of a happy marriage remains a secret.
-Henny Youngman

Whether or not you are inclined to agree with comedy legend Henny Youngman (1906-1998), most married people would agree that marriage is work. Marriage is work in the sense that when people choose to marry (or otherwise partner) they have to make accommodations and compromises for one another. However, good marriages are not *hard* work. They are not hard work because they are founded upon solid principles of positive interpersonal transaction. Good marriages, while not perfect, are loving, supportive, functional, and rewarding.

Marriage

There are many types of marriage. Social anthropologists have identified various marriage arrangements in various cultures throughout the world. These include polygamy-polygyny (one husband-more than one wife), polygamy-polyandry (one wife-more than one husband), group marriage (more than one husband-more than one wife), and monogamy (one husband-one wife). In America, monogamy is the civil and legal standard for marriage (Schultz & Lavenda, 2006). However, as in other parts of the world, alternative forms of marriage are known to exist within the United States. Polygamy-polygyny appears to be the most common.

Although many aspects of the following discussion apply to all intimate relationships, it is presented in terms of a male/female monogamous marriage. The term "spouse" is used to mean any intimate partner in a committed relationship.

Marriage Roman Style

In the Julian marriage laws of 18 BCE, No.120, *Men Must Marry*, Roman emperor Augustus Caesar (63 BCE-14 AD) declared, "If we could survive without a wife, citizens of Rome, all of us would do without that nuisance; but since nature has so decreed that we cannot manage comfortably with them, nor live in any way without them, we must plan for our lasting preservation rather than for our temporary pleasure" (Lefkowitz & Fant, n.d.,1). The first part of this sounds a bit like the modern expression "can't live with them, can't live without them" used by some men when discussing women. Can it be that not much has changed in over two thousand years? The second part was an attempt on the part of Augustus Caesar to increase the number of children born to citizens of Rome.

Hopefully, in the twenty-first century, men do not continue to think of marriage and having a wife in the same manner as the emperor!

Families

Married couples have at least three families: the *immediate family*, the *family of origin*, and the *extended family*. The immediate family is comprised of husbands, wives, and any children. The family of origin is the family from which one came, for example, a person's mother, father, and siblings. The extended family is comprised of all other relatives such as aunts, uncles, cousins, in-laws, and so forth.

Reconciling one's family of origin values and practices with the family of origin values and practices of a spouse is a primary task of married couples. Without some degree of reconciliation, differences in family of origin values and practices can negatively impact or even eventually destroy immediate family relationships.

Problems arise when one's values, loyalties, and so forth (often developed in the family of origin) conflict with those of the spouse. These conflicts frequently surface in marriage therapy. In the defense of their respective positions, spouses say things like, "I can't help it. It's how I was raised" "I can't disappoint my mother" or "I don't housework. It's women's work." Much of the work of marriage counseling involves helping the couple see that they are no longer bound by family-of-origin mandates. They can now decide for themselves how they will transact with one another.

Learning new ways to transact within the immediate family may require confronting members of the family of origin – quite the challenge. To better understand this, consider the following hypothetical "women's work" example. A man was taught by his father, who did not do housework, that housework is woman's work. Because of this, and being a male child in his family of origin, he did not do housework. Now, as a married man, he continues to follow this family-of-origin "rule" and refuses to help his wife with household chores. For him, it is all he knows. It does not matter that she works full time, cares for the kids, and manages the finances. Men do not do housework. For her, because she is so busy, she has little time to spend on housekeeping. She is exhausted and becomes frustrated by his complaints of an untidy house and his unwillingness to help. The conflict grows, they argue about it, but there is no resolution. They decide to enter therapy. Housekeeping becomes a point of discussion. Following discussion, and to his credit, he eventually overcomes this edict of his childhood. He becomes quite the helper around the house. His wife recognizes and appreciates the change. Their relationship improves. Both are happier. One day, his father is visiting and notices that his son clears the table and starts washing dishes. The father says "What are you doing? I've never washed dishes. What kind of man are you?" He is embarrassed, unsure how to respond.

What has happened? To provide much needed assistance to his wife and to improve his marriage relationship, the man has had to reconsider a family-of-origin rule. For this, he has been chastised by his father, the man that generated and enforced the rule. Now he must learn a new way to transact with his father. He must do so because he has decided against a family-of-origin rule that, for him, has outlived its usefulness. He has decided to improve his immediate-family relationship by "violating" a family-of-origin rule. In the end, he has come to realize that he can now decide for himself what is good for him and his family, that he is not bound by family-of-origin rules, and that he may need to re-define his relationship with his father.

Family Culture

Families are culturally diverse. They are multi-generational, evolve a system homeostasis, and have various structures, combinations, alliances, coalitions, rules, and myths. The homeostasis (steady-state) of a family system is reflected in how the family functions. It relates to the behavior of family members, their interactions, family values, and so on. Some families have a high-functioning homeostasis; others are quite dysfunctional. Regardless of the level of family functionality, all default to a homeostasis.

The homeostatic level of functionality can be altered by inputting energy into the family system. Such energy is represented by efforts to change unwanted or dysfunctional interactional patterns. If successful, family systems move from a default homeostatic position to a homeostatic system by design. But altering a family system is not easy. Theoretically, there are system forces that operate to maintain the family homeostasis, regardless of whether it is functional or dysfunctional (Lebow, 2005).

Family Rules, Myths, Alliances, Rituals, and Relationships

Rules are common in families. One of the most important rules is, "Who makes the rules?" The answer to this question defines the power broker(s) in families. Rules can be explicit (men do not do housework) or implicit (do not discuss feelings). Myths too are common. They are comprised of family beliefs that are exaggerated or mostly false. They get passed from one generation to another. Some of the more common family myths have to do with how the family conceptualizes itself, such as "We are special and better than others" and "We don't have problems." Rules and myths function to define and govern a family unit.

Alliances and coalitions describe the relationships of some family members. For instance, a father and daughter might be allied together against the wife-mother. Such an alliance would "triangulate" the family, where the father and daughter represent a coalition. This would permit joint action against the wife-mother. In this dysfunctional scenario, the daughter has been elevated to the level of a spouse, and the wife has been relegated to the position of a child. The position of the daughter is empowered by the father. This would make even appropriate mother-to-daughter guidance, influence, and discipline nearly impossible. In such cases, the parent-child structure of the family has been damaged, sometimes irrevocably.

Rituals are family events that serve to communicate or reinforce family bonds. Having a family dinner every evening serves as a bonding ritual for some families. Rituals can look a lot like rules, depending on how non-participation in the ritual is managed by the family. Rules, myths, alliances, and rituals are observed in all family systems. They may be functional or dysfunctional.

An interesting perspective on family rules, the parent-child relationship, and the structure of family was provided by actor Ricardo Montalban (1920-2009). In a column of syndicated writer Ann Landers circa 1975, he penned this letter to his son:

> Dear Son: As long as you live in this house you will follow the rules. When you have your own house, you can make your own rules. In this house we do not have a democracy. I did not campaign to be your father. You did not vote for me. We are father and son by the grace of God, and I accept that privilege and awesome responsibility. In accepting it, I have an obligation to perform the role of a father. I am not your pal. Our ages are too different. We can be many things, but we are not pals. I am your father. This is 100 times more than what a pal is. I am also your friend, but we are on entirely different levels. You will do, in this house, as I say, and you cannot question me because whatever I ask you to do is motivated by love. This will be hard for you to understand until you have a son of your own. Until then, trust me. Your father.

Premarital Mentality

Some persons approach marriage with the *safety valve* mentality. The safety valve mentality is "If I don't like marriage or if it doesn't work out, I can always get divorced." Is this a good thought for couples considering marriage? It implies a degree of uncertainty and a lack of commitment. It is very different from the *marriage commitment* mentality, "There is no issue that we cannot resolve." If a couple has this thought prior to marriage, and maintains the thought throughout their relationship, the probability of staying happily married is greatly enhanced. If a couple once had a commitment mentality and somehow lost it, it may not be too late for reclamation.

Marriage, Emotional Divorce, and Reclamation

Ever wonder why things seem to go so well at the beginning of a romantic relationship? In the beginning, couples enjoy each other's company, can talk to one another for hours, and miss each other when apart. For many, things go so well for so long that they are convinced they have found "the one," and if things go well enough for long enough, they declare their love and decide to marry. A storybook saga.

After marriage, there is the honeymoon period. And like the time before marriage, it seems to be characterized by the best behavior of each person. This period can last from months to years, and if lucky, for a lifetime. But this is not the case for all couples. For some, the storybook tale ends. They find themselves at odds much of the time. Dissatisfaction increases. As a result, they place greater demands on one another, become less flexible, and have less tolerance for differences. Any compromises made for disparities in family-of-origin values begin to fade. Anger and frustration increase. To avoid conflict, the couple begins to live more independently. As years pass, they spend less time together. Almost without noticing, they drift apart. As the drift increases, their emotional connection diminishes. They feel less connected to one another. If there is still sex, it is somewhat cold and mechanical. If there are children, they may still be good parents, but both recognize that something in their relationship has changed. They wonder "where has the love gone?"

Couples in this state sometimes describe their marriage as having become emotionally flat. In more serious cases, the couple becomes *emotionally divorced,* a condition wherein the couple remains married but there exists little or no emotional connection. Emotionally divorced couples will sometimes stay married to co-parent or because of finances or religious beliefs. Some emotionally divorced couples have gone so far as to set a date for actual divorce. It usually coincides with their youngest child's eighteenth birthday or graduation from high school.

Being married and emotionally divorced is a difficult way to spend years of life. It is like being suspended in marriage limbo - being married but not enjoying it, while not being ready or feeling able to move on. As a result, emotionally divorced couples live fairly separate lives and come together only when necessary. Most report being unhappy, but not knowing what to do about it. They sometimes say things like, "This is my life" and "Where would I go if I left?"

If none of this describes your relationship, congratulations. If it is descriptive of your relationship, and your marriage is not beyond saving, it is time to do something about it. It is time to reinvest in your relationship and rekindle your emotional connection. If you had a good marriage and somehow lost it, you can work with your spouse to recover it. Do this by looking back to the time when the relationship was good. How is the relationship different now? How is your behavior different now? This historical survey is the first step toward relationship recovery.

What can you do to reestablish the positive in your relationship? Try opening up dormant lines of communication, schedule a date night, show an interest in your spouse's activities, and do more things together. Seek professional help if necessary. Most importantly, as in all life-by-design strategies, *reclaim your marriage.*

Marriage and the Three Relationship Counseling Positions

When a couple initiates marriage counseling, they usually start in one of three positions: (1) we are committed to staying together, help us to make our relationship better, (2) we have decided to separate, help us to separate in the best way possible, or (3) we are unsure if we want to stay together, help us figure this out. The position of the couple often determines the course of therapy.

It is possible for persons in a couple to be in different positions. The most common is a combination of position one and three:

one person reports being committed to the relationship, while the other is unsure about continuing. In this mixed position, it is usually the emotional connection which has eroded for the person who is uncertain. They say things like, "I love him, but I'm not in love with him," "I haven't felt anything in this relationship for a long time" and "I'm just here to give it one more chance."

In counseling, some couples are able to find what they once had; a loving, functional relationship. This is because everything necessary to improve the marriage still resides within them. Other marriages have moved too far down the dysfunctional relationship track. Their relationship is a train wreck waiting to happen. Dysfunction or loss of emotional connection has gained too much momentum and cannot be stopped. In such cases, at least one of the couple will conclude that there is no option but to separate.

Functional Relationships

Functional relationships are characterized by a balance between relationship rights and relationship responsibilities. The importance of this balance cannot be overstated. It is best achieved by maintaining a solid relationship foundation. The stronger the foundation, the more balanced and functional the relationship. This is true not only of marriages but of all relationships. The Foundation Building Blocks of Functional Relationships describes the primary components of functional relationships.

Foundation Building Blocks of Functional Relationships

1. *Emotional connection.* All relationships are characterized by feelings or the emotional connections that exist between or among relationship members. Feelings frequently alter or influence perceptions and behaviors. Love is a common emotional connection. The emotional connection established between persons can alter or be altered by any or all of the other blocks.
2. *Trust.* Trust is a fundamental building block of all functional relationships. Trust is related to many other components

of functional relationships including fidelity, dependability, and honesty.

3. *Honesty.* Functional relationships are characterized by a high degree of caring honesty. There is a place for not hurting others feelings and not addressing every issue. However, consistent misrepresentation or avoidance to avoid short-term conflict often results in the establishment of negative outcomes such as long-term resentment and invalidation.

4. *Assumption of honesty.* With trust, we can assume honesty in others. A relationship in which honesty cannot be assumed is plagued with suspicion. Such relationships are characterized by trying to mind-read the "real" meaning of various interactions.

5. *Respect.* Respect is demonstrated in all areas of functional relationships—verbal communication, nonverbal behaviors, openness for discussion, conflict resolution, and so on. Without respect, relationships cannot remain functional and problem resolution communication is not possible.

6. *Tolerance.* The acceptance of personal differences and individual preferences, and having *patience* with one another are vital to keeping relationships working well. A degree of mutual tolerance facilitates forgiveness when there is perceived transgression, reduces points of conflict, and makes relationships more pleasant. Avoid becoming irritated by minor perceived transgressions and innocuous idiosyncrasies.

7. *Responsiveness.* Your responsiveness to others helps to validate their importance to you. It reflects your commitment and demonstrates relationship meaningfulness. Responsiveness is especially important in families and in hierarchical work relationships.

8. *Flexibility.* Personal rigidity frequently strains relationships and limits potential functional boundaries. Highly functional relationships are characterized by reasonable flexibility so that when stressed, they bend without breaking. Many things are not as serious as they first seem. Develop and maintain a sense of humor as part of flexibility.

9. *Communication.* Make it safe for communication. Speak and listen in a calm manner. Allow others to express thoughts and feelings without interruption. Stay mindful of the difference between *hearing* and *listening*. Safe and functional communication is characterized by listening.

10. *Commitment.* Long term functional relationships are characterized by commitment and a willingness to work on problems. This is accomplished by acceptance of personal responsibility, attempts to see things from other perspectives, conflict resolution, and the ability to move beyond perceived transgressions.

> Foundation reinforcers of functional relationships: (1) the assumption of good faith in your partner and (2) the absence of intentional harm.

In troubled relationships, the fundamental blocks have been damaged. Because the blocks are the foundation upon which the relationship is built, the damage in the foundation is reflected in the relationship. Persons will experience a degree of relationship discord commensurate to the amount of foundation damage. Conceptually, the relationship is supported by the foundation blocks, while the foundation blocks can be damaged or repaired by the relationship they support.

Most persons in troubled relationships do not seek help until the dysfunction reaches some crisis. By this time, the foundation may have sustained too much damage for the relationship to be repaired.

Special Status

All of us have *special status* people in our lives. In monogamous relationships the person with the highest special status is the spouse. Spouses are the only persons in the entire universe that hold the "spouse" status...special indeed. It is ok to do some things differently for spouses, like yielding an argument even if you do not normally do this with others. Doing this for your spouse recognizes their special status and increases the likelihood that they will do likewise sometime in the future. A useful way to remember this is, *you often get what you give.*

When talking or otherwise interacting with special status people (especially your spouse), do not forget with whom you are interacting. Remaining mindful that you talking to or interacting with a special person in your life will help you to moderate your behavior and maintain a "mindful of foundation blocks" (MOB) mentality. This will help you to remain calm, respectful, and measured in potentially emotionally charged situations. As a result, you will be able to better avoid behavior that you may later regret. For example, if you have ever found yourself apologizing following a conversation with someone you care about by saying something like "I'm sorry, I shouldn't have spoken to you that way" you did not maintain a MOB mentality during the conversation.

To maintain good relationships and to improve those that are strained, model the behavior that you wish in return. This is a contemporary way to restate the golden rule: treat others as you wish to be treated. Modeling appropriate behavior does not always bring about change in others but it will maintain the self-satisfaction that comes with acting within your personal values.

Sex and Intimacy: Intimacy Enhancing – Intimacy Distancing

Sex is not intimacy. Intimacy is not sex. Sex is a behavior. Intimacy is an emotion. People can have sex without intimacy and be intimate without sex. Intimacy involves a feeling of closeness and connection. The closer a person feels to another person, the more intimate the relationship. High functioning relationships are characterized by a high degree of intimacy. In high functioning marriages, this makes sex with intimacy possible—a very good situation.

Intimacy enhancing

Many behaviors are intimacy enhancing. Intimacy enhancing behaviors are those that encourage feelings of interpersonal connectedness. Intimacy enhancing behaviors are limited only by the imagination. A kiss on the cheek, a thoughtful gift, a well-timed wink, and establishing a date night are all examples of intimacy enhancing behaviors. Just about any gesture that expresses love, caring, or concern enhances intimacy.

Special occasions such as birthdays, anniversaries, Valentine's Day, and so on are ideal times for enhancing intimacy. Thoughtful gifts, activities, and cards on special occasions are often much appreciated and work to enhance intimacy. Forgetting or minimizing special occasions will often distance intimacy (in spite of your spouse's statements to the contrary). So, remain mindful of special dates. Also, do not underestimate the intimacy enhancing power of the occasional card or gift for no reason other than spousal appreciation (often a "sticky note" with a caring message will do). These seemingly simple things keep relationships fresh, interesting, and rewarding.

Intimacy distancing

Many behaviors are intimacy distancing. These behaviors are emotional wedges that force people apart. Yelling, criticizing, minimizing, threats, and physical violence are examples of intimacy distancing behaviors. Intimacy distancing behaviors are common in dysfunctional relationships. They comprise and describe the dysfunction in dysfunctional relationships.

Relationships can be improved by avoiding intimacy distancing behaviors and increasing the frequency of intimacy enhancing behaviors.

Relationships and Communication

Communication is vital to functional relationships. There are many thoughts about and conceptions of human communication. There are theories about verbal communication, nonverbal communication, mass communication, persuasion, the list goes on. Some theories are simple, others quite complex. A simple, easy to remember and useful way to think about verbal communication is the triad *content-message-delivery*.

Content-message-delivery

Within the content-message-delivery triad, content refers to the actual words chosen to send a message. The message is the meaning, while delivery refers to how the content is spoken. Delivery includes nonverbal behavior when the verbal communication is in-person. Nonverbal behavior during in-person communication helps to define or emphasize the message. For example, pointing a finger at someone while saying, "I'm talking to you" intensifies the message. Proxemics is also an important feature of nonverbal behavior. Proxemics have to do with interpersonal spacing. In American culture, body contact to about twelve inches distant is considered "intimate space." Any incursion into this area by those not part of an intimate relationship will increase discomfort, raise anxiety, and alter any accompanying verbal communication - a fact well-known by military boot camp drill instructors and experienced police interrogators. And while there are social circumstances where such intrusion is tolerated, like being in a crowded elevator, it nonetheless remains uncomfortable.

The content of verbal communication can impart various messages. This is because many words, phrases, and sentences have inherently differential meanings. These meanings are far from static. They change with time, contemporary usage, and underlying socio-cultural influences. For instance, the word "gay" meant something very different in the 1920's than it does today. And words like "bum" and "boot" mean very different things depending upon whether one is in the USA or the UK. Additionally, new words are constantly being invented. Words like "microplastics" and "antivaxxer" have only recently come into existence. Such words carry their own meaning and contribute to available verbal content.

A person can use the same content to send different messages. This is accomplished by altering the delivery. For instance, "That was smart!" said in an approving, enthusiastic, voice would send a complementary message, while the same sentence said in a criticizing, disapproving tone, would mean just the opposite.

A person can also use different content to send the same message. For example, when speaking to someone who has recently completed a difficult task, "I think you've done a great job" sends a similar message (one of approval) as "I'm impressed with your work and how well this turned out."

It is clear that delivery can alter the message of content. Most police officers are well familiar with this feature of communication. Many reported citizen complaints against police officers are founded in the grievance, "It's not what he said (content), it's how he said it" (delivery).

A fundamental component of delivery is *intensity*. Intensity can be thought of as ranging from a low of 1 to a high of 10. For most couples, verbal communication in excess of intensity level 5 brings the conversation out of "problem solving territory." In conversations with an intensity higher than 5, the focus usually changes from the issue being discussed to the issue of power. Once people start yelling at one another, the core of the exchange becomes an argument over who is dominant. When the argument changes to a fight for dominance, spouses are arguing for their place in the relationship. So, a complaint about not replacing the toothpaste cap after brushing becomes, "Who are you to tell me what to do!" Interestingly, once a conversation evolves into a power fight, the issue that initiated the discussion seldom gets addressed. It becomes lost in the greater argument.

Infrequently straying out of problem-solving territory will not likely permanently damage a relationship, but it can happen. It depends upon the couple and actual circumstances. In any event, moving out of problem-solving territory is almost certain to increase intimacy distance, even if only temporarily.

Ironically, some couples with a history of verbal "knock-down, drag out" yelling fights appear to do well together. Such relationships endure in spite of such exchanges, with both parties reporting being happy with one another. How is this possible? Like many things in a relationship, much seems to depend on the couple and the strength of their fundamental relationship blocks.

To keep discussions in problem solving territory, couples must monitor their verbal intensity. This involves remaining mindful of one's emotional state, vocal emphasis, and vocal volume.

Verbal intensity

It is not possible to demonstrate verbal intensity on the pages of a book, but varying communication intensities can also be expressed in writing. Written intensity involves text selection (content), semantics (meaning and message), letter case, fonts, underlining, and punctuation (delivery). For example, which sentence reads with greater intensity? "Leave me alone" or "LEAVE ME ALONE!" What about "Leave *me* alone" and "Leave me alone?" Most of us can literally "hear" the differences among these identical sentences. It is the same for verbal communication. Volume and emphasis can determine the message of identical content. Combine this with nonverbal behaviors and environmental context, and the framework for communication is complete.

Overall, and especially in marriage, communication improves when content aligns with the intended message and the intensity of the delivery is respectful and appropriate.

Message-to-Content

A dysfunctional content-message-delivery communication pattern which can cause considerable distress for couples is the "message-to-content" transaction. This negative behavioral pattern involves using benign or even complimentary content, but delivering it in a way that sends an insulting or attacking message. Then, if the sender is confronted on the attacking nature of the message, the sender defends it by referring to the content. An example will help to illustrate this pattern: A husband walks into the couple's messy kitchen, looks around, and sarcastically says to his wife, "I see that you've been working on keeping the house clean." The wife, responding to the criticizing message sent by the sarcastic delivery, responds, "Stop picking on me! I'm doing the best I can. It wouldn't hurt you to help out more!" The husband, now reacting to his wife's challenge, takes on the innocent, good guy role. He responds, "What's wrong with you? All I said was that I saw that you've been working on the house. I was giving you a compliment! You must be crazy!"

The message-to-content pattern of communication is very destructive, especially when engaged repetitively. In its severe form it is a type of *gaslighting,* a kind of psychological abuse that attempts to undermine another's perception of reality. The message-to-content pattern is an intimacy-distancing behavior which damages several blocks of the couple's relationship foundation.

But what if in the example above, the husband was actually trying to give his wife a compliment? After all, isn't it possible that his good intention might have been misinterpreted? Of course this is possible. However, if it were true, the husband would not have been sarcastic in his delivery. The delivery of the content would have been different, appreciative.

The Communication Imperative

In communication, the possibility of being misunderstood is ever present. This is because communication is transactional. This means that the message you intend to send may not be the message received by the listener. Likewise, any message you receive, may not be that intended by the sender. It is the message received, as interpreted, that will determine or influence your response. It is this imperfection in communication that makes feedback so important. Feedback, in the form of communication clarification, is sometimes necessary to avoid misunderstandings and improve communication accuracy.

To avoid miscommunication, you should remember the communication imperative: *a person will respond to the message received and not necessarily the message you intended to send.* This is also true for you. You will respond to the message you receive and not necessarily the message intended by the sender. If you are unclear about the message you received, or if it is upsetting or seemingly unjustified, you can ask the sender to clarify the meaning.

To improve communication, and thereby improve the baseline of any relationship, think about speaking in suggestions, proposals, and preferences. For instance, which would you rather hear, "We're staying in tonight because I'm tired." or "I'm a little tired tonight. What do you think about staying in?" The first sentence uses content that can be perceived as domineering and controlling. If the listener is sensitive to these issues, this sentence will trigger an argument or result in quiet resentment. The latter sentences are more likely to be received non-defensively, regardless of whether the listener is sensitive to being ordered about. Instead, the content of the latter sentences validates the listener as a factor in decision making. From this point, the couple can negotiate the evening's activities.

Negotiation, Bad Behavior, and Intimacy

A word about negotiation. If during negotiation you agree to something, you forfeit your right to complain about it later. The time to argue and complain is during the negotiation, not afterward. Once you agree to something, stand by your agreement. Do not punish others by agreeing to do something, such as going out for dinner when you wanted to stay home, and during dinner do little more than "display attitude" and act badly. Such poor behavior reduces or eliminates the intimacy-enhancing value of doing something nice for someone else, especially if the "someone else" is your spouse. Acting badly after agreeing to something is not reflective of good faith negotiation. It is not standing by your agreement. Instead, it is part of a dysfunctional behavior pattern that increases intimacy distance.

The good news is that this intimacy distancing pattern can be easily avoided. Avoid this pattern by negotiating in good faith, agreeing to an option, and standing by your agreement. Doing this improves poor relationships and helps to sustain good ones. Another way of thinking about this is, once you agree to do something that is not your choice but is the preference of another, why not try to enjoy yourself and pick up a few intimacy-enhancing "kindness points." The payoff for you is two-fold: the relationship bond is strengthened and the other person will likely return the favor at some point in the future.

If all this seems too complicated, remember that good communication and intimacy-enhancing behavior may require a bit more energy than poor communication and intimacy-distancing behavior, at least at first. Once more functional patterns are established and gain habit-strength, it takes little energy to maintain them.

Interpersonal Behaviors and Communication

There are several distinct interpersonal behaviors that can impede good communication. These are best described as hijacking the conversation, dominating the conversation, simultaneous talking, talking over, formulating the response, intentional inattention, and the pause jump.

- *Hijacking the conversation* occurs when someone abruptly takes a discussion from the current topic to something about themselves. When a conversation is hijacked, the original discussion is lost. The hijacker continues talking and often goes on to dominate the conversation.
- *Dominating the conversation* is nearly continuous talking without regard for others. Although the person talking achieves expression, no one else is provided this opportunity. Dominating the conversation monopolizes the transaction, fatigues listeners, and shuts down conversation.
- In *simultaneous talking*, if everyone is talking, who is listening? Everyone is so concerned about making their point that there is no consideration for the views of others. Is this communication? Not really. It is more like a struggle to establish interaction dominance.
- *Talking over* is a singular form of simultaneous talking. It is the occasional cutting off the communication of another by interjecting your response over their communication. It does not matter if they are mid-sentence, just making a point, and so on. Talking over can be a feature of superior rank or dominance in a relationship. It invalidates the speaker and prevents a positive mutual exchange.
- *Formulating the response* is a communication pitfall. It is characterized by not listening. In the place of listening, the person is mentally formulating how to respond to make a point, regardless of the speaker's information. While formulating the response, vital pieces of the speaker's communication may be missed. This is because most of us cannot fully attend to another's communication while actively thinking about making our point.

- *Intentional inattention* is characterized by disinterest. Being disinterested in what a speaker is saying is not in itself dysfunctional. It only becomes dysfunctional when it is wielded as a weapon designed to shut down or discount another person. It does not allow another person to appropriately discuss a point or position with which you disagree. Intentional inattention is often reflected in nonverbal facial expressions. Observation of these expressions sometimes prompts the speaker to ask, "Are you listening to me?"
- The last of the communication-impeding interactions is the *pause jump*. The pause jump occurs when a listener perceives even the slightest pause in the communication of others as an opportunity to jump in. This often provokes the response, "I wasn't finished!" or worse, "You never let me finish talking." To avoid the pause jump, persons must realize that different communication styles are composed of different length pauses within verbal communication. Some communication styles maintain very brief pauses. When all parties are such communicators, this is not much of a concern. It can be annoying, but at least everyone is on the same hectic page. When persons differ in the duration of what they view as normal pauses, it can become a problem. The problems are often similar to those seen in talking over. Good listeners are patient and allow for variations of pauses during discussions.

Police Marriages

Many police marriages are highly functional. In these relationships, the couple works together in ways that support one another. Regardless of whether the officer is the husband, wife, or both are officers, straight or gay, married or living together, many officers report a high degree of satisfaction in their relationships. This is reflected in police officer marriage statistics.

The U.S. Department of Health and Human Services reports that on average, from 40 to 50 percent of first marriages end in divorce. Although some police marriages end in divorce, there is growing evidence that the divorce rate for police officers is similar to or maybe less than that for the general population. This is counter to the long-held belief that police officers experience a higher-than-average divorce rate.

In one study which compared the divorce rates of those in various occupations, several occupations had divorce rates higher than police officers. These included dancers, bartenders, massage workers, and telemarketers. Police officers, optometrists, clergy, and podiatrists, were characterized by lower-than-average divorce rates. The factor that emerged as the most significant influence on the probability of divorce was the state of residence (McCoy & Aamodt, 2009). It is likely that the higher-than-average divorce rates historically reported for police officers originated out of several poorly conducted studies and the occupational tales of the 1980s (Honig, 2007).

Police marriages have much in common with other marriages. When police marriages become troubled, they are troubled by the same issues present in many marriages. The usual suspects include the loss of emotional connection, money, sex, alcohol and drug use, child discipline, and infidelity.

Occasionally, occupational stressors will surface as the primary problem in police marriages. These stressors often involve the officer's work schedule, the officer's behavior at home (acting like a cop with family members—most family members do not like being treated as suspects), the officer prioritizing the job over family, and less commonly, having firearms in the house.

Rarely, spouses of officers are upset by the risks inherent in policing. This is because most police spouses manage any existing fear by trusting the officers' ability "to come home" after every shift. However, for a small number of spouses, the fear that the officer will be injured or killed on the job becomes unbearable. This sometimes occurs after the officer's involvement in a shooting or other life-threatening work-related incident. In extreme cases the spousal fear is transformed into an ultimatum "it's me or the job." In response, some officers will end their police career.

Environmental Stimulation, Work Stress, and the Police Family

The desire for, and tolerance of, environmental stimulation is relative. Some persons enjoy a great deal of environmental stimulation. Others find minimal outside stimulation desirable (a factor to be reckoned with in marriages where individual stimulation preferences are widely different). For most persons, there is a personal optimal range of stimulation. If they fall much below their optimum, they become bored and restless. If they are much above the optimum, they become overstimulated, overstressed, and irritable.

Work stress and the police family

Work can be stressful. Police officers (and others) should avoid returning home from work without any fuel in their *stressor management gas tank* (SMGT). The idea of SMGT helps us gauge the amount of coping energy available for continued stressor management following our work shift. With some practice, anyone can become adept at assessing after-work SMGT levels. The goal is to have enough after-work fuel in your SMGT so that you can appropriately cope with the stressors of home life. The hypothetical example of Officer D will help clarify the notion and usefulness of the SMGT concept.

Officer D has had a difficult workday. During his shift, he made two arrests, investigated five crime reports, investigated a vehicle accident, and wrote three traffic tickets. During one of the arrests, he was slightly injured. During another, the suspect spewed out insult after insult. One of the recipients of traffic tickets told him he should be out catching real criminals. One questioned why he was picking on the honest citizens who pay his salary. To top things off, his sergeant mentioned that a citizen had filed a complaint in reference to one of his traffic stops the week before...the driver did not like his "tone of voice" when, after issuing a citation, he closed the conversation with "have a nice day." As the day wore on, Officer D was becoming increasingly frustrated. He needed greater amounts of self-restraint to remain professional. By the end of his shift, Officer D had pretty much reached his limit. His coping energy, the energy needed to deal with others in a positive way, was nearly depleted. This meant that his SMGT was precariously low. He has been overstimulated. He has experienced too many demands in too short a period of time. There is little fuel remaining in his SMGT. By the end of his shift, he is a raw nerve, a powder keg ready to explode at the least of provocations. And now he is going home.

Once home, it would not take much to ignite family conflict. In fact, something as simple as his child asking him to play might do it. Imagine this. Officer D's child, happy to see her dad, asks him to play catch. Normally, this would not be a problem. However, in his current SMGT-depleted condition, where his toleration for additional demands is nearly zero, he snaps at her, "Not right now!" The child walks away disappointed and confused. At eight years old she cannot understand what she did to make daddy angry. Officer D's wife, having watched the exchange, yells at him, "What's wrong with you! Why are you treating her that way?" Officer D responds, "You don't know anything. Back off!" He stomps to the refrigerator, grabs a beer, and walks outside. This is not good, and the evening has just begun.

Fortunately for Officer D and his family, future similar scenarios are avoidable. In order to prevent similar future occurrences, Officer D needs to renegotiate his *internal* and *external* interface.

Internal and External Interface

The internal and external interface is a theoretical, but practical and useful way to think about ourselves and our environment. The internal interface represents the relationship that we have with ourselves. It is related to the ideas of self-concept, self-esteem, personal values, and self-control. The internal interface is made possible by the complexities of human consciousness. By renegotiating his internal interface, Officer D can learn to practice techniques and use strategies that help to prevent or manage stimulus overload (see next section). This will help maintain adequate SMGT levels.

In the event that internal interface strategies occasionally prove insufficient, he can renegotiate his external interface. The external interface is best described by how a person relates to everything outside of self, including other people. By renegotiating his external interface (altering the environment), he would have replenished his SMGT prior to arriving home.

Police officers, SMGT, and self-awareness

As a police officer, if you have had a stressful workday, your SMGT may be nearly depleted. You can learn to recognize low levels of coping energy by increasing your self-awareness. If you feel that you cannot handle much more without an angry outburst, you have little left in your SMGT. What should you do? You should engage internal and external interface management strategies. You should do this to keep from arriving home in a stressed out, no tolerance, state of mind.

Internal and External Interface Management

When you feel stressed out after a workday, and you recognize that you have little fuel in your SMGT, *do not go home,* at least not immediately. (1) Stop. Hang around the station for a few minutes. Practice relaxation breathing. Talk to friends. Talk about something other than police work. Calm yourself. Decompress. (2) Think about your family. Think about the fact that you will need to continue to cope with stressors when you get home. If you have children, keep in mind that they may be waiting for you...and happy to see you. Consider that when you get home, your spouse may need a break from the kids. This means that you may need to go from police officer to parent as soon as you arrive. (3) Think about all that is good in your life. By accessing these thoughts, you add some fuel to your SMGT. (4) On your way home, listen to some favorite music. Continue your relaxation breathing. Think about a recent pleasant family outing. (5) Stay out of the bars. When feeling burnt out after a work shift, spending time in a bar drinking before you go home is not a positive way to manage yourself. Worse than going home stressed is going home stressed and intoxicated. This is hardly a good way to improve family transactions. (6) Upon arrival home, *check yourself.* Checking yourself involves calming down and preparing yourself for family transactions. Tap into your replenished SMGT. It is now time to transition from police officer to partner and parent. (7) Refuse to allow the stressors of your workday to follow you home. Really, would you want the suspect that you arrested today to affect you in ways that cause you marital or family problems? You might as well bring the suspect home! We do not bring suspects home physically, and we cannot afford to bring them home psychologically. Keep the bad guys out of your head, out of your home, and out of your family. The same holds true for all work stressors. (8) At home, if needed, ask your family for a few minutes down time. Always follow up this request with something like, "I'll be back shortly. Then we can catch up on things." During your down time, recharge, then reengage. (9) Try to think outside yourself. You are an important figure in your family's life. It is important for your family to have you available. Having a family that is happy to see you after a work shift, even though it has the potential to contribute to stimuli saturation, is not a bad thing. (10) If you are a parent, *remember that your behavior today is creating your children's future childhood memories.* What kind of childhood memories would you like your adult children to have? Certainly, coming home from work and terrorizing the family is not one of them. *The worst of who we are should never be acted out against those whom we care for the most.*

Engagement—Disengagement

Related to optimal levels of environmental stimulation are the concepts of *engagement* and *disengagement*. These are useful ideas when trying to understand stimulation-based difficulties. Simply stated, when persons are overstimulated, they seek disengagement from environmental stimuli, including people. When understimulated, they seek to increase stimuli and engage others. On any given day, officers that have been overstimulated at work may return home to a spouse that has been understimulated (or vice versa). This creates a substrate for conflict. For example, after a stressful day, an officer might seek solitude at home. Meanwhile the spouse, being bored most of the day, might seek social contact and interaction once the officer arrives home. The worst cases of such a circumstance might end in heated exchanges such as "Talk to me!" (an attempt to engage) and "Get out of my face!" (an attempt to disengage).

Of course, most engagement/disengagement conflicts are not this severe; however, couples should be on guard for the difficulties that can arise out of engagement/disengagement conflicts. Because anyone can become overstimulated or understimulated, these situations can arise even when spouses are nearly identical in their overall preference for environmental stimulation.

Love Is Not Enough – Myths of Marriage

One of the myths of marriage is that love will keep the couple together. Love can keep a marriage together, but there are no guarantees.

Love can keep a marriage together even when the marriage becomes dangerous. Every police officer is familiar with the response of some battered women when asked, "Why do you stay with this guy?" She often replies, "Because I love him." This is usually followed up with something like "He's not always bad. He just loses his temper. He promised that he won't do it again." In seriously dysfunctional relationships, officers sometimes hear "It's my fault that he hits me."

In cases like this, there is always the question of whether the woman is truly speaking of love. It could be that she is unknowingly describing suppressed fear or emotional dependency. Regardless, couples like this are in need of immediate intervention. Left untreated, this kind of relationship represents a significant threat to the woman, and too many times ends in serious injury or death.

Associated with the myth of love keeping a marriage together is the myth that love will keep the couple happy. Love is not sufficient to create a happy marriage. Imagine being in love with a person that cannot be trusted. Happy? Not likely. To have a happy marriage, all of the relationship foundation blocks must be present. In happy marriages, each of the foundation blocks is strong and sturdy.

A third myth of marriage is that the other person will never leave. The fact is that anyone can treat another so badly for so long, that most persons will consider leaving. This marriage myth is founded within denial and narcissism.

A person that believes their spouse would never leave, despite chronic awful treatment, is convinced that the spouse is so in love or so dependent that the thought of leaving is not possible (denial). And even if the spouse thought about leaving, how could they leave a person as special as me? It just could not happen (narcissism).

Case in point: a police officer in a metro police department had engaged in numerous affairs during the past several years of his marriage. One of his affairs produced a child with a local prostitute for which he and his wife were paying child support. His wife begged him to stop the extramarital relationships. She had begged him for years. They entered marriage counseling on at least three separate occasions. On each occasion, the wife would tell him that she loved him and wanted the marriage to work. He would promise to be faithful. On each occasion, the officer terminated counseling after a few sessions, dismissing it as "not helpful."

Several months after the officer terminated their most recent marriage counseling, his wife discovered that he had begun a new affair. This time she had reached her limit. She contacted an attorney and filed for divorce. Upon learning this, the officer went into a psychological tailspin. His friends became so concerned for his welfare that they arranged for him to see the police department psychologist. In counseling, he said that he could not believe that she would actually leave. He asked, "What's going on? Why did she spring this on me? I had no warning!"

It got worse. The serving of the divorce papers functioned as a critical stimulus. This act punctured his wall of denial. It became clear to him that he could not undo or fix things this time. He had lost her. The divorce papers also stripped away his narcissistic defenses. He became very depressed and suicidal. He had to be relieved of duty. His firearms were collected and placed into lockdown due to concerns for his safety. Because of the severity of his depression, he was hospitalized. He did not reengage the department's psychological services.

Marriage, love, and separation

Some couples separate despite confessing their love for one another. When "loving" couples divorce, it is usually because of a violation of the marriage agreement. For many couples, infidelity is one such violation; bad behavior associated with alcohol or other drugs is another. Some couples separate due to the sheer exhaustion of trying to live together when significant personality or preference differences exist.

Police Couples Counseling

In counseling, wives of police officers often discuss their husband's at-home behavior in less than flattering terms. In these troubled marriages, officers are described as angry much of the time, over-controlling, suspicious, demanding, verbally abusive, impatient, and intimidating. Such descriptions frequently (not always) conflict with the work reputation of these officers. At work, they are known to be professional, competent, compassionate, caring, and kind. They exercise good judgment and authoritative discretion. They are respected and well-liked by their peers. They seldom receive citizen complaints. So how is it that very little of this behavior is seen at home? When asked this question, officers respond nearly universally, "There are consequences at work. I don't want to lose my job or get in trouble. I want to get promoted. If I feel angry or frustrated at work, I handle it. I want to look good. Work is work. When I get home, I want to be myself. I don't want to have to watch how I act."

These officers are describing *role driven* behavior. The role is *police officer,* and the behavior is that which they see as appropriate for the role. This way of thinking is not in itself dysfunctional. All of us alter our behavior to some degree when acting in particular roles. However, within the officers' responses, there are three interesting and clinically significant underlying implications:

- The first implication is that the officer believes there are no or minor consequences for behavior at home ("There are consequences at work..."). No consequences? The officer is sitting in the office of the department psychologist due to relationship problems. He may be close to losing his family. *This is an extreme consequence.*
- The second implication is that the "real" person, when not being driven by the role of police officer, is not a very nice person ("When I get home, I want to be myself..."). Is this true? Can it be that the compassionate, understanding,

coping professional person seen at work is nothing more than a sham. No. *If the officer is a kind and compassionate person at work, he can be a kind and compassionate person at home.*

- The third implication is that stress coping strategies can stop at home ("If I feel angry or frustrated at work, I handle it...") *Where did police officers ever get the idea that stress coping strategies can stop at home?* This idea has no merit whatsoever. Officers must continue to utilize stress coping strategies at home. They must present their best thoughts, feelings, and behaviors to those they care about most.

For happier marriages, officers must avoid getting caught in the police role-driven behavior trap. It is an unfortunate reality that some officers treat peers, citizens, and even suspects kinder than they treat their spouses, children, family, and others. But it does not have to be this way.

The Popeye Philosophy and Prove You Love Me

There is another trap lying in wait for police (and other) couples. This is the *Popeye philosophy*. The Popeye philosophy is represented within the cartoon character's often stated declaration, "I yam what I yam." Well, everyone is what they are, and there is something to be said for simply accepting oneself. This is normal and can be healthy. However, if it gets carried to an extreme or is the cause of undesired outcomes, it becomes a rationalization for dysfunctional behavior. The Popeye philosophy can destroy efforts to improve behavior and it can destroy relationships. In essence, the extreme of the Popeye philosophy is another way of saying, "I'll behave as I want, and you'll just have to deal with it." This is seldom a good way to maintain a happy marriage.

Just how far should persons go in self-acceptance? It seems to depend upon values and goals. Sorting out what is appropriate for self-acceptance and what should be targeted for improvement is a major challenge to everyone living a life-by-design. When confronting this challenge, it is important to keep in mind that self-acceptance and self-improvement are not mutually exclusive. It is possible to accept yourself for who you are *and* target behaviors or traits for improvement. This helps to maintain self-esteem while continuing efforts for desired change. Remember, living with another person necessitates some change and compromise.

Frequently observed within the Popeye philosophy is the *prove you love me* (PYLM) transaction. PYLM transactions are characterized by behavior in which one member of the couple seems to consistently test the loyalty and love of the other. This is done by behaving badly and watching the other's response. This bad behavior can range from pouting to outright challenges, "If I'm so bad, why don't you leave!?" Following the bad behavior, the perpetrator waits and observes the other's reaction. If the other's response is satisfactory, like sufficiently consoling, submissive, apologetic, and so on, the goal has been accomplished. The other has "proved" their love and met the dysfunctional needs of the perpetrator. If the response is not satisfactory, the intensity of the PYLM transaction is increased until the desired "proof" is presented. PYLM transactions are most often motivated by an internal and sometimes repressed sense of relationship or personal insecurity. They also involve elements of dominance, manipulation, and control.

PYLM transactions undermine relationship authenticity and are therefore undesirable. They can be significantly destructive. The issues that underlie PYLM transactions can be serious and are best confronted directly, with professional assistance if necessary.

My Job—Your Job

In addition to the Popeye philosophy and PYLM, there is the *my job-your job* (MJYJ) transactional pattern. Officers must be aware of MJYJ because it can cause significant relationship difficulties. The MJYJ pattern is being played out when the officer diminishes or disregards the occupational stressors of the spouse, based on the intensity of the stressors inherent in policing. For officers and their wives, it goes something like this. The wife expresses a work frustration. The officer responds "I can't get excited because some janitor didn't clean your office. It's not a big thing. Do you realize what I deal with every day?"

Note that in the MJYJ pattern, the focus of conversation quickly changes. It starts with the wife expressing a work frustration and ends with the officer talking about his job. The conversation has been hijacked.

In the full expression of MJYJ, the officer continues to tell his wife of his work stressors. The wife, who came to her husband for discussion and support, must now comfort him. Her issue has been lost within the dysfunction of MJYJ.

The MJYJ comes in many forms but all minimize the importance of the issues presented by the spouse. It frequently leads to the spouse feeling invalidated and unimportant in the relationship. This is intimacy distancing and thereby dysfunctional. Many times, the MJYJ pattern is not overtly expressed. It can surface through nonverbal behaviors and a general dismissive attitude.

Although policing includes unavoidable stressors and personal risk, listening to and supporting spouses when they are upset or overwhelmed by their job stressors, including the stressors of being a stay-at-home spouse or parent, is a fundamental feature of functional police marriages.

Marriage, Housekeeping, and Sloppy Factor

A major complaint in some officers' marriages is housekeeping. This may sound like a minor problem, but it can have serious consequences. This problem often gets expressed in statements like "I work all day, and I have to come home to a pigsty." It is easy to see in statements like this that some relationship foundation damage has already occurred. This issue can be especially difficult when the spouse does not work outside the home. For the officer, there is often a sense that the other "does nothing all day."

Even in relationships where housekeeping is not a major problem, there exists the *sloppy factor*. Sloppy factors differ for most couples. Spouses with the least tolerance for sloppiness often find themselves doing most of the housework. This is because their tolerance for sloppiness is exceeded before it reaches critical levels for their spouses. Therefore, the spouse with the least tolerance for sloppiness is constantly picking up the house. This may occur with or without resentment. If there is no resentment, there is little problem. If there is resentment, more destructive patterns develop. These patterns are usually characterized by criticism and dysfunction. For example, a husband might say something like, "I can't take this mess." This normally leads the wife to respond, "I'll clean the house, but does it always have to be on your timetable?" Frustrated, the husband begins to clean. The wife, angered by her husband's cleaning because it implies that she is an inadequate housekeeper, yells, "I'm gonna do it. Leave it alone!" To which the husband responds, "When? I told you I can't take this mess! And I'm tired of you never doing anything around here!" (The exchange has now become the housekeeping argument.) The argument goes on until it reaches its predictable end. Exchanges like this are intimacy distancing and do nothing to solve the problem. In situations like this, couples improve their chances of successful resolution if they calmly discuss their complaints and avoid personal criticisms. Only then does the couple have an opportunity to productively address the issue and bring about a satisfactory outcome.

Protect Less-Communicate More

In highly functional relationships, there is less protecting and more communicating. So, *protect less-communicate more.* This is accomplished by a reduced effort to protect the relationship from disagreement and a greater willingness to calmly discuss sensitive topics. In combination, these factors increase the probability of successful problem resolution.

Protecting less and communicating more does not mean becoming hypersensitive (see Gottman's Marriage Tips, *Edit yourself*). In all relationships there is a place for letting things go and moving on. Do not get caught up in the minor and unimportant aspects of everyday living. It is not necessary to confront every issue, even if mildly annoying.

However, if an issue is important to you, you should open a discussion. This also applies to your spouse. If your spouse approaches you with something important to them, remain open minded. If the issue involves your behavior, it may be difficult to listen to how your actions hurt or otherwise affected them. Even if you disagree with what is presented, "That would not have bothered me" or "You're too sensitive" is seldom a good response. Instead, focus on listening. Work together to resolve the concern and to prevent similar future occurrences. Apologize—it should not be difficult to apologize to your special status person. In the end, make an effort to alter your behavior based on the discussion. This is a wonderful courtesy that can be extended. Remember, a courtesy rendered frequently results in a courtesy returned.

Protecting less and communicating more is also a functional way to avoid getting stuck in the *silent treatment.* The silent treatment is often used to punish someone or passively express anger. Becoming upset, taking a break, calming down, and remaining quiet for a short period of time will not normally damage a relationship. Especially if the couple reengages to discuss the issue. However, long periods of silence, days or weeks of silence, place the relationship on a very undesirable intimacy-distancing course. When there is an issue to address, it is better to appropriately confront it than to bury it in angry silence.

Intentional and Unintentional Harm

Some couples will intentionally harm one another. They do this psychologically, emotionally, and physically. They look to harm one another to get their way, punish, even a score, or teach a lesson. Such behaviors are hallmarks of marital discord and dysfunction.

Fortunately, most couples do not intentionally harm one another in any significant way, even when angry, frustrated, or disappointed. This is an important characteristic of most marriages, and it has clinical significance for couples in counseling. *If a couple would not intentionally harm one another, then it makes sense to believe that any harm experienced must be unintentional.* This realization can move a couple forward not only in counseling, but also in everyday life.

Unintentional harm

When considering unintentional harm, two points should always be kept in mind: (1) you do not have to intend harm to do harm (this is the very definition of unintentional harm), and (2) if you feel harmed, you should talk about it. Do not let the feeling of being harmed, even unintentionally, build resentment or lead you to unfounded conclusions.

If you feel harmed by the actions of your spouse, open a discussion. Choose where, when, and how you will initiate it. Confront the issue gently. It is reasonable to assume good faith and good intention on the part of your spouse. Therefore, inform them that you believe the harm was either unintentional or had a motivation other than harm (many jokes or attempts at humor can unintentionally harm others). If during the discussion it is determined that your spouse intended to harm you, this becomes the issue to be addressed.

If your spouse confronts you about something you did that harmed them, regardless of how you feel about it, remain open minded, listen non-defensively, and commit to make necessary changes. Do not make things worse by criticizing their perceptions or trying to justify your behavior.

In the end, if your partner informs you that your behavior has caused harm, it is incumbent upon you to stop or alter the harming behavior. This is true even if you had no intention to harm, were just "joking around," or think that your spouse is being too sensitive. *In functional relationships, one spouse does not continue to engage in behavior that they know harms the other.*

Playing the relationship card

One pattern of intentional harm involves consistently playing the *relationship card*. The relationship card is played when a person implicitly or explicitly threatens to leave the relationship unless the other does what is desired. It has several variations including, "If you don't do this, I'll leave" "If you don't like it, there's the door" and "I'm not sure I'm coming home tonight." The relationship card is used to manipulate, dominate, and control. It is intimacy distancing and risks the relationship.

Sometimes a spouse will "call" the player, "Leave if want, and don't come back." When this happens, player reactions can range widely. Much depends upon the circumstances and the persons involved.

The use of the relationship card is one level below the threatened use of violence, which is one level below actual violence to obtain what is desired in a relationship.

Playing the relationship card is categorically different from being dissatisfied with the relationship and honestly discussing the possibility of separation.

Complaint versus Criticism

Every person has a right to complain. Let's consider a husband and wife. If the husband says he will do something, and he fails to do it, the wife can register a complaint, "You said that you were going to get the car washed, and you didn't. I'm disappointed that the car is not clean." Complaints are valid and are factually based. They differ from criticism. Criticism attacks the person, "You said that you were going to get the car washed, and you didn't. You always let me down. You can't be trusted to do anything!"

Notice that in complaint, the wife (as complainant) identifies the issue then talks about herself, "*I'm* disappointed that the car is not clean." In criticism, the wife (as criticizer) identifies the issue then talks about her husband, "*You* always let me down. *You* can't be trusted to do anything."

The outcomes of complaint versus criticism are often very different. Registering a complaint increases the probability of continued discussion and positive resolution. Criticism frequently leads to defensive behavior and off-topic heated arguments (in this case, the exchange would likely move from getting the car washed to husband reliability).

Successfully addressing a complaint is intimacy enhancing and thereby strengthens the couple's bond. Criticism is intimacy distancing and will weaken it (Gottman & Silver, 1999).

The best way to avoid becoming a critic is to keep the difference between complaint and criticism in mind. The best way to avoid a complaint is to follow through on what you say.

Disrupting Dysfunctional Relationship Patterns

Dysfunctional relationship patterns are repetitive and predictable sequences of behavior which result in undesirable or negative outcomes. For instance, have you ever wondered why you *always* end up leaving the house in a rage when you and your spouse try to discuss a sensitive topic? If this or something similar describes your relationship, you are playing out a dysfunctional relationship pattern.

When couples are locked into dysfunctional patterns, they often see each other as adversaries. It feels as if it is husband against wife, wife against husband, partner against partner. This feeling energizes the dysfunction, contributes to its maintenance, and increases intimacy distance. Couples can better alter undesirable and predictable patterns if they think about teaming up against them – "Let's confront the pattern and not one another. It's us against the pattern and not us against each other." This approach allies the couple in an effort to disrupt and defeat the pattern. It works like this: whenever either perceives the startup or presence of the dysfunctional pattern (usually marked by increasing feelings of anger, frustration, resentment, not being heard, and so on), it is brought to the attention of the other. This communication acts as the signal for the couple to engage previously designed pattern-disruption strategies.

Pattern-disruption strategies include a myriad of interventions. They include taking a short break and reengaging, calming down and reengaging, lowering the intensity of the communication, and increasing attentive listening. In this way, the old pattern is disrupted and the probability for a better outcome is increased. When a couple thinks about attacking a dysfunctional pattern instead of each other, it changes the focus from *prevailing over each other* to *prevailing over the pattern.* As they succeed in their efforts, a new, more functional pattern is reinforced. With continued practice, the previously dysfunctional pattern is eventually replaced with a more functional and intimacy-enhancing interaction.

To increase the probability of dysfunctional pattern replacement, both persons must agree beforehand to engage coping responses upon the request of the other. This is sometimes initiated by the use of a prearranged codeword. Such agreement is necessary because as the dysfunctional pattern unfolds, its habit strength will naturally carry the couple to its undesirable outcome. In other words, *the pattern resists change!*

At first, a call for disrupting a dysfunctional pattern from one member of the couple may feel frustrating to the other. This is because the other person has grown accustomed to the pattern. Any deviation may feel uncomfortable.

To overcome this, the couple must trust one another to use dysfunctional pattern disruption coping strategies only when appropriate and not as a means to exert control, avoid unpleasant topics, or otherwise manipulate the other. The coping strategy of dysfunctional-pattern-disruption must not be transformed into another element of relationship dysfunction.

Sometimes the person who identifies the dysfunctional pattern and first calls for coping responses may feel weak, as if it is tantamount to backing down. That is, by refusing to fight or to participate in acting out the old pattern, it may feel that the other person has somehow "won." While the feeling of backing down in pattern disruption is common, it is not truly reflective of the circumstances. When dysfunctional patterns are interrupted and improved outcomes achieved, both persons win. The reward is an improved relationship. In fact, it is usually the stronger person in the couple that first breaks the habit-strength of the dysfunctional pattern.

Change

People do not change easily (think about what happened to your last dieting effort or planned exercise regimen). In order for persons to bring about consistent change, effort must be applied throughout the change process. Initial effort must be applied to achieve what is desired; secondary effort must be applied to maintain the result. It is effort for change and effort for consistency.

The process for change involves (1) accepting responsibility for your behavior, (2) identifying what you want to change, (3) developing a plan for change, (4) implementing the plan, (5) evaluating for success, and (6) altering the plan or means of implementation if not successful.

As it pertains to couples, a plan for change can involve one or both of the couple. It can also involve skills to be learned. For instance, spouses can learn to be better mates, fathers, mothers, and partners. And individually, persons can learn how to alter dysfunctional thoughts, feelings, and behaviors.

When it comes to change, keep in mind that good intentions and plans, while necessary, are not sufficient for change. Like a blueprint for construction, even the best intentions and the most detailed of plans must be put into action before any results are seen. Another way of expressing this is *blueprints do not build a house.*

The Relationship Imperative – Make it Safe!

Do not forget the Relationship Imperative: *Make it safe!* Making it safe involves remaining calm and attentive, even when discussing sensitive topics. A single conversation wherein you "blew your top" or appeared disinterested can discourage communication for years. Making it safe means that persons are able to come to one another with *any* issue and expect respectful discussion. It does not mean you must agree. Discussing and successfully resolving a difference, apologizing for any harm even if unintended, or agreeing to disagree, is intimacy enhancing.

Psychological Defense Mechanisms and Police Marriages

Psychological defense mechanisms were first discussed by Sigmund Freud as part of his approach to the treatment of anxiety (1920). As mentioned in chapter 4, psychological defense mechanisms are thought to operate unconsciously and therefore outside of conscious awareness.

Defense mechanisms protect us from undue psychological harm. They allow us to cope with stressful circumstances without actually changing them. The defense mechanisms of suppression, denial, and rationalization have been previously discussed. Recall that suppression pushes anxiety-producing thoughts out of awareness; in denial, we fail to acknowledge ego-threatening thoughts and behaviors that are obvious to others; and rationalization allows us to create questionable semi-credible explanations for problem-causing thoughts and behaviors. Other defense mechanisms include *intellectualization, projection,* and *displacement,* to name a few.

Intellectualization is the process by which we use theoretical thinking to justify our thoughts and behavior. Projection is the process by which we attribute to others our own unacceptable thoughts and feelings. Displacement is the transfer of emotional reactions, like anger, away from the proper object, like the boss, and redirecting them toward a "safer" target, like your spouse.

In themselves, there is nothing pathological about psychological defense mechanisms. In fact, they can be thought of as adaptive in many ways. It is only with their overdevelopment that problems result. Because defense mechanisms operate unconsciously, persons struggling with difficulties caused by defense mechanism overdevelopment have no insight into the cause of their problems.

Emotional Insulation and Police Officers

One particularly interesting psychological defense mechanism is *emotional insulation.* Emotional insulation is the process whereby feelings and emotional reactions are dampened. It is especially useful for police officers because they are required to remain calm in emotionally charged situations. Remaining calm in such situations permits police officers to better process information and achieve resolutions based upon actual circumstances and fact, not emotion. Emotional insulation helps to make this possible.

There are several factors that encourage the development of emotional insulation in police officers. The first is the unavoidable stressors of police work. In policing, unavoidable stressors include repeated exposure to violence, injury, danger, and death. Without some sort of psychological protection against the negative effects of such exposure, officers would soon overload their coping capacity.

The second is the police culture. There exists a social value among police officers for calmness in situations which would normally evoke strong emotion. It is not that officers never express emotion, but only that there is a value placed on remaining cool and calm, especially in stressful situations. Case in point: an officer contacted two suspects for a minor violation. The suspects became uncooperative and attacked the police officer. During the altercation, the officer was able to radio for assistance. As other police units arrived and the suspects were taken into custody, the first thing the slightly injured and roughed up officer said was "How did I sound on the radio?" Many officers have suffered the taunts of other officers for "freaking out" or screaming into the radio. And one of the last things that officers want is to be seen by their peers as fearful, excitable, or overly emotional.

The third is the court system. The court system encourages police-officer emotional insulation by placing a premium upon objective, uninvolved, and unemotional behavior. In fact, if an opposing attorney can demonstrate officer-emotional behavior in reference to a case, the officer's testimony is discredited. Such attorney arguments usually center on, "Officer, isn't it true that you were upset and angry? And isn't it true that your actions were based more on your anger than on appropriate police procedure?"

Another way that an officer's testimony can be impeached in court is if the opposing attorney can show some emotional connection between the officer and anyone involved in the case. This last circumstance is not quite the same as emotional insulation, but it is another example of the testimonial standard of objectivity expected of police officers.

So, emotional insulation helps officers to function non-emotionally in stressful situations. Its development is encouraged by the factors mentioned. What then is the problem? Is not emotional insulation a good thing for police officers? Not always. Much depends upon the degree or "thickness" of the insulation.

Protection: payoff and cost

The payoff of emotional insulation for police officers is psychological protection. Emotional insulation protects officers from *experiencing* emotional responses to external stressors, making it more likely they can meet the demands of the job. But this protection comes at a cost. It also dampens the *expression* of emotion on and off the job. Therefore, emotional insulation can be thought of as an emotional shield from normally emotion-provoking external events and a barrier to the expression of emotion.

For an officer with overdeveloped emotional insulation, any experience of emotion, produces discomfort. As a result, emotion becomes further repressed, further insulated. If any emotional connections remain, they are often only with peers, not citizens, not family.

Although the overdevelopment of emotional insulation is subtle and occurs slowly over time, it does not take long for spouses to notice a change. Spouses of overdeveloped emotionally insulated officers complain that their relationship has become cold and unfeeling. Sex, if it is occurring at all, seems mechanical. One wife described it as "Wham bam, thank you, ma'am." Other family activities are also affected. Family transactions become brief and disturbingly neutral. If there is any emotion expressed by the officer, it is usually anger. This is because not much of any other emotion can penetrate the insulation. Over time, in response to lack of feelings expressed by the officer, spouses find themselves withdrawing emotionally. This widens the intimacy gap between the couple and sets the relationship on a collision course.

Living with an overly insulated officer is difficult. Spouses of over emotionally insulated police officers complain that "This is not the person I married" and "I don't know who this is." The officers say little in response until some comment provokes an angry outburst.

On the other side, emotionally insulated officers complain that their spouses do not understand them. They say that their wives expect too much, have become intolerant, and "bitchy." One wife so criticized, responded that her husband has become an "asshole" who treats her nicely only when he wants sex. After sex, he reverts to the cold, detached, unfeeling robot he has become, until he wants sex again. Officers and spouses that have reached this point are at an impasse. They are frustrated and do not know what to do about it. They only know that the relationship is in trouble. When asked if things were always this way, both reply no. They once had a much more loving and compassionate relationship. Neither knows where that relationship went. Neither knows how they got to where they are. Such is the insidious progression of emotional insulation.

The course of therapy for such couples depends upon actual circumstances. Generally, it is helpful to explore relationship history, discuss emotional insulation, and explore ways to reduce it. With this, the couple can emotionally reconnect and reclaim their marriage.

Police officers must remain on guard to avoid the overdevelopment of emotional insulation. Good communication helps. Talking to spouses, staying involved in family life, and having interests or hobbies outside of policing are excellent buffers against the development of excessive emotional insulation. Taking time for one another and engaging in some fun activities without the kids are also important. Good work/home boundaries are imperative. Happily married police officers strive to maintain a healthy work/family balance. This helps officer-spouse relationships to remain satisfying, interesting, and functional.

Marriage and Marital Fidelity

There is a true test of marital fidelity. The test has three components: (1) you are attracted to a person not your spouse, who is also attracted to you, (2) the person makes it known to you that they are available and willing to engage in romantic or sexual activities, and (3) you believe that you can engage in such activities and not be discovered. You pass the test if you walk away and redirect your emotional energies to your spouse and into your marriage.

What happens if you fail the test? Failing the test means engaging in romantic or sexual activities outside of your marriage...*an affair.*

Extramarital Affairs

Some marriages are troubled most of the time. Some marriages are troubled some of the time. Many marriages are not troubled at all. Having an extramarital affair will normally cause trouble for most marriages most of the time.

Although affairs can be the result of an unhappy marriage, they also occur within "good" and "happy" marriages. Ironically, many persons who are having an affair or have had affairs often report being "in love" and happy with their spouse. As one such serial-affair person explained "I just like some strange once in a while."

No matter how a marriage is described, happy or otherwise, an affair has the potential to destroy the relationship.

Marriages can survive affairs. However, for most, following the affair, the marriage is changed forever. This is because the emotional wounds caused by affairs seldom completely heal. These emotional injuries, often deeply repressed, will remain with the offended person for life. These feelings are often so much a part of the offended person that they will continue to exert their influence even after the death of the unfaithful spouse.

Some couples say things like, "The affair was a good thing. It helped us seek counseling and focus on our problems." Although an affair may be responsible for the initiation of counseling and the focusing on problems, an affair is seldom a good thing for a marriage. For most, statements like this help to rationalize the affair and distribute responsibility ("It's part your fault that I had an affair because you . . ." or "It's part my fault that you had an affair because I . . ."). Rationalization serves the purpose of allowing the couple to move forward, and in this sense is useful. Unfortunately for some relationships, once this initial purpose is served, at least one of the couple will decide that the marriage is over.

In some marriages, both spouses have had affairs. These can occur concurrently or years apart, and for various reasons. Sometimes, an affair is initiated by one spouse in response to an affair of the other. Such affairs may be the result of a diminished sense of obligated fidelity or as a component of revenge or "getting even." No matter. Both spell trouble for the marriage.

Is it possible for a person to have an affair and afterward find a renewed commitment to their marriage? Yes. Many persons that have had an affair, or even multiple affairs, (discovered or undiscovered) move past such behavior and become completely committed to their marriage. This is possible due to the complexity of human experience, conceptualization, and emotion. In such cases, newly formed thoughts or the experience of feelings previously non-existent, or rediscovery of feelings thought long-lost can last a lifetime. But in some cases, especially in discovered affairs, this comes too late. The affair has damaged the relationship foundation beyond the point of repair and the marriage collapses.

Types of extramarital affairs

There are at least three general types of extramarital affairs: the emotional affair, the infamous one-night stand affair, and the ongoing affair.

The emotional affair - the exact meaning of "emotional affair" is difficult to define. In general, an extramarital emotional affair exists when a person develops a romantic intimate relationship with a person not their spouse. This relationship often fills some emotional need that is not being met within the marriage. Emotional affairs involve no or little physical contact. Instead, they place a third person in an emotional role normally occupied by the spouse. Emotional affairs do not need to take place in-person. They can be carried out on electronic devices with participants being thousands of miles apart.

Some marriages do not survive emotional affairs, in spite of claims from the offending spouse that "I didn't do anything wrong" (did not have sexual contact). When marriages do not survive emotional affairs, it is often the sense of emotional betrayal that causes the breakup.

The one-night stand affair - the one-night stand affair is a sexual encounter with a partner that you have no intention of seeing again. It is sex without intimacy. In addition to the danger one-night stand affairs present to a marriage, they also include risks of sexually transmitted diseases and unplanned pregnancy.

The ongoing affair - ongoing affairs are pretty much self-described. They are sexual encounters with a partner that spans a period of time. Ongoing affairs can last days, years, or a lifetime. They may or may not involve a degree of intimacy. Like the one-night stand, there are risks of sexually transmitted diseases and unplanned pregnancy.

Known marital infidelity

Some marriages seem to endure even after years of known marital infidelity. The reasons for this are too numerous to specify here. Suffice it to say that the actual effect and outcome that known affairs have on a marriage is dependent upon several complex interactions among various psychological, emotional, economic, and social factors. One does not have look very far to find examples of known and sometimes continuing affairs in marriages that endure. While many of these seem to involve financially or politically powerful men, such affairs are known to exist across socio-political and gender lines.

Known affairs are different from "open" marriages. In open marriages, also known as *consensual non-monogamy* (CNM), spouses agree to allow one another to have relationships and/or sex with persons outside the marriage.

There are many versions of CNM, including swinging, double-dating, solo dating, and various other interpersonal arrangements. Most include consent for spouses to engage in extramarital sexual activities. It is this permission and the fact that both spouses are involved that differentiates CNM from the known marital affairs previously mentioned.

It appears that CNM is becoming more popular. A 2017 Kinsey Institute research poll estimated that about 20% of American married couples had engaged in some form of CNM. This is an increase over previous estimates. There is also some evidence that younger adults are more open to CNM and the notion of polyamory, the idea that a person can romantically love more than one person.

Advocates of CNM maintain that traditional monogamy is an unnatural condition imposed by antiquated religious and political institutions. And while monogamous marriage may work well for some, it does not work well for everyone. They argue that CNM is morally proper, more ethical, and less threatening to marriages than engaging in secretive extramarital affairs, especially those meant to "save" a marriage.

Rationales for affairs

There are various rationales for having an affair. One of the most common is "I had an affair to save my marriage." It goes like this, "I am unhappy in my marriage (may include, exclude, or be exclusively about sex). If I act on my unhappiness, I'll have to ask for a divorce. I don't want to divorce (may include a declaration of love for the spouse). So, I had an affair to compensate for what is missing in my marriage. This way, I meet my needs and my marriage is saved."

Another affair rationale is "If I can get it (sex), why not take it. You only live once." This rationale is readily understood and has to do with self-centeredness and the pursuit of personal pleasure. It disregards any sense of marital commitment and the emotional well-being of the spouse.

A third rationale is "It just happened." It is difficult to make sense of this rationale. Clearly, the person is not accepting responsibility for personal behavior. While this type of affair may have been unplanned, affairs do not "just happen." Intentional behaviors must be engaged to have an affair.

There are other rationales for affairs, including "I was drunk" and "It didn't mean anything." Regardless of the rationale, extramarital affairs are difficult to overcome. For most couples, this is true whether the couple seeks counseling, remains married, or chooses "temporary" separation. For some persons, an affair on the part of their spouse can be so emotionally overwhelming that they resort to violence, including homicide, suicide, or both after learning of the affair.

Pressured into sex

Rationales for voluntarily engaging in affairs are categorically different from being pressured into sex by those in power positions. Having sex under pressure frequently involves a sense of career or other survival. Victims of pressured sex often say things like "What choice did I have" "I need this job" "I just wanted the pressure to stop" or "It's the only way to advance here." In spite of laws and regulations against unwanted advances, being pressured into sex remains a problem in many organizations, including police departments and family systems.

For perpetrators of pressured sex, the interaction is viewed as consensual, no matter the degree of victim reluctance. It is the claim of "victim consent" that allows these perpetrators to nearly always avoid criminal prosecution or conviction when held accountable for their abhorrent behavior.

Marital Fidelity, Consequence, and "Prosequence"

When it comes to marital fidelity, ongoing decisions must be made. If you find yourself confronted with circumstances that test your fidelity, you have decisions to make. If your commitment to your marriage is intact, the decision is easy and predetermined. You decide in favor of your marriage. If your commitment is not intact, you can still decide in favor of your marriage, or you can decide to have an affair.

All decisions have consequences. The *marital* consequence of deciding in favor of marriage is clear - fidelity continues. The marital consequences of deciding to have an affair range from none (the affair is not discovered) to complete marriage "blow up."

In cases where an affair is not discovered, there may be personal consequences. These include a sense of guilt, fear of disease or pregnancy, anxiety over future revelation, and fear of harassment or blackmail. In some cases, there is actual harassment or blackmail, often leading to confession or other affair discovery.

Marriage blow-up

There are many ways for an affair to blow up a marriage. This can happen even in situations where a person has no intention of leaving the marriage or continuing the affair, as in a one-night stand.

At times, the consequences of having an affair are not well thought out. When an affair is discovered and persons are confronted with all that comes with discovery, they sometimes say things like "what was I thinking?" and "why didn't I think of this before?" Certainly good questions. The answer? The person failed to engage *prosequence.*

Prosequence

Prosequence is a two-fold process. It consists of: (1) imagining the likely consequences of your decision, and (2) imagining that those consequences are now real. Concerning marital fidelity, it is imagining having to cope with the consequences of having an affair before engaging in one. For example, before deciding whether or not to have an affair, imagine that you had an affair and it became known. Think through its likely effect on your spouse, children, job, family, friends, and *yourself*! Such reflection does not mean you will decide against the affair. It means only that you will have a clearer idea of what you might be getting yourself into. Is it worth it?

In summary, "prosequence" is a coined word created to help persons consider the likely or eventual consequences of particular decisions *before* they occur.

Affairs and Sex Addiction

Are some affairs related to an addiction to sex? Can a person be addicted to sex? There are some clinicians that advocate for the authenticity of sex addiction. They specialize in treating persons considered to be sex addicts. Supporters of this position not only maintain that sex addiction is real but also feel that it is acted out in various ways, including affairs.

Opponents of sex addiction argue that it fails to meet accepted definitions of addiction. They contend that sex addiction is a myth applied primarily by rich and powerful men when they are caught in sex scandals. This makes these men victims of their disease and allows them to avoid responsibility for their behavior. In essence, by confessing their "addiction" they become victims deserving of sympathy, instead of perpetrators of misogynistic or other condemnable behavior.

The current Diagnostic and Statistical Manual of Mental Disorders, DSM-5-TR (APA, 2022), does not recognize sex as an addiction. The DSM-5-TR explains why sex addiction is not currently a diagnosis; "...groups of repetitive behaviors, which some term *behavioral addictions* (with such subcategories such as "sex addiction," "exercise addiction,", and "shopping addiction"), are not included because there is insufficient peer-reviewed evidence to establish the diagnostic criteria and course descriptions needed to identify these behaviors as mental disorders" (543). Whether this will change in the future remains an open question.

For those clinicians that support the idea of behavioral addictions (formerly called *process* addictions), sex is considered an addiction even though there is no specific diagnosis within the DSM-5-TR. In such cases, clinicians may specify the DSM-5-TR classification, *Focus of Clinical Attention, sex counseling*. Sex counseling is not a mental disorder.

In 2018 the World Health Organization International Classification of Diseases (ICD), 11th edition included a new diagnosis, *compulsive sexual behaviour disorder* (CSBD). While the diagnosis of CSBD formally recognizes various compulsive sex-related behaviors, it is classified as an impulse-control disorder. It stops short of identifying compulsive sexual behavior as an addiction. Additionally, CSBD can only be diagnosed if the behaviors cause clinically significant distress (excluding distress caused by moral judgement) or personal or social impairment. In this way, alternative or unusual sexual practices are not pathologized. CSBD replaced the "excessive sex drive" specified in the historical ICD diagnoses of *nymphomania* (uncontrollable sexual desire in a woman) and *satyriasis* (uncontrollable sexual desire in a man). Unfortunately, CSBD is sometimes "referred to as sexual addiction or hypersexuality" (Grant, 2018, 34). Bottom line: while the reality of addiction to sex remains controversial, there is currently no formal medical or professional recognition of sex addiction.

Incidentally, in contrast to an excessive sexual drive, it is also possible to experience a less than normal sex drive. While it is normal for sex drive to wax and wane, if low sex drive is persistent and certain other conditions are present, *female sexual interest/ arousal disorder* or *male hypoactive sexual desire disorder* may be diagnosed (DSM-5-TR).

When considering sex drive, you may have heard that "sex is ninety-five percent psychological and five percent physical." While this statement captures the importance of being "turned on" when it comes to sex, low sex drive and sexual performance difficulties can have their origin in physiology (this is also true for excessive sexual drive). One of the most common physical causes for low sex drive and an inability to perform sexually is the inadequate endogenous production of sex-related hormones. This condition can be readily diagnosed and treated by qualified physicians.

The treatment of low sex drive often includes the administration of supplemental hormones, a treatment not without risk. Persons experiencing low sex drive or other sexual difficulties should discuss the possible benefits and risks of available treatments with qualified physicians.

Healthy Marriages and Gottman's Marriage Tips

Couples researcher, psychologist John Gottman identified seven tips for keeping marriages healthy. In combination with the Foundation Blocks of Functional Relationships and Some Things to Remember, they provide an excellent framework for those wishing to maintain or enhance their marriage.

- *Seek help early.* The average couple waits six years before seeking help for marital problems (and keep in mind, half of all marriages that end do so in the first seven years). This means the average couple lives with unhappiness for far too long.
- *Edit yourself.* Couples who avoid saying every critical thought when discussing touchy topics are consistently the happiest.
- *Soften your "start up."* Arguments first "start up" because a spouse sometimes escalates the conflict from the get-go by making a critical or contemptuous remark in a confrontational tone. Bring up problems gently and without blame.
- *Accept influence.* A marriage succeeds to the extent that the husband can accept influence from his wife. If a woman says, "Do you have to work Thursday night? My mother is coming that weekend, and I need your help getting ready," and her husband replies, "My plans are set, and I'm not changing them". This guy is in a shaky marriage. A husband's ability to be influenced by his wife (rather than vice-versa) is crucial because research shows women are already well practiced

at accepting influence from men, and a true partnership only occurs when a husband can do so as well.

- *Have high standards.* Happy couples have high standards for each other even as newlyweds. The most successful couples are those who, even as newlyweds, refused to accept hurtful behavior from one another. The lower the level of tolerance for bad behavior in the beginning of a relationship, the happier the couple is down the road.

- *Learn to repair and exit the argument.* Successful couples know how to exit an argument. Happy couples know how to repair the situation before an argument gets completely out of control. Successful repair attempts include: changing the topic to something completely unrelated; using humor; stroking your partner with a caring remark ("I understand that this is hard for you"); making it clear you're on common ground ("This is our problem"); backing down (in marriage, as in the martial art Aikido, you have to yield to win); and, in general, offering signs of appreciation for your partner and his or her feelings along the way ("I really appreciate and want to thank you for . . ."). If an argument gets too heated, take a 20-minute break, and agree to approach the topic again when you are both calm.

- *Focus on the bright side.* In a happy marriage, while discussing problems, couples make at least five times as many positive statements to and about each other and their relationship as negative ones. For example, "We laugh a lot;" not, "We never have any fun". A good marriage must have a rich climate of positivity. Make deposits to your emotional bank account. (Copyright 2000-2010 by John M. Gottman. Reprinted with permission from the website of the Gottman Institute at www.gottman.com). And as recommended by the Gottman Institute, "Never stop dating your partner" (ibid. 2022,1).

In summary, a good marriage is like a traditional mechanical clock. Wind it up, input positive energy to keep it going, and it ticks away faithfully for years.

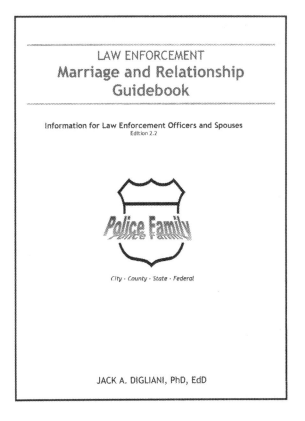

LAW ENFORCEMENT
Marriage and Relationship
Guidebook

Information for Law Enforcement Officers and Spouses
Edition 2.2

City · County · State · Federal

JACK A. DIGLIANI, PhD, EdD

The Law Enforcement Marriage and Relationship Guidebook is comprised of most of the information included in this chapter, the Marriage and Couples Exercise, an article by police psychologist Ellen Kirschman titled *Think It's Hard Being a Cop? Try Being Married to One*, and more. It can be used as a concise review, a couples resource, or forwarded to interested officers and spouses.

The Law Enforcement Marriage and Relationship Guidebook is available without cost at www.jackdigliani.com.

Chapter 8

Coping with Death and Mourning

The life of the dead is placed in the memory of the living.
-Marcus Tullius Cicero (106-43 BCE)

In general, America is a death denying society. Cemeteries are "memorial gardens" and "burial parks." Most Americans "pass on" or "pass away" instead of dying. This is because most of us are uncomfortable thinking about or discussing death. Want to be a hit at your next party? Initiate a discussion about death. The popularity of this topic will soon reveal itself.

In most technological societies, even the death of food animals is uncomfortable. We are familiar only with neatly packaged animal body parts enclosed in plastic wrap. We do not care to see or become familiar with the living animal that will end up on our dinner plate. It is fortunate for those who enjoy the consumption of animals that there are some persons who are capable of working in the food-animal industry.

When thinking about death, we occasionally think about those in the funeral business. Our thoughts often include wondering how they do it. It certainly takes a special kind of person to deal with death on a regular basis. Funeral directors, coroners, medical examiners, and many physicians seem to be among those special kinds of persons. They provide services that most others would find unpleasant. While it may be possible for nearly everyone to develop a greater tolerance for death exposure if circumstances required, if given a choice, most of us are content to keep a healthy distance from the reality of death.

Humans are probably the only species that knows it will die. This knowledge has led to the development of a number of religious, philosophical, and psychological belief systems. All societies, whether considered primitive or advanced, have belief systems and accompanying rituals that help members address and cope with the reality of death. To manage the seemingly ubiquitous anxiety around death, many such belief systems conceptualize physical death not as an end of life, but as a transition to another form of life.

Death Exposure

Exposure to death is an unavoidable stressor of policing. Police officers must have or must develop some ability to cope with the stress of death exposure. The psychological effects of exposure to death range from mild to severe. Much depends upon personal variables and the frequency, duration, and intensity of exposure.

Death exposure response spectrum

The *death exposure response spectrum* is a hypothetical continuum that identifies the possible emotional reactions to death. At one end of the spectrum lie the emotional responses of sensitization and traumatization. Such traumatization frequently includes the experience of death anxiety, fear, and depression. At the other end lie emotional numbing, indifference, and insensitivity - resulting in an almost robot-like response to death. In the middle of these extremes are the more psychologically healthy responses to death.

Death exposure and the job

For police officers, death is a more-than-usual topic for thought. Police training encourages officers to think about death; their own as well as others. Every police officer is trained to recognize circumstances wherein their life or the life of others may be in jeopardy. In such circumstances, lethal force for self-defense or defense of others may become necessary.

Police officers are also prone to think about death by the very nature of their work. Street and investigative experience expose officers to death in various ways, including homicide, suicide, natural death, auto crashes, pedestrian accidents, fires, and industrial accidents.

If some police officers have not been personally exposed to death, they almost certainly will be. For most, it is just a matter of time. And even if it happens that they are never exposed, they certainly know coworkers that have. This creates a type of vicarious death exposure. Either way, direct or indirect exposure to death seems a common aspect of the psychology of police officers.

Regardless of how officers encounter death, it is possible for them to develop feelings of having seen too much of it. This is especially true if there is a high frequency of exposure. It can become more difficult if the deaths involve children, "didn't have to happen", or appear "meaningless."

If death exposure is managed in a healthy way, it can result in enhanced coping abilities. These provide some psychological protection against the possible negative effects of death exposure. But nothing is perfect. No matter how officers conceptualize death or how well they cope with exposure, there is the ever-present risk of *death imprint*.

Death imprint

When officers experience anxiety about death, it often involves one or more of the following:

- thoughts about their death
- thoughts about the death of others
- the inevitability of death
- seeing a deceased person that reminds them of a living or dead loved one
- the future death of loved ones
- memories of those that have already died.

These and other experiences can emotionally overwhelm even the best prepared officers. Becoming overwhelmed can occur (1) due to the circumstances of a particular case, (2) when a particular case causes a *tipping point* in the ability to manage death anxiety, (3) when a recent death reactivates feelings about a historical loss, or (4) gradually over time with continued death exposure. Regardless of the cause(s) of death anxiety, the result of this emotional decompensation is *death imprint*. Death imprint becomes possible when psychological coping defenses weaken. This allows the normally suppressed anxiety and depression associated with thoughts of death to reach some degree of expression.

It is sometimes helpful for officers to remember that no one can prevent the possibility of death. This is especially important for officers on the brink of death imprint. When nearing their capacity of death tolerance, officers say things like "nobody dies on my watch today." It would be fortunate if saying it made it so. A more accurate thought would be "I will do my best to prevent anyone from dying today."

Although police officers have saved countless lives by protecting others, applying first aid, administering CPR, and completing rescues, there is no way to eliminate the possibility of death. This makes death exposure and the risk of death imprint an occupational hazard for police officers.

Officers are sometimes surprised by their feelings following a particular death exposure. They say things like "I don't know why this hit me so hard" and "This one really got to me." In such cases, death exposure has tapped into something deep within the officer. This often results in feelings of sadness and grief.

Grief and Mourning

Grief and mourning are not identical. Grief is the personal, emotional response to loss. Mourning represents the public, culture-specific way of expressing loss. There are varied mourning rituals that are characteristic of various cultures. For example, it is not uncommon for deceased Italian-Americans to have items that were important to them during life placed in their casket prior to burial. My grandfather was buried with a bottle of whiskey; my father with a cigar. This practice is hardly new, and it is not limited to any single culture. It has its multicultural roots in antiquity, as far back as pre-homo sapiens and Egyptian pharaohs.

Grief

There are many expressions of grief. A person's grief can be somewhat unique, and therefore difficult for others to understand. Upon a loss, some persons may express little outward sentiment, while others will be consumed by uncontrollable bouts of expressed emotion.

It is difficult to predict how a person will respond to death; and more difficult to predict how a person will respond to the death of a loved one. For instance, a woman who had been married for many years expediently cleared the entire house of everything owned by her deceased husband. This included clothes, bedding, tools, and so on. She accomplished this within one week of his death. There are also cases wherein houses, or a room in the house, are kept intact for years after the death, just as the deceased left it, including cigarette butts in an ashtray.

There are varying lengths of time needed to grieve. It depends on the person. One thing seems certain. For any specific person, grieving cannot be rushed. Grieving appears to have a timeline of its own, and it can last a lifetime.

In several ways, loss can be viewed as an emotional and psychological injury. Much like a physical wound, these injuries need time to heal. If you broke a bone in your arm yesterday, you would not expect it to be healed today. So it is with grief. The loss of yesterday is not likely to be healed today.

Tasks of Grieving and Mourning

After the death of a loved one, survivors are confronted with the completion of at least four tasks before they can once again fully engage life. (1) The first task is to fully accept the reality of the loss. To complete this task, survivors must accept the loss emotionally. The disbelief which often accompanies the denial of the loss must be processed. Accepting the loss involves confronting the vacuum left in your life by the person's death. (2) The second task of grieving is to experience the pain of the loss. This means that persons must accept and work through their feelings, and avoid conscious efforts to suppress their sadness. (3) The third task is to adjust to the environment in which the deceased is missing. This involves adjusting to even the simplest of tasks, such as who will now take out the trash. Many survivors say that they did not realize how much the deceased did until they had to assume their everyday responsibilities. (4) The fourth task is to withdraw the emotional investment in the deceased and recover the ability to reinvest in other relationships (Worden, 1982). This is sometimes referred to as "learning to love again." It can be especially difficult for widows, widowers, and partners.

Upon the death of a loved one, some persons act out in various uncharacteristic ways. This behavior is frequently an attempt to manage the powerful emotions associated with the loss. For example, sexual promiscuity is sometimes observed upon the death of a spouse; and the inappropriate coddling of another's child may be seen upon the death of a child.

Isolation, the opposite of acting out, is also observed in grief. Even after an extended period of time, some people will continue to socially and emotionally isolate themselves. This is most often seen in persons who have lost a beloved spouse. In their isolation, becoming platonically involved with another person is avoided for any number of reasons. Becoming romantically involved with another person is unimaginable. This causes a suspension of any relationship-developing behavior. If this situation remains unchanged, task four is never completed. This has significant implications for the remainder of the survivor's life.

Survivor loneliness is another likely result of death, especially when a spouse dies. Loneliness is often a component of grief, and it can last long after the experience of grief subsides. For surviving spouses, even if their relationships were contentious, there was, at the least, another person around. Having another person around, even in dysfunctional relationships, provides a degree of companionship and helps to structure time.

The loss of a spouse often creates a "social and time" vacuum, long periods of time within which the survivor has no or little interaction with others. This is sometimes seen when one of an elderly couple dies. This situation is more likely to be experienced by women than men. This is because women are more likely to become widows than men are to become widowers. The reason?

The life expectancy of women is greater than that of men, and men tend to marry women younger than themselves. These factors combine to make it more likely that a woman will outlive her male mate. Statistically, the loss of a male spouse is a "built in" life stressor for most women.

When a spouse dies, some friends and family may do their best to maintain a connection with the survivor. Even so, some degree of survivor loneliness is nearly inevitable. It becomes worse if there are no friends and if family members are either not present or have little concern.

Being alone after the death of a spouse can sometimes bring forward deep-seated fears previously buffered by the presence of the spouse. Regardless of age, when alone after death, some people experience long-standing or newly developed childlike fears such as fear of the dark, thunderstorms, strange noises, imagined monsters, ghosts, and so on.

An interesting phenomenon sometimes seen after the death of loved one is the idea that the deceased has acquired abilities in death not possible during life. Examples of this are the notions that the deceased is ever-present, constantly watching, and influencing personal and environmental events in ways not possible when living.

Death and Guilt

The experience of guilt is common for human beings. There are two types of guilt normally associated with death, *real guilt* and *survivor guilt*. Real guilt is generated by behavior and/or thoughts. Real guilt for behavior involves something done or not done. For instance, real guilt for something done might involve a recent conversation with the deceased wherein there was an angry exchange of words. Real guilt for something not done might involve a failure to visit a sick relative in the hospital who suddenly died. Real guilt for thoughts involves current or past thinking. For example, a person might feel guilty about having thought that the deceased feigned symptoms for attention or exaggerated the sickness that eventually caused death. Real guilt is associated with a perceived violation of personal values, a standard of behavior, or some moral code. Because individual morals and values differ, one person may experience real guilt in circumstances where another does not. It is important to remember that real guilt is relative. It describes only the fact that a person is feeling guilty for some perceived reason. It has little to do with whether anyone else believes that there are justifiable reasons for the person's guilty feeling. Additionally, it is possible to feel guilty and not understand why. Have you ever said to yourself, or heard someone else say, "I shouldn't feel guilty, but I do," or "I don't know why I'm feeling guilty, I didn't do anything wrong." Such circumstances normally represent an internal unaddressed or unresolved issue.

Survivor guilt is different than real guilt. Survivor guilt is the term used to describe the feeling associated with surviving while others died. It is common among airplane crash survivors, survivors of natural disasters, and soldiers who have returned from war. The question often asked is, "Why did I live and not them?" Pursuing an answer to this question can lead to a lifelong quest and, unfortunately in some cases, lifelong difficulty.

Real and survivor guilt can occur in combination. A combination of real and survivor guilt might be observed in the following hypothetical situation: a father, driving while accompanied by his infant daughter, is late for an appointment. He is driving faster than the speed limit. As he approaches a curve in the road, he loses control of the vehicle and strikes a highway abutment. The crash kills his daughter while he walks away without serious injury. In this imagined tragic scenario, it is very likely that the father would experience real and survivor guilt.

Guilt is often unwanted, uncontrollable, and difficult to understand. Because guilt can be punishing, it can cause significant difficulties. It can drive abnormal behavior and generate destructive thoughts.

To outside observers, a person's guilt may seem out of proportion to the circumstances. No matter, such guilt often leads to or is a component of depression. If serious enough, thoughts of suicide develop. The father in the aforementioned hypothetical car crash represents a significant risk for intense guilt, depression, and suicide. Persons suffering from this degree of guilt require support, immediate intervention, and professional treatment.

To manage or avoid feelings of guilt, especially those associated with the suicide of another, some persons sterilize their memory and "re-write" the history they had with the deceased. This can occur consciously, where authentic recall is actively re-interpreted, or unconsciously, where the process occurs outside of personal intention and awareness.

Guilt, Death, and Connection

Guilt is an emotion that can help us to feel we are still connected to the person that has died. By feeling guilty, the connection remains prominent. Many persons unconsciously fear that losing the guilt will cause them to lose the connection. Actually, guilt and the feeling of connection are quite independent. Healthy grieving involves letting go of guilt while maintaining the connection through an understanding of the person's legacy.

Guilt as a Positive Force

The feeling of guilt can be used as a behavioral guide. It can be seen as a factor in moral and value development. If morals and values are developed by design, the experience of guilt can be a signal that there has been a deviation from the selected path. Make the appropriate amends and corrections, and guilt feelings normally subside. Understanding the inevitability of death and the guilt that can follow the loss of those important to us, serves as a reminder to conduct ourselves in a self-determined appropriate manner while loved ones are still with us.

Healing from Loss

Healing from loss involves feeling good again. After the death of a loved one, some persons feel that it is disrespectful to the deceased to again have fun, enjoy life, and move forward. This feeling is normal and usually diminishes over time. To heal, survivors must acknowledge that it is not disrespectful to the deceased to once again enjoy life. To accomplish this, it is sometimes comforting to remember that the deceased also confronted the death of loved ones (in most cases) and also had to move forward.

Healing and Psychological Legacy

Honoring the legacy of the deceased is necessary for healing. Legacies are complex, multifaceted, and unique to each survivor. Simply stated, a legacy is what you feel the deceased has contributed to your life. There are several types of legacies. One of the most important for survivors is the psychological legacy. Psychological legacies have nothing to do with financial legacies which involve wills, houses, money, and other property.

Psychological legacies are unique because they are developed out of the emotional and particular relationship a person had with the deceased. This is why the psychological legacy experienced by one person can be very different from that experienced by another.

Like photographs, psychological legacies come *in-the-positive* and *in-the-negative*. Both contribute positively to our lives.

Psychological legacies in-the-positive are what you perceive as the valued contributions the person made to your life. They involve what you consider "good lessons learned" and those things about the deceased that you wish to emulate. For example, you may have admired how the person treated family members and resolved to do likewise. In this way, you want to be like the deceased person.

Psychological legacies in-the-negative contribute positively to our lives by teaching us what not to do. For example, you may not have admired how the person treated family members and committed yourself to doing something different. In this way, you want to be different than the deceased person, but the lesson is valuable nonetheless.

Psychological legacies are not considered inherently good or bad. Psychological legacies in-the-positive and in-the-negative teach you something valuable relative to your value system. Psychological legacies become good or bad only when evaluated against an independent value system.

If you have difficulty finding the psychological legacy of the deceased, consider looking at photographs or other reminders. You can do this alone or with someone you trust. Think about and talk about the memories they represent. In this way, the psychological legacy can be discovered. Ask yourself how the deceased contributed to your life. The answers to this question will help clarify their psychological legacy.

For a personal journey, consider writing a journal about what the deceased meant to you. Start with your earliest memory of the person. Include the good and the not so good. No one is perfect. There is no disrespect in understanding and expressing your feelings. This will help you to process the emotional loss caused by the death.

If you have unfinished business with the deceased, finish it in your journal. As part of your journey, consider writing your thoughts on a separate paper. Write down what you feel is unfinished. Include your feelings and things that you wished you said while the person was alive. Say goodbye. When completed, burn the paper. This keeps your thoughts and feelings private and sends smoke upward. Some persons feel that this also sends the message upward. For most, this is a psychologically healing activity. For some it is a spiritual or religious experience. For nearly all, it helps to provide closure.

Your journey is complete when you can think of the deceased, accept the good and the not so good, appreciate the psychological legacy, and smile through any tears. This is the highest honor that you can bestow on someone who was once a part of your life.

Death, Loss, and Survivorship

The following is a summary of issues involved in death, loss, and survivorship.

1. *Learning of the death.* Shock and denial are common initial responses to death, especially if the death is sudden and unexpected. Disbelief and confusion are frequently experienced.
2. *Reactions to death.* Many factors influence how intensely we feel the loss. Among these are the nature of attachment, spiritual views, the age of the deceased, how the person died, the similarity of the deceased to others we love, and the extent of the void that the person's absence leaves in our life. The death of another can also trigger our own

fears of death and memories of previous traumatic events or losses.

3. *Grief and mourning.* Grieving takes time. This is important to remember because American culture is not readily accepting of lengthy grieving or mourning periods. Instead, there is the idea that a person needs to put the loss behind them and get on with life. There is no correct way to grieve. People deal with loss in different ways for different periods of time.

4. *Coping with loss.* It is common to experience powerful emotions. Confront emotions openly. Strong emotion may feel overwhelming. Breathe through it. Remember the "ocean wave" (chapter 4).

5. *Specific reactions to loss.* There are many possible reactions to loss. Common and normal reactions include sadness, crying, numbness, loss of appetite, inability to sleep, fatigue, anger, frustration, finding it difficult to be alone, or wanting to be alone. Utilizing your support system is the best way to deal with the pain of grieving. It is also possible that none of these reactions occur. The absence of commonly experienced grief reactions does not necessarily indicate repression or pathology. Many persons, grateful for the relationship with the deceased and understanding the inevitability of death, accept the loss and continue with life.

6. *Stages of grief.* Some clinicians have identified what they refer to as stages of grief. Although such stages differ in terminology, the basic structure of the stages involve (1) an initial shock and denial, (2) a subsequent impact and suffering period, followed by (3) some adjustment and degree of recovery (similar to exposure to any traumatizing event). However, grieving is a complex process; it does not progress clearly from one stage to another. It is normal to once again have feelings long thought to have disappeared.

7. *Healing.* Acknowledge and accept your feelings. You may experience seemingly contradictory feelings such as relief and sadness (for example, relief that a burden of care or the person's suffering has ended, and sadness due to the loss). This is normal. Keep in mind that your emotional attachment does not end upon the death of someone you care about.

Remember, bereavement is the normal process by which human beings deal with loss.

8. *Surviving the loss.* Surviving the death of someone you care about involves honoring the memory and legacy of the person by acknowledging what the person contributed to your life. From here, you can further honor the person by reengaging life.

It is important to remember that similar feelings can follow the death or loss of pets, non-pet animals, and even plants and inanimate objects, especially if they have acquired some special meaning (like losing a family heirloom). Brain studies show that the same neural pathways of grief are activated regardless of the loss.

Grief, Uncomplicated Bereavement, Prolonged Grief Disorder, and Major Depression Disorder

If a person seeks professional counseling for normal issues involved in grief, *uncomplicated bereavement* is specified. Uncomplicated bereavement is not a mental disorder. It is a focus for psychological support. If a person is struggling with a persistent grief response after at least one year (six months for children and adolescents) following a death, and the response creates clinically significant distress or impairment, *prolonged grief disorder* (PGD) is diagnosed. PGD first appeared as a diagnosis in 2022 (DSM-5-TR). If a person becomes significantly depressed in response to someone's death, *major depressive disorder* may be diagnosed.

Memorials and Legacy

Memorials are common throughout the world. Some memorials start as recognition of the achievements of the living. For example, *America* was named for the then living Italian explorer Amerigo Vespucci (1454-1512) in 1507. Others are dedicated after death.

In America, memorials are ever present in our street names (Eisenhower Avenue), waterways (Hudson River), and government structures (Kennedy Space Center). Memorials honor the dead and keep their legacy connected to the living. They may be public and grand, like the Washington Monument, or private and personal, like the planting of a backyard tree.

Personal memorials help to fill the void left by the death of a loved one. They serve to ameliorate the pain of the loss. One type of personal memorial seen more frequently today is the tattoo. Due to the current sophistication of tattooing, actual photographs of the deceased can be reproduced in ink on human skin. These images, now possible in 3-D, as well as dates of birth and death, reproduced signatures, and special designs and symbols comprise many of these very personal memorials.

Personal memorials can be just about anything. Regardless of the form of any personal memorial, all have one thing in common: all personal memorials feel special to the survivor - and therein lies their power.

Chapter 9

Interacting with Persons that are Mentally Ill

Mental illnesses take many forms. Some are mild and only interfere in limited ways with daily life...other mental health conditions are so severe that a person may need care in a hospital.

-American Psychiatric Association

Conceptions of mental illness vary widely. From ancient cultures to modern societies, humans have struggled to define, understand, and treat illnesses of the mind. Ancient explanations for today's mental disorders included the influence of spirits and demons, punishment from the gods, or the results of witchcraft spells and magic. Interestingly, there are twenty-first century cultures where some or all of these remain the primary explanations of mental illness.

In the nineteenth century, theories of mental illness were based on a developing understanding of the brain. As part of this advance, mental illnesses came to be understood as primarily organic or functional.

Organic mental illnesses were characterized as: (1) a defect in brain structure, (2) chemical intoxication or withdrawal, (3) medical conditions, or (4) brain injury. This class of mental illness represented those cases wherein the cause of the disorder was traced to the brain — the organ of the mind (hence *organic*). These were the diseases of the so-called "psychobiologic unit" (APA, 1952, 1).

Functional mental illnesses were those in which there was a mental disturbance; however, based on the science of the day, the brain appeared to be intact, with no known defect, intoxication, or medical condition. In this class of mental illness, the structure of the brain appeared normal but the brain did not appear to be working normally. These illnesses were thought to be caused by impairment in brain function (hence *functional*). The conception of functional mental illness generated various theories to explain and treat the conditions associated with the impairment.

Although the organic and functional terminology is seldom used today, many of the most serious mental disorders once thought to be functional are now known to be caused by a brain disorder.

The Concept of Mental Illness

The concept of mental illness has normative features and is culturally relative. It changes as cultural norms evolve. The clearest example of how culture effects what is considered a mental illness is homosexuality. The evolution of homosexuality from a mental disorder to non-disorder can be traced through the various editions of the current diagnostic manual.

In America, the Diagnostic and Statistical Manual of Mental Disorders (DSM) has been the primary text for the classification, statistical data, and diagnosis of mental disorders. The DSM was first published in 1952, and has since undergone several revisions. The original DSM included the diagnosis *sexual deviation* and specified homosexuality as a mental disorder. This diagnosis was carried into the DSM-II, published in 1968. But things were changing.

The 1960s and 1970s characterized a period of unrest in America. There was the Vietnam War and all it entailed, and the civil rights movement. The previous standards and acceptances of American society were being challenged. Included in this challenge was the historical view of homosexuality. In response to changing times, the trustees of the American Psychiatric Association voted to eliminate homosexuality *per se* as a mental disorder. In December of 1973, upon the seventh printing of DSM-II, *sexual deviation* was replaced with the diagnosis *sexual orientation disturbance*. Sexual orientation disturbance described "individuals whose sexual interests are directed primarily toward people of the same sex and who are either disturbed by, in conflict with, or wish to change their sexual orientation. This diagnostic category is distinguished from homosexuality, which by itself does not constitute a psychiatric disorder" (44). This represented a significant change in the clinical conception of homosexuality.

The third revision of the DSM, DSM-III (1980) eliminated sexual orientation disturbance as a diagnosis. It was replaced with *ego-dystonic homosexuality*. The diagnostic criteria of ego-dystonic homosexuality consisted of two elements: "The individual complains that heterosexual arousal is persistently absent or weak and significantly interferes with initiating or maintaining wanted heterosexual relationships" and "There is a sustained pattern of homosexual arousal that the individual explicitly states has been unwanted and a persistent source of distress" (282).

The diagnosis of ego-dystonic homosexuality was never widely accepted by clinicians, likely because it lacked adequately descriptive criteria. It was also determined that many homosexual persons were distressed by their homosexual arousal, at least at first. This weakened the discriminatory value of the diagnosis. In 1987, with the publication of the DSM-III-R (revised), the diagnosis *ego-dystonic homosexuality* was eliminated. There was no replacement diagnosis.

Today, if a person sought psychological counseling for any issue regarding homosexuality, clinicians would specify the focus of clinical attention as *sex counseling* (DSM-5-TR, 2022). Sex counseling is not a mental disorder.

Types of Mental Disorders

There are several major categories used to specify the various types of mental disorders. Contemporary classification of mental disorders include neurodevelopmental disorders; schizophrenia spectrum and other psychotic disorders; bipolar and related disorders; depressive disorders; anxiety disorders; obsessive-compulsive and related disorders; trauma and stressor related disorders; dissociative disorders; somatic symptom and related disorders; feeding and eating disorders; elimination disorders; sleep-wake disorders; sexual dysfunctions; gender dysphoria; disruptive, impulse-control, and conduct disorders; substance-related and addictive disorders; neurocognitive disorders; personality disorders; and paraphilic disorders (DSM-5-TR, 2022). As psychological research continues and brain science advances, these categories and the specific diagnoses within them are likely to change.

Diagnoses, Signs, and Symptoms

Diagnoses are made when the diagnostic criteria for a specific condition are met. Clinicians use *signs* and *symptoms* to assess diagnostic criteria. Signs are things that you can observe or otherwise perceive. They include another's behavior, dress, appearance, odor, activity in context, and so forth. For example, the observations of flattened emotion, stunted activity, and a blank stare are some signs of depression. Signs are different than symptoms. Symptoms are conditions reported by the person. For example, a person saying "My head really hurts" is reporting a symptom (pain). If he is also holding his head while saying this, he is presenting a sign along with reporting a symptom. Many persons will speak of symptoms and include both signs and symptoms within their description.

Mental disorders have diagnostic criteria. The criteria for each officially recognized mental disorder are specified in either the DSM or the International Classification of Diseases (ICD). Most mental disorder diagnoses are comprised of:

1. specific elements of the diagnosis.
2. a specified length of time that the elements must be present (e.g., "minimum of three days," "for one month,").
3. a particular level of impairment or distress (the condition causes clinically significant impairment or distress).
4. positive or negative symptoms (positive symptoms are those that are not present in healthy persons—such as hallucinations. Negative symptoms are those conditions that are present in healthy persons but are lacking in persons that qualify for the diagnosis—such as lacking the ability to experience pleasure).
5. the condition is not caused by substance intoxication, medical condition, or better accounted for by another mental diagnosis.

The classifications and specific conceptions of mental disorders serve purposes other than diagnosis. They also assist in the gathering of statistical data and in the development of effective treatments.

Although diagnostic manuals are written in a manner that can be understood or interpreted by many, self-diagnosis or diagnosis by unqualified persons must be avoided.

Mental Disorders, Insanity, and Nervous Breakdown

Mental disorders are clinical conditions defined by specific diagnostic criteria. Diagnostic manuals of mental disorders do not include a diagnosis of *insanity*. This is because insanity is a legal concept and not a mental disorder. Therefore, a person may be adjudicated insane but not diagnosed insane.

In most states, when persons are adjudicated insane, it means that they have been arrested for the commission of a crime but cannot be held criminally liable due to mental illness. They are not held criminally liable because of the determination that at the time of the offense, the person was mentally ill and due to the mental illness was either incapable of distinguishing right from wrong, incapable of understanding the consequences of their actions, or incapable of controlling their behavior.

Attorneys representing clients charged with criminal offenses sometimes enter pleas of *not guilty by reason of insanity* (NGRI). In America, attorneys for serial killers are the most likely to proffer the NGRI defense. During the years from 1992 to 2007, 474 serial killers are known to have been criminally charged in the U.S. Of these, 85 (17.6 percent) entered a plea of NGRI. Of the 85, 15 (16.5 percent) were found NGRI (Moberg & Aamodt, 2007).

NGRI and President Reagan

On March 30, 1981, 25-year-old John Hinckley Jr. attempted to assassinate then President Ronald Reagan (1911-2004). During the attempt, Hinckley fired six .22 caliber "Devastator" bullets, designed to detonate on contact, in the direction of Reagan. The first of Hinckley's shots struck Reagan's press secretary James Brady above the left eye. The second struck Washington D.C. police officer

Thomas Delahanty in the back of the neck. Hinckley's fourth shot hit secret service agent Timothy McCarthy in the lower abdomen. The sixth bullet Hinckley fired ricocheted off the presidential limousine and struck Reagan in the left underarm.

President Reagan survived his wounds, as did Delahanty and McCarthy. James Brady sustained severe brain damage and died 33 years after the incident. He died in 2014 of complications related to his 1981 gunshot wound. The cause of his death was ruled homicide. The Devastator bullet that struck Brady was the only one of the six fired by Hinckley that exploded.

After apprehension, Hinckley stated that his attempt on Reagan's life was an attempt to impress actress Jodie Foster, with whom he had developed an erotomanic obsession. In various court appearances, attorneys for Hinckley argued that he was not responsible for his actions due to obsessional and delusional mental illness. Following lengthy legal proceedings, Hinckley was determined to be "not guilty by reason of insanity" on all thirteen federal charges.

Having been found NGRI, Hinckley avoided prison and was committed to institutional psychiatric care. In July 2016, after decades of hospital detention and treatment, a federal judge found that he was no longer a threat to himself or others and ruled that he could be released. He was released with conditions in September 2016. In June 2022, his release became unconditional.

The public outrage at the NGRI verdict in the Hinckley case led to the passage of the Insanity Defense Reform Act of 1984. This Act revised the standards of the NGRI defense in the federal court system and shifted the burden of proof of insanity to the defense. Although this modified version of the NGRI plea remains available in the federal court system, several states have completely abolished NGRI. These states have replaced NGRI with pleas of "guilty but insane" "guilty but mentally ill" or "guilty except for insanity."

Like Hinckley, most persons judged NGRI are committed to psychiatric hospitals for treatment. Being "not guilty" they are not sentenced to prison. This does not mean that the person will soon go free. A person judged NGRI will often be confined for a greater length of time in a psychiatric hospital than they would have in prison. "In fact, the average stay in a locked mental institution for insanity acquitees is 35 *years*, whereas the prison term for these same crimes would be 20 years...A successful NGRI plea doesn't mean the defendant got away with a thing. In fact, he often pays a higher price for the crime committed" (Rubinstein, 2016, 1).

Some people facing criminal charges plead not guilty by reason of *temporary* insanity. In this version of the NGRI plea, persons claim that they were mentally ill and not responsible for their behavior at the time the crime was committed, but are not now mentally ill.

Nervous breakdown

Like insanity, *nervous breakdown* is not a clinical diagnosis. It is a generic term used by non-clinicians to describe a measure of depression, anxiety, and stressor-related distress. While the intensity of these conditions may not reach the level required to diagnose a mental disorder, they are often sufficient to impair a person's ability to function normally.

The term reached a pinnacle of popularity in 1965-1966 when it became part of the lyrics of a number one song by the English rock band Rolling Stones. The song was titled "19th Nervous Breakdown."

Recognizing Mental Illness

Person suffering from serious mental disorders such as schizophrenia, major depression, and bipolar disorder (manic, hypomanic, and depressive episodes), when severe, are easily recognized. When the intensity of these disorders is less than severe, impairment becomes less obvious. Generally speaking, the more moderate the person's impairment, the more difficult it is to recognize.

When assessing for mental illness, officers must evaluate a person's behavior within context. It is not difficult to imagine that behaviors which might indicate mental illness in one situation may not be so indicative in another.

Defining Mental Illness

Every state provides a legal definition of mental illness or mental disorder. In Colorado, the statutory definition of a "person with a mental illness" was replaced with "mental health disorder" in 2017:

"Mental health disorder" includes one or more substantial disorders of the cognitive, volitional, or emotional processes that grossly impairs judgment or capacity to recognize reality or to control behavior. An intellectual or developmental disability is insufficient to either justify or exclude a finding of a mental health disorder pursuant to the provisions of this article 65. (C.R.S.27-65-102 (11.5) Definitions).

Under the law and in clinical conceptualizations, intellectual disability (formerly known as *mental retardation*) and developmental disability are different than mental illness. This difference is especially important in the distinctions that must be made in emergency situations where officers might invoke an involuntary detention due to mental illness. It is important for police officers to understand the legal definition of intellectual and developmental disability as well as that of mental illness or disorder (see Modern History of Intellectual Development Disorder below).

Voluntary and Involuntary Compliance

The goal of all police interactions is voluntary compliance. Police officers seek, desire, and should be trained in methods of interpersonal communication which improve the probability of voluntary compliance. During police interactions, when there is voluntary compliance, the interaction moves in the direction desired by the officer (for example, when an officer asks someone to move along and the person leaves the area). When there is noncompliance, and depending upon the circumstances, officers may be justified in using force to compel compliance. This type of compliance is involuntary. In cases of involuntary compliance, persons do not willingly follow the directions of officers. During involuntary compliance, the police ethic for the use of force is to engage only the degree necessary to accomplish the task. Depending on the circumstances, it can include deadly force.

Human behavior is ultimately unpredictable. This is true because the most we can do is predict the probability of behavior. No matter how high the probability that persons will behave in a particular way, they can always act otherwise. This is true under the best of circumstances.

The odds of predicting human behavior are confounded by mental illness. In practical terms, this means that when officers are interacting with a person that is mentally ill, they must always engage appropriate officer safety measures. Officers must avoid a false sense of security due to initially cooperative behavior. Every officer knows that behavior can change in an instant. This is true of all persons. Research shows that statistically, persons that are mentally ill represent about the same level of threat to police officers as those not mentally ill. Having said this, keep in mind that based upon the actual symptoms of particular mental illnesses, *some mentally ill persons may represent a significant threat to the safety of police officers and others.*

In summary, police officers should never bet their lives on the probability that any person, mentally ill or otherwise, will act as expected.

Field Assessments for Mental Illness

Police officers must be capable of conducting field assessments for mental illness. The standards for police officer field assessments are different from those assessments conducted by mental health professionals. In field assessments, police officers need only to determine (1) whether reasonable cause exists to believe that a person is mentally ill, and (2) due to the mental illness, does the person represents a danger to self, others, or is gravely disabled. To accomplish this task, officers rely on their personal observations, information gathered from reliable others, and information obtained from the person being assessed. The ability of officers to conduct accurate field assessments leads to better decision-making and improved call or case resolution.

Speech and field assessment

Speech is a form of behavior that can provide significant information during field assessments, especially when assessing for psychotic disorders. During psychotic episodes, a person's speech can be marked by several unusual phenomena:

Loose associations. Loose associations are verbal responses which do not follow any logical sequence (sometimes referred to as *word salad*). They are reflective of disorganized thinking and a deficit in the ability to form ongoing coherent thoughts.

Clanging. Clanging, also known as *clang association* is a condition wherein words are put together based on their sound and not their meaning, like "I'm going home for dome to find foam." In clanging, the words spoken do not express a coherent thought.

Echolalia. This is indicated by repetition of a word, phrase, or sentence spoken by someone else. For example, to the inquiry, "Are you ok?" the person responds, "Are you ok, are you ok."

Perseveration. Perseveration is repeating words in an unusual manner such as "*I like candy, candy, candy.*" Such responses can also be expressed in answer to different questions, "What is your name? *I like candy.* Are you ok? *I like candy.* How did you get here? *I like candy.*"

Neologisms (invented words). For example, "I need to find my *timbrycer.*" Strings of nonsense words or meaningless mumblings may also be present.

The speech abnormalities of psychotic disorders are frequently accompanied by odd or unusual behaviors or conditions such as inappropriate clothing for the context or temperature, eating odd substances, manipulation of feces, a failure to maintain personal hygiene, assuming unusual postures, and body movements consistent with responding to internal voices or delusional beliefs. The more police officers understand the behavioral expressions and symptoms of mental disorders, the more likely they are to make accurate field assessments.

Of the more serious mental disorders, persons suffering from a psychotic disorder, major depression, and bipolar disorder are most likely to come to the attention of police. When officers are interacting with persons suffering from a mental illness, they must always remember that serious mental illness is a disease and that *it is not against the law to be mentally ill.* Therefore, police options for resolution are intentionally limited.

Psychotic Disorders

Psychotic disorders are some of the most debilitating of the mental disorders. Schizophrenia is the most widely known psychotic disorder. It is characterized by impairment in several critical areas of normal functioning. Schizophrenia represents a condition wherein the person experiences odd and sometimes bizarre hallucinations, delusions, disorganized thinking, and emotional disturbances. These cause the person to behave in very strange and unusual ways. Historically, persons experiencing a psychotic disorder were considered as having "lost contact with reality." This continues to be an apt description, as a person suffering from schizophrenia will often appear to be lost in the aberrant world of hallucination, delusion, thinking difficulties, and emotional distress.

Hallucination

Hallucination is a disorder of perception. Persons experiencing hallucinations may see things that are not there, hear things that no one else hears, and often respond to these stimuli in ways that are confusing or frightening to others. Hallucinations can occur in all five senses. In schizophrenia the most common type of hallucination is auditory. Persons afflicted with schizophrenia most often hear voices, although hearing sounds other than voices is possible. The voices can be perceived as coming from the environment or from inside the head. They can be the perceived voices of strangers, dead relatives, or deities. "You're shit" and "You want to f—k your mother" are two actual auditory hallucinations reported by persons diagnosed with schizophrenia. The person that reported the auditory hallucination "you're shit" also reported constantly smelling manure, an olfactory hallucination. The person experiencing the auditory hallucination involving his mother was aged in his 30s and shared a house with her. For him, this unwanted and uncontrollable voice was very disturbing.

In a percentage of cases, the voices of auditory hallucinations are at least partly flattering or complementary. Some persons report that the voices they hear tell them they are beautiful, should be made king or queen, and so forth.

Auditory hallucinations can order persons to do things. These are known as *command hallucinations*. Depending upon their content, they can cause persons to engage in violent behaviors, including killing themselves or harming others. The first thing police officers need to do if they suspect a person is experiencing auditory voice hallucinations is to determine what the voice is saying. This is because officers can interact with a hallucinating person quite differently if the person informs the officer that the voice is saying, "You'll never amount to anything" as opposed to "Cops are dangerous and should be hurt."

Command hallucinations in schizophrenia are more common than previously thought. In one group of patients diagnosed with schizophrenia, auditory hallucinations commanding harm to others was reported by 30 percent of those assessed. Twenty-two percent of these patients reported that they had complied with the commands (McNiel et al., 2000). In another study, command hallucinations were documented in 50 percent of outpatients with schizophrenia; however, not all of the commands were violent in content (Zisook et al., 1995). Complying with commands, violent or otherwise, is more likely if the hallucinated voice is recognized and if the commands are related to a specific delusion (Hersh & Borum, 1998).

A lethal combination of hallucination and delusion was seen in the well-publicized Son of Sam serial killings in New York City during 1976 and 1977. During this time, six people were murdered and seven others were wounded. The crimes were carried out by David Berkowitz (born Richard David Falco) who claimed that he acted on command of his neighbor's (Sam Carr) demon-possessed dog, a Labrador retriever named Harvey.

As we have seen, hallucinations can occur in sense combination. A person with paranoid schizophrenia might hear voices and taste poison in their food, smell noxious odors, or see strange and spying faces. About twenty percent of persons with schizophrenia hear voices and experience tactile hallucinations. One of the most frightening tactile hallucinations is *formication* (from the Latin *formica,* meaning ant). Formication is feeling bugs walking on or crawling under the skin. Persons experiencing formication often need to be temporarily restrained to keep them from harming themselves in an effort to remove the surface or subdermal insects.

Hallucination, illusion, and, vivid image

Hallucinations are different from *illusions.* Illusions involve misperception or misinterpretation of actual visual stimuli. Illusions are relatively common in human experience and are not considered a feature of psychotic disorders or mental illness (nearly everyone is familiar with the idea of "optical illusion").

In fact, police officers are very familiar with the illusion phenomenon. Most officers, tired on a midnight shift, have experienced the late-night perception of a "crouching man," which upon closer inspection turns out to be a fire hydrant or a small shrub. Illusions are different from vivid images (chapter 4) in their etiology. Illusions are not considered a high-stress, critical incident visual phenomenon.

Charles Bonnet syndrome

The visual hallucinations sometimes reported in schizophrenia must be distinguished from the visions associated with *Charles Bonnet syndrome* (CBS). In CBS, mentally healthy persons with significant vision loss experience complex visual phenomena. The visions of CBS are most frequently comprised of lines and color patterns; vague, nondescript, disembodied faces; people and animals; plants and trees; and various inanimate objects. The visions can be animated and move about the person's visual field – in one case, miniature people running about tipping their hats and waving their arms. CBS is predominately observed in the elderly suffering from macular degeneration and glaucoma, but can appear in others who are visually impaired (Vukicevic & Fitzmaurice, 2008).

Many persons experiencing CBS know nothing about it. They may become frightened by the visions or fear that they are mentally ill. For the latter reason, they often keep their experiences secret.

Although there are no known effective treatments for CBS, intentional blinking or staring directly at the vision can sometimes help. Remaining in stimulating social environments and well-lit areas may also produce some improvement. Police officers can help visually impaired persons reporting such visions by referring them to their physician. Write down "Charles Bonnet syndrome" for the person so that they may bring the note to their doctor—this should be done because many physicians are unfamiliar with CBS.

Once the causes of CBS are understood by those afflicted, any associated anxiety normally diminishes. Keep in mind that the symptoms of CBS are not indicative of schizophrenia or any other mental disorder. There are no auditory hallucinations in CBS. The visions of people sometimes seen in CBS do not speak.

Delusion

Delusion is a disorder of thinking. Delusions differ from thoughts or beliefs that are simply incorrect. For instance, if you thought there was a wolf in a closet and I arranged for you to look in the closet and you did not see a wolf, you would change your belief. This is not the case for those experiencing delusions.

Case study: The case of Miss M demonstrates delusional thinking. Miss M was a psychiatric patient diagnosed with paranoid schizophrenia. She was being treated with medications and psychotherapy. Her delusional system involved the belief that wild animals seeking to harm her were hiding in various spaces. There was one particular closet of the psychiatric unit that caused her great dismay. She was fearful of a wolf which she believed was hiding there. One day, upon encouragement from hospital staff, she chose to confront her fear and examine the closet. She slowly walked up to the closet. Upon her permission and with staff support, a staff member slowly opened the closet door. With great courage, she looked into the closet. When asked about her observations, she said that she did not see a wolf. When asked if she now felt safer, she quickly answered, "No! The wolf disappears when anyone looks at it, and it comes back as soon as you look away!" Responses like this are common in delusional thinking. Delusions cannot be altered by reality testing. They have a magical quality that resists alteration.

For Miss M, after some time and with proper treatment, the wild animal delusion vanished. Once in remission, she discussed her delusion openly, realized it was a false belief, and remembered everything about her closet confrontation.

The most common types of delusion are paranoid or persecutory, referential, grandiose, and bizarre. Paranoid or persecutory delusions involve thoughts of being persecuted, singled-out, and marked for harm. Referential delusions involve the thought that certain behaviors are directed at oneself, like believing the TV news broadcaster is speaking directly to you. Grandiose delusions are thoughts and beliefs of self-importance, greatness, and superiority. Bizarre delusions are characterized by strange and odd beliefs such as the belief that your home attic is occupied by invisible interstellar aliens. Other types of delusions include nihilistic, erotomanic, and somatic. Delusional thinking can include a combination of the major types, or represent something altogether different.

Just what constitutes a delusion is not always easy to determine. As stated in the DSM-5-TR, "The distinction between a delusion and a strongly held idea is sometimes difficult to determine and depends in part on the degree of conviction with which the belief is held despite clear or reasonable contradictory evidence regarding its veracity" (101). A situation too often seen in modern-day politics.

Of the more interesting specific features of delusional thinking are *thought insertion* – the belief that others are inserting thoughts into your head; *thought broadcasting* - where it is believed your thoughts are being broadcast to others; and *thoughts of influence* - where you believe that you can influence the external world by the mere act of thinking.

Although delusion is frequently observed in conjunction with hallucination, delusions can exist in the absence or non-prominence of hallucinations. In cases where delusions are present and there is no history of hallucination or schizophrenia, *delusional disorder* is diagnosed.

Emotional Disturbance and Behavior

The emotional and behavioral disturbances associated with schizophrenia and other psychotic disorders include the negative symptom of anhedonia (an inability to experience pleasure), emotional lability (lack of emotional stability), depression, anxiety, poor impulse control, and unusual behaviors, such as eating cigarette butts, standing naked in public places, and odd body posturing.

Psychotic Disorders and Memory

It is common for previously psychotic patients to remember their hallucinations and delusions. Like the woman with the wolf-in-the-closet delusion, most patients retain full recall of their experiences during the symptom phase of psychotic episodes, including how they were treated by clinical staff and police officers. These memories endure long after symptoms disappear.

Diagnosis of Psychotic Disorders

Currently, there are no definitive laboratory or psychometric tests for the diagnosis of the psychotic disorders. Therefore, the diagnoses of specific psychotic disorders are dependent upon presenting signs and symptoms, and their duration.

In addition to schizophrenia (symptoms for at least six months), the class of psychotic disorders includes *brief psychotic disorder* (symptoms for at least one day and less than one month), *schizophreniform disorder* (symptoms for at least one month but less than six months), and *schizoaffective disorder* (symptoms of schizophrenia and a major mood episode) (DSM-5-TR, 2022).

Summary of Field Assessment for Psychotic Disorders

In a field assessment for psychotic disorders, police officers should observe the person and engage in discussion.

Observe the person's behavior and appearance to determine:

1. if behavior is appropriate for context.
2. if clothing is appropriate for temperature.
3. if behavior is strange, bizarre, or otherwise odd.
4. if there are issues of personal hygiene.

Engage in discussion to:

1. determine the presence of hallucinations and delusions. Rule out command hallucination.
2. determine the presence of disorganized thinking, loose or unusual verbal associations, odd verbal patterns, and any accompanying bizarre thoughts.
3. assess emotional disturbance.
4. assess if the person is a danger to self, others, or gravely disabled.
5. rule out the possibility of a medical condition. If medical concerns are present, request medical assistance.
6. determine degree of impairment in social, occupational, and personal environments.
7. assess for necessity of emergency detention and treatment.

Suggestions for Police Officers Interacting with Persons who are Psychotic or Otherwise Mentally Ill

Always be cautious and remain alert. Be mindful of your level of awareness. Keep in mind that human behavior is ultimately unpredictable. Assessment of mental illness and threat level is further complicated by alcohol and other drug intoxication.

Take time to consider the situation. Request backup. Interacting with a person that is mentally ill is not the time to go it alone. Another officer may better relate to the person for reasons that are not immediately apparent. Also, a team approach offers a greater margin of officer safety. Unless *duty bound to take action*, proceed slowly and thoughtfully.

Communication. Talk to the person in a way that encourages communication. Speak in simple language but do not talk down to the person. Try to develop rapport and trust. When appropriate, consider deemphasizing your authority by using first names. This often helps to reduce the person's anxiety. *Do not deemphasize officer safety.* State your purpose: "I am here to help." Avoid abusive language and threatening behavior. If appropriate under the circumstances, explain what you are going to do before you do it.

This also decreases anxiety. Additionally, it lessens the probability that the person will act out. Avoid insults, challenges, and profanity. Keep providing rational verbal stimuli until you achieve voluntary compliance or you assess that the person is too mentally ill or otherwise incapable of being influenced in this manner.

Interaction. Many mentally ill persons are or become frightened, especially upon arrival of the police. Most will respond positively to a caring attitude. Ask for the person's help to accomplish your goals. Build upon the time that you are in contact. For example, "We have been talking for ten minutes. We have done well together. Let's keep working as a team. How about (specify your request)." Consider the *short order* if necessary or if rapport fails. A short order is a brief, authoritative order aimed at gaining compliance or interrupting dangerous or undesirable behaviors. STOP! SHOW ME YOUR HANDS! and DO IT NOW! are examples of short orders. Compliance with short orders is founded upon a presumed history of a person complying with authority figures.

Appropriate supportive touch. Some mentally ill persons respond well to *appropriate* supportive touch such as a pat on the back or a handshake. Apply an appropriate supportive touch only if you assess that it is safe for you and the person to do so. If you use an appropriate supportive touch to calm or reassure a person with mental illness, be certain that the person cannot easily access your police equipment. Appropriate supportive touch is best used when there is more than one officer on scene. Keep in mind that even the best-intended supportive physical contact can trigger an anxiety, aggressive, or violent response, so use with caution.

Mentally ill does not mean unintelligent. Never assume that the person cannot understand you. Be particularly careful of what you say during side conversations with other officers.

Do not allow yourself to be angered. Try to remain calm. The person may be very adept at provoking anger (name calling, threats, and so on). For many persons with mental illness, anger directed at others is often displaced. The person's anger responses are frequently the result of frustration, anxiety, or fear. If you remain calm, you increase the probability that the person will be voluntarily compliant. Some persons will mildly resist to a point and cooperate after a degree of rapport is established.

Avoid excitement. As a general rule, limit outside stimulation. A quiet, more stable environment tends to decrease anxiety. Ask the person to move to another, quieter location if necessary. Lessened anxiety increases the probability of voluntary compliance.

Avoid deception. It is sometimes tempting to lie to bring about a resolution; however, deception is often unnecessary and may be harmful. Exception: when life is at risk, any strategy or technique that you reasonably think might accomplish your goal is justified.

Disposition. Contact relatives or friends of the person if necessary. Leave them in place if there is no reason to do otherwise. If, due to mental illness, the person is a threat to self or others, or is gravely disabled, ask for cooperation and initiate voluntary intervention. If the person will not consent to voluntary intervention, initiate the procedure for involuntary evaluation and treatment (Reiser, 1982).

Mood Disorders: Depression and Bipolar Disorder

Mood disorders are mental illnesses that are characterized by disturbances in *affect*. Affect refers to emotions and feelings. For example, the profound sadness in depression and the feelings of euphoria in mania are disorders of affect. Disturbances of sleep, appetite, concentration, cognitive ability, sexual interest, and behavior are often observed in the mood disorders. *Major depressive disorder* and *bipolar disorder* are two of the more well-known mood disorders.

Major Depressive Disorder

Major depressive disorder is characterized by feelings of sadness, flat affect, loss of interest in previously enjoyed activities, sleep disturbances (either insomnia or hypersomnia), appetite disturbances (either no appetite or overeating), loss of interest in sex, impairment in memory and concentration, unintended weight loss or gain, feelings of guilt or worthlessness, thoughts of death, suicidal thinking, suicidal behavior, and psychomotor retardation. There are several course specifiers for the diagnosis of major depressive disorder: mild, moderate, severe, with psychotic features, in partial remission, in full remission, and unspecified.

Other specifiers include, with anxious distress, with melancholic features, with catatonia, with peripartum onset, and with seasonal pattern.

If a person experiences clinically significant distress or impairment due to depression, and does not meet the criteria for major depressive disorder or the bipolar disorders, *persistent depressive disorder* may be diagnosed.

Bipolar Disorder

Bipolar disorder evolved out of the former *manic-depressive disorder*. As a diagnosis, bipolar disorder first appeared in DSM-III (1980). Bipolar I and bipolar II were specified.

To be diagnosed with bipolar I disorder, persons have to be experiencing, or have at some previous time experienced, a manic episode. Manic episodes cause marked impairment in normal functioning and can include all or several of the following: feelings of euphoria, loss of need to sleep, expansive thinking, increased interest in sex, poor impulse control (travel, spending, and so on), pressured speech, racing thoughts, irritability, distractibility, grandiose delusions, loss of judgment, high energy levels, behaving in uncharacteristic ways, the presence of psychotic features, and the need for hospitalization. Overall, the person appears "revved up" and unable to effectively manage life's demands. Manic episodes may be mild, moderate, or severe. A person may or may not have experienced a major depressive episode or a hypomanic episode. A manic episode in the absence of a depressive episode or hypomanic episode is sufficient to diagnose bipolar I.

Bipolar II disorder is comprised of at least one past or present hypomanic episode and a major depressive episode. Hypomanic episodes, while similar to manic episodes, differ from them in that they do not include psychotic features and are "not severe enough to cause marked impairment in social or occupational functioning or to necessitate hospitalization" (DSM-5-TR, 151). Like manic episodes, hypomanic episodes may be mild, moderate or severe.

Mixed features may be present in bipolar I and bipolar II. Mixed features are characterized by the simultaneous presence of symptoms associated with a manic or hypomanic episode and a major depressive episode.

Bipolar disorders may cycle. The person may experience recurring, alternating manic or hypomanic episodes and major depressive episodes. If there are at least four manic, hypomanic, mixed, or major depressive episodes within the past 12 months, *rapid-cycling* is specified.

While the major depressive episodes involved in bipolar disorder and in major depressive disorder appear similar, they often need to be treated differently. This is because some of the medications used to treat major depressive disorder will trigger a manic or hypomanic episode in those with bipolar disorder depression. The underlying mechanism by which this occurs is not yet fully understood. Other substances known to trigger manic or hypomanic episodes in those with bipolar disorder include steroids, cocaine, and cannabis (Williams, 2006).

Bipolar II disorder is considered an independent diagnosis and not a milder form of bipolar I disorder.

If a person experiences clinically significant distress or impairment due to mood aberrations that do not meet the criteria for the bipolar disorders, *cyclothymic disorder* may be diagnosed.

Mental Illness, Alcohol, and Drugs

Some persons with mental illness abuse alcohol and other drugs. Some persons that are mentally ill are also substance addicted. The intake of alcohol and other drugs may be an attempt to cope with the symptoms of the underlying mental disorder, especially in cases of psychotic and anxiety disorders. Regardless of the reason for substance use, if continued, it is not long before substance use becomes a problem and an independent focus for treatment. In such cases, the person is said to have a *dual diagnosis* (mental illness and substance use disorder). The presence of a substance use disorder significantly complicates the treatment of any simultaneously occurring mental illness.

There is a major controversy within the field of alcohol and drug use disorder. This controversy is expressed by (1) those experts who feel that substance use disorder is a disease and out of the control of the person and (2) those who conceptualize substance use as a choice. The fact that some persons are able to stop using their preferred substance is seen by choice supporters as evidence for their position. They oppose the disease hypothesis by arguing that a person can choose not to use their preferred substance, whereas in a true disease, like diabetes, a person cannot choose not to have the disease.

Mental Illness and Medical Conditions

There are many medical conditions that can produce psychiatric symptoms. Police officers must remain aware that some persons who appear mentally ill or intoxicated may be suffering from a medical condition requiring immediate medical attention.

Mental Illness and Medication

Great advances in the pharmacological treatment of mental disorders have been made since the synthesis of chlorpromazine in 1950 (sold in America under the brand name Thorazine). The success of Thorazine in the treatment of schizophrenia and other mental disorders revolutionized the practice of psychiatry. Today, much more is known about the neurobiology of the brain, the physiology of mental illness, and the medications that best treat mental illnesses.

Like all medications, psychoactive medications have *main effects* and *side effects*. The main effect of a medication is that which treats or ameliorates the disorder or symptom. Main effects are useful and desirable. Side effects are mostly undesirable. They are effects of medication that do not treat targeted symptoms and often cause additional difficulties.

Some side effects of medications used to treat one condition have gained a main effect to treat another. The common aspirin is a good example. Aspirin is an effective analgesic; its main effect being pain reduction. It has long been known that a side effect of aspirin is stopping blood platelets from forming clots. This side effect of aspirin is now used as a modern-day main effect to help prevent the recurrence of heart attack.

The side effects of some psychoactive medications are serious enough that other medications are needed to manage them. Without these ancillary medications, the person might not be able to continue taking the primary medication. Thorazine is good example of this. Without the simultaneous administration of an anticholinergic medication, the side effects of Thorazine are normally too serious to continue its use.

Sometimes the side effects of a medication are so severe or undesirable that the medication must be discontinued. If the medication is stopped, the side effects normally subside, however the symptoms for which the medication was prescribed usually reappear. Some symptoms worsen significantly when primary medications are discontinued.

For police officers, knowing something about psychoactive medications can greatly aid field assessments. Knowledge of the more widely prescribed antipsychotics, antidepressants, and anxiolytics is especially useful. This is because knowledge of a person's past or present medications provides a short-cut source of information about their condition and likely diagnosis. A list of medications used to treat various mental disorders has been published by the National Institute of Mental Health. It can be accessed at *www.nimh.nih.gov.*

Treatments for Mental Illness

There are many treatments for mental illness. Treatments for mental illness have changed dramatically since the days of chained confinement, spinning chairs, ice baths, and strait jackets. Modern conceptions of mental illness and a greater understanding of the etiologies of mental disorders have improved therapies and therapeutic outcomes for millions of people.

Today, there are two primary treatments for mental disorders: psychotherapy (counseling) and psychopharmacology (medication). There are also additional treatments including the electrotherapies, "new age" practices, and psychosurgery. All have as their goal the alleviation of symptoms associated with mental illness.

Psychotherapy

There are several theories or "schools" of psychology. These include psychoanalysis, behaviorism, cognitive-behaviorism, gestalt, humanism, existentialism, the list goes on and on. Each has its own orientation for psychotherapy. The psychotherapeutic interventions based upon the various schools are similar in some cases and quite different in others. Therefore, strategies for psychotherapy can vary greatly.

Psychotherapy involves communication between a mental health professional and a person seeking assistance. It differs from casual conversation in that it includes a trained therapist and is focused to address identified difficulties.

While psychotherapy is a major component of the treatment of mental illness, many persons also find psychotherapy helpful when dealing with the stressors of everyday living, such as work stress, grief, marriage, and other personal relationships.

Some counseling approaches are tied to the theory of one school of psychology. Others are not. Many psychologists and other clinicians practice eclectic psychotherapy, a combination and blending of several therapies and techniques originating from several schools of psychology.

Comprehensive psychotherapy programs often include elements of proper nutrition (diet) and appropriate physical activity (exercise).

Psychopharmacology

Psychopharmacology has a long history. The use of substances to influence consciousness, mood, mental conditions, and psychological ailments has been known since ancient times. Various societies have made use of the over four thousand plants known to include psychoactive substances. At least sixty of these plants or plant derived substances have been in common use for millennia, including cannabis, opium, coca, tea, coffee, tobacco, and alcohol (Malcolm, 1972).

Modern psychopharmacology is directed at treating various mental disorders. The development of psychoactive drugs with high efficacy and low or no side effects is the primary goal of psychoactive drug research laboratories. Their efforts have proven beneficial. There is little doubt that modern psychoactive medications make it possible for many persons to live a better life. In many cases of mental illness, symptom improvement brought about by psychopharmacological treatment is remarkable.

Some psychoactive medications seem to have staying power, such as the *selective serotonin reuptake inhibitor* (SSRI) Prozac (FDA approved in 1987). Prozac remains one the most prescribed antidepressant medications in America. Others seem to come and go. Of these medications, some are removed from the market following unanticipated health risks, some remain unpopular because of troubling side effects, and some simply never seem to catch on.

What of psychotherapeutic approaches that combine psychotherapy and psychopharmacology? Interestingly, research outcome studies have shown that psychotherapy is at least as effective as medication in the treatment of mild to moderate depression. However, research indicates that neither psychotherapy nor antidepressant medication alone appears to be as effective as both combined (Keller et al., 2000). Psychotherapy has also been shown to enhance the treatment outcomes of medication regimens for psychotic and other mental disorders (Smith, 2003).

How do antidepressant medications work? While the various classes of antidepressants work via various intercellular mechanisms, the SSRIs are thought to work by increasing the amount of serotonin (a chemical neurotransmitter) in the brain. The development of SSRI medication was spurred on by the notion that at least some depressions were caused by the lack of sufficient levels of brain serotonin. This theory came to be known as the *serotonin-hypothesis* of depression. It fit nicely with the idea that depression was caused by a chemical imbalance in the brain.

Several studies have challenged the authenticity of the serotonin-hypothesis of depression. These studies concluded that while some depressed persons seemed to improve on SSRI and other antidepressant medication, the improvement was statistically similar to that reported by depressed persons that received pills which were chemically benign (Kirsch, 2009). Their improvement was attributed to the *placebo effect*, the ability of expectation and hope to change the way a person feels. The placebo effect for SSRI and other antidepressants was stronger in cases of mild to moderate depression than severe depression. In severe cases, the chemical effects of antidepressants may yield an actual benefit although that effect was reportedly slight (Begley, 2010).

Why do some people improve after being provided placebos? One theory is that the placebo effect may be due to the body's ability to respond to its own naturally occurring substances. For this to occur, it appears necessary that a person believes the medication may help. If this is true, it represents an interesting explanation of how antidepressants, and likely some other medications, work.

Recent critics of the notion that SSRI and other antidepressants do not work maintain that studies such as those cited above "didn't so much show that antidepressants don't work, but rather that placebos often work just as well when the person taking them is enrolled in a research study and has only mild to moderate depressive symptoms" (Pierre, 2018,1).

The question of SSRI-antidepressant efficacy was most recently addressed in a systematic review of existing SSRI-antidepressant research by psychiatrist Joanna Moncrieff and her colleagues. Following this review, the authors concluded that while SSRIs were found to numb emotion, "Our comprehensive review of the major strands of research on serotonin shows there is no convincing evidence that depression is associated with, or caused by, lower serotonin concentrations or activity" ... "We suggest it is time to acknowledge that the serotonin theory of depression is not empirically substantiated" (2022,1).

As it stands, there remains controversy and some confusion in this area. Many clinicians feel that the issue has been settled - the serotonin and chemical imbalance theory of depression has been debunked (Lane, 2022). Others maintain that this information is nothing new..."very few scientists actually subscribe to such a simplistic version of the serotonin theory at this point" (Gorman & Gorman, 2022,1). Psychiatrist Tracy Marks expressed this view, "We see depression to be much more complicated than a chemical imbalance, but involving neuroplastic changes—the ability for the brain to rewire itself and change pathways" (as cited in Weg, 2022).

But if chemical imbalances or low levels of serotonin do not cause depression, what does? Candidates for the cause(s) of depression include the constant rewiring of brain neurons, brain inflammation, the gut-brain connection, and hormonal changes (Perlmutter, 2022). Additional research will eventually clarify the science. In the meantime, debate over whether antidepressants work due to placebo effect, brain chemical alteration, an unknown secondary process, or a combination of these, continues.

A disturbing finding involving antidepressant medication is that in some children, adolescents, and young adults, treatment with antidepressants was found to *increase* suicidal thinking and behavior. This finding quickly prompted controversy, with some clinicians believing that it was the result of unconvincing research. Nonetheless, in October, 2004 the FDA issued a "black box" label warning indicating that the use of some SSRI-antidepressant medication prescribed for some conditions may cause an increase in the suicidality of young people.

St. John's Wort

There is some evidence that the popular mood-enhancing botanical, St. John's wort (an extract from the flowering plant *Hypericum perforatum*) may have a therapeutic effect on mild to moderate depression. There is also evidence that it can dangerously interact or interfere with the effects of several classes of prescribed medications, especially antidepressants. Persons taking prescribed medications and/or oral contraceptives should consult with their physicians before initiating a course of St. John's wort or any herbal remedy (NIMH, 2010). Research conducted into the use of St. John's wort demonstrated that it could produce a number of undesirable side-effects including agitation and anxiety, dizziness, diarrhea, dry mouth, headache, and fatigue. The safety of using St. John's wort during pregnancy or while breastfeeding has yet to be established.

Electroconvulsive and Transcranial Therapy

Electroconvulsive therapy (ECT) (formerly called *electroshock*) evolved out of the work of several persons, including Hungarian neuropathologist Ladislas J. Meduna (1896-1964). In 1934, his research led him suspect that epilepsy and schizophrenia were antagonistic – that they could not occur together. From this, he reasoned that seizures might somehow protect those with epilepsy from developing schizophrenia. If this were true, he wondered if inducing seizures would treat those suffering from schizophrenia. He decided to test his theory. He injected several schizophrenic patients with camphor, an epileptogenic organic compound. As expected, the camphor produced seizures. He repeated the process several times with the same patients over several days. After a course of multiple induced seizures, most patients showed remarkable improvement (Suleman, 2020).

Meduna's seizure-treatment successes launched a profession-wide effort to find more efficient ways to produce seizure. In 1935, the seizure-producing drug *metrazol* and the hormone *insulin* were being widely used in Europe for this purpose. While metrazol and insulin-induced seizure continued to produce positive outcomes, there remained serious drawbacks. A better method to produce seizures was needed.

In 1938 in Italy, neurophysiologist Ugo Cerletti and psychiatrist Lucio Bini were the first to use electricity as a stimulus for human convulsive (seizure) therapy. It is said that Cerletti came upon the idea after watching pigs being anesthetized by electroshock prior to slaughter. He began experimenting with electroshock on dogs. He soon refined the procedure and began using electricity to induce seizures in patients. The results were gratifying. Many patients diagnosed with serious mental illnesses improved significantly following electricity-induced seizure treatment.

The news of electroconvulsive therapy (ECT) and its effectiveness spread rapidly throughout Europe and to the United States. ECT had found its place in the treatment of mental disorders and was initially used to treat a wide variety of mental conditions. This is not the case today.

Modern ECT is used primarily to treat life threatening depression and select other conditions when medications and alternative therapies have failed. It is also used as a first-line intervention, but usually only when lesser therapies are contraindicated. In the United States, ECT is normally conducted in series – two to three treatments per week for three to four weeks.

ECT looks much different today than it did when first developed. The early practice of applying high-dosage electricity to fully conscious patients (which immediately rendered them unconscious), resulted in some seizures so violent as to cause broken bones. This no longer occurs. Present-day ECT seizures are significantly attenuated. Patients are anesthetized and administered muscle-relaxant medication prior to the procedure. Blood pressure, oxygen levels, heart rhythm, and brain activity is monitored. Low dosage electricity is applied. In combination, these factors make modern ECT much safer than it once was. While safer, just how ECT brings about mental improvement remains unknown. Most theories suggest that it affects brain neurotransmitters, connections between brain cells, brain proteins, and "turning on" of genes.

Critics of ECT argue that real ECT is only marginally more effective than placebo ECT, and that the possible side effects of ECT outweigh its benefits (Ross, 2006). Despite these criticisms, ECT is still in use and remains an option for the treatment of certain mental disorders.

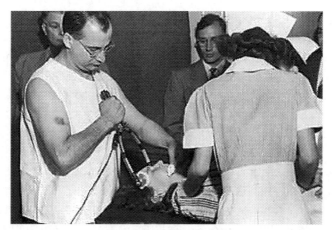

James G. Shanklin, M.D. performs ECT at Western State Hospital in Virginia in 1949 in preparation for a Walter Freeman lobotomy.

A milder and more recently developed electro-treatment for depression is *transcranial direct current stimulation* (tDCS). This treatment involves the application of a very weak electrical current to specific areas of the brain via electrodes placed on the scalp. Unlike traditional ECT, tDCS does not produce seizures.

Transcranial magnetic stimulation (TMS) differs from electro-treatments in that no electrodes are applied to the patient. Instead, the procedure utilizes a changing magnetic field to induce changes in brain functioning. TMS received FDA approval for the treatment of depression in 2008, and as a treatment for migraine in 2013.

New age therapies

New age therapies are comprised of those interventions that lie outside the currently accepted norms of psychotherapeutic intervention. They have no or little scientific evidence of efficacy. Certain energy-alteration and specific-technique body therapies fall within this category.

Psychosurgery

Psychosurgery is surgery performed on the brain which has as its goal the treatment of a diagnosed mental disorder. This is different from other forms of brain surgery, which have as their goal the treatment of various neurological conditions.

The oldest known form of psychosurgery, *trepanation*, was practiced as early as 6500 BCE (Restak, 2000). Trepanation is the act of drilling a hole in the skull. Historically it was used to treat headache, seizures, and what would come to be called mental illness. Trepanation is still used to treat subdural hematomas and several other medical conditions. There remain some groups that believe there is benefit in "venting" the brain and continue to practice trepanation, however there is no modern application of trepanation for the treatment of mental illness.

During the heyday of psychosurgery, the most often performed procedure was the pre-frontal lobotomy. A significant figure in the American history of lobotomy was Walter J. Freeman II, M.D. (1895-1972). Although Freeman did not invent the lobotomy, he developed the transorbital lobotomy – a procedure wherein an ice pick-type instrument called an orbitoclast (sometimes called a leucotome) was inserted under each eyelid and pounded through the thin bone of the eye socket. Once the orbitoclasts entered the braincase, they were pushed into the brain about one and one-half inches and moved in a preplanned manner. This motion severed the fibers of the prefrontal lobes, separating them from the rest of the brain. Once this was accomplished, the instruments were withdrawn. The lobotomy was completed.

Of the estimated 40,000 to 50,000 lobotomies performed in the United States from the 1940s through the 1960s, Freeman recorded performing 3,439 of them; most by using the "ice pick" method. His fee for performing an ice pick lobotomy, $25.00; his anesthesia, electroconvulsive shock (Cordingly, 2005). Freeman performed his last lobotomy in 1967 on long-time patient, 52-year-old Helen Mortensen. She died of a cerebral hemorrhage following the procedure. It was her third Freeman lobotomy (NPR, 2005). Following the death of Mortensen, Freeman's license to practice medicine was revoked.

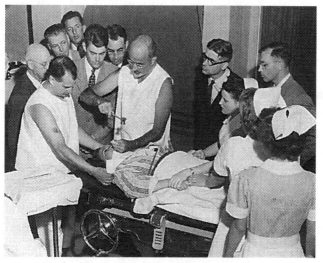

Walter Freeman performing an "ice pick" lobotomy on a patient previously anesthetized with ECT by James G. Shanklin.

The lobotomy rapidly fell out of favor when serious side effects were noted and new medications were developed, especially the anti-psychotic drug chlorpromazine (Thorazine).

The lobotomy, once touted as a cure-all for serious and chronic mental illness, has no current application in the present-day treatment of mental disorders.

Modern and more recently developed psychosurgery performed to treat intractable mood and obsessive-compulsive disorders include cingulotomy, subcaudate tractotomy, and limbic leucotomy.

Dementia and Delirium

Dementia is a neurocognitive disorder which causes impairment in brain function. It has multiple causes and results in generalized cognitive deterioration. The primary symptoms of dementia are memory loss, moodiness, communication problems, and confusion. In dementia, *executive function* is impaired. Executive function is the term used to describe the highest cognitive abilities of the human being, including information processing and reasoning. If the impairment is significant, the person may not be able to safely live independently. Dementia normally worsens over time. There are many types of dementia. Alzheimer's disease is the most common and likely the most well-known dementia (Geldmacher, 2003). According to the Alzheimer's Association about 1 in 9 Americans over 65 years of age are living with Alzheimer's disease. Women represent about two-thirds of those diagnosed (2022).

Delirium is also a neurocognitive disorder, but different from dementia. Delirium is an impairment of consciousness characterized by reduced awareness of the environment. It normally has a rapid onset. Persons with delirium are disoriented (lack of awareness of date, time, and place), confused, have difficulties paying attention, and may experience hallucinations (mostly visual and tactile). Delirium is often temporary and reversible. Its most likely cause is drugs, prescription or otherwise. Delirium is common after surgery, due to anesthesia and pain control medications. It is sometimes observed in the elderly without a drug etiology, often the result of an underlying health condition such as dehydration or urinary tract or other infection.

Some deliriums are irreversible. Irreversible delirium may be caused by brain injury, stroke, or other physical trauma. Delirium is a serious condition and requires immediate medical assessment and treatment.

Dementia and delirium are not mutually exclusive. Persons with dementia may also experience delirium. For some persons with delirium, the condition evolves into a chronic brain dysfunction similar to dementia (Anton et al., 2006).

Factitious Disorder and Tourette's Disorder

Police officers must know something about factitious disorder and Tourette's disorder.

There are two factitious disorders – *factitious disorder imposed on self* and *factitious disorder imposed on another* (previously called Munchausen syndrome and Munchausen by proxy).

Factitious disorder imposed-on-self involves the falsification, faking, or otherwise intentionally producing medical conditions for the assumed goal of being a patient. Persons with this disorder present themselves to care providers as ill, impaired, or injured. They may inflict harm upon themselves and "doctor shop" in order to continue to receive medical attention. They willingly undergo invasive medical procedures and in the most serious cases, have multiple surgical scars as a result. This behavior can continue even in the absence of obvious external rewards.

Factitious disorder imposed-on-another is diagnosed when a caregiver falsely presents another as ill, injured, or impaired. Persons with this disorder may cause harm to someone else, most often a child, to satisfy their needs. In such circumstances, the condition, illness, or injury is real, but caused by the perpetrator. In several well-known cases, mothers were eventually arrested for poisoning their children with feces, overdosing them with salt, and double-dosing prescribed medications to create their child's illness. Factitious disorder imposed-on-another is a serious condition that has resulted in the death of the victim. Police officers should consider it as a possible factor in all child abuse investigations.

Tourette's is a neurodevelopmental brain disorder which produces multiple involuntary motor tics and one or more verbal tics, with onset before the age of eighteen. The verbal tics can be comprised of throat-clearing sounds, grunts, screams, and words. Sometimes the word vocalizations of a person with Tourette's disorder include profanity and socially inappropriate phrases. A person suffering from Tourette's and engaging in such outbursts due to the disorder must be distinguished from a person intentionally behaving badly.

Myths of Mental Illness

The American Psychiatric Association published the following information in an effort to dispel the myths associated with mental illness.

1. *Mental illness doesn't affect the average person.*
   * Fact: No one is immune to mental illness.
2. *Children do not get mental illnesses.*
   * Fact: In reality, millions of children—from infants through 18-year-olds suffer from diagnosable mental disorders such as depression, attention deficit disorder, and pervasive development disorders. While mental illness can occur at any age, three-fourths of all mental illness begins by age 24.
3. *All people suffering from mental illness receive treatment.*
   * Fact: Only about one in five people dealing with a diagnosable mental disorder seek treatment.
4. *All mentally Ill people are dangerous.*
   * Fact: People suffering from mental illness are statistically about as dangerous as those people without mental illness. People with serious mental illness are more likely to be victims of crime than perpetrators of crime.
5. *If you have a mental illness, you are crazy all the time.*
   * Fact: The course of serious mental illness such as schizophrenia, bi-polar disorder, depression and other mental disorders often "wax and wane" and are influenced by several factors including life circumstances, severity of the illness, and type of treatment (if any) that a person is receiving.
6. *If I am diagnosed with a mental illness, I will have to take drugs or electroshock.*
   * Fact: There are various treatments for mental illness. The recommended type and course of treatment varies with the type and severity of the particular disorder. Mental illnesses take many forms. Some are mild and only interfere with daily life in limited

ways, such as certain phobias (abnormal fears). Other mental health conditions are so severe that a person may need hospital care.

7. *If I go to see a mental health professional, people will look down on me or think I'm crazy, strange, or weird.*
   - Fact: Many people who have a mental illness do not want to talk about it. But mental illness is nothing to be ashamed of! Great strides have been made in public education about the nature of mental illness. As people have begun to understand more about mental illness, the past stigma of visiting with a mental health professional has significantly declined. The fact is that most of us will need some help at some point in our lives.

8. *People never recover from mental illnesses.*
   - Fact: As many as eight in ten people suffering from mental illness can effectively return to normal, productive lives with appropriate treatment. It is a medical condition, just like heart disease or diabetes. And mental health conditions are treatable (includes information from R. Parekh, 2018).

Intellectual Developmental Disorder and Mental Illness

Intellectual developmental disorder (IDD), also referred to as *intellectual disability* (formerly *mental retardation*), is different from mental illness. Whereas mental illness is characterized by signs, symptoms, and additional criteria, the essential features of IDD are deficits in intellectual and adaptive functioning in various domains of social and life skills.

Intellectual developmental disorder and mental illness are not mutually exclusive. It is possible for a person to meet the criteria of IDD and one or more mental disorders.

History of Intellectual Developmental Disorder

Historically, the intelligence quotient (IQ) of a person was derived by dividing their mental age score, determined by standardized intelligence testing, by their chronological age, and multiplying by 100. Therefore, a person 10 years old with an assessed mental age of 10 years would have an IQ of 100. Similarly, a person 10 years old with an assessed mental age of 8 would have an IQ of 80, and so on.

Using this formula, in the early 1900s, American psychologist Henry Goddard (1866-1957) proposed and popularized the following classifications of those determined to be "feeble-minded": *moron* (IQ 70-51), *imbecile* (IQ 50-26), and *idiot* (IQ 25-0). This nomenclature was first presented on May 18, 1910, at a meeting of the American Association for the Study of the Feeble Minded. These diagnostic categories were used for several decades.

The notion of feeble-mindedness and the classifications of moron, imbecile, and idiot fell out of favor toward the end of the 1940s. They were not included in the first DSM (1952). Instead, the DSM utilized a new diagnosis, *mental deficiency.* Mental deficiency was defined as "primarily a defect of intelligence existing since birth, without demonstrated organic brain disease or known prenatal cause" (23). Mental deficiency could be mild, moderate, or severe.

The diagnosis of mental deficiency was replaced by *mental retardation* in the DSM-II (1968). Mental retardation could be borderline, mild, moderate, severe, or profound, depending upon assessed IQ. Years later, in the DSM-III (1980) the "borderline" specifier was deleted. The DSM-IV (1994) and DSM-IV-TR (2000) retained mental retardation as a diagnosis. Mild mental retardation was diagnosed at IQ levels of 50-55 to approximately 70. Moderate mental retardation was specified at IQ levels of 35-40 to 50-55. Severe mental retardation was characterized by IQ levels of 20-25 to 35-40, while profound mental retardation was diagnosed at IQ levels below 20-25.

Mental retardation remained a diagnosis until the publication of DSM-5 (2013). In DSM-5, the diagnosis of mental retardation was replaced by *intellectual developmental disorder (intellectual disability)* (IDD). Intellectual developmental disorder (intellectual disability) was defined as "a disorder with onset during the developmental period that includes both intellectual and adaptive functioning deficits in conceptual, social, and practical domains" (33). This is unchanged in DSM-5-TR (2022) (37).

Standardized intelligence testing continues to be used in the diagnosis of IDD. However, the severity of IDD, *mild, moderate, severe,* or *profound,* is now determined by degree of adaptive functioning and not IQ. This represents a significant departure from the traditional way in which intellectual impairment was assessed.

When the focus of clinical attention is intellectual abilities but the diagnostic criteria of intellectual developmental disorder are not present, *borderline intellectual functioning* is specified. Borderline intellectual functioning is not considered a mental disorder.

Recognizing Intellectual Development Disorder

The ability to appropriately interact with persons with an intellectual disability is an important skill for police officers. This is because some intellectually impaired persons may look adult but cannot act in the manner suggested by their appearance.

Adults who are intellectually impaired:

- may dress, communicate, and comprehend as a child.
- may dress and appear as an adult but be incapable of responding or processing information as an adult.
- may not comply with police commands because they cannot fully understand them or appreciate the gravity of noncompliance. There have been incidents where intellectually impaired persons have attacked police out a sense of anger, fear, or frustration, much like a child with poor impulse or temper control might. In unfortunate circumstances, some officers have had to defend themselves with deadly force.
- may be easily influenced by others. When this happens, they may get into trouble due to a lack of judgment or wanting to belong.
- may be sensitive to their perceived deficits. As compensation, some may become street toughs or thugs. Those persons with abilities closest to average are most likely to come to the attention of police for this reason.

- may wander around the community watching or otherwise interacting with children. This may be because children can be better understood by the person and the person feels better understood by them.
- may come to attention of other adults because of their preference to be in the company of children, especially around playgrounds and parks. This may prompt a call to police.
- may struggle with adult emotional and sexual drives while having only a limited cognitive ability to express them in appropriate ways.
- may be able to live independently with proper assistance.

Police Stress and Exposure to Persons Who are Mentally Ill and/or Intellectually Impaired

Interacting with persons who are mentally ill and/or intellectually impaired can be stressful. Sadly, during these interactions, there is the potential for tragic outcomes (similar to the interactions involving non-mentally ill and non-intellectually impaired persons). If officers find themselves struggling with an issue arising out of an experience with a person who is mentally ill and/or intellectually impaired it often helps to:

- talk it out with a trusted person
- contact a member of the Peer Support Team
- contact the police psychologist, chaplain, or other support person
- contact the Employee Assistance Program

Most importantly, remember that you do not have to go it alone.

Chapter 10

Suicide, Family, and Police Officers

It is during our darkest moments that we must focus to see the light.
-Aristotle *(384-322 BCE)*

Suicide is the intentional act of self-killing. Human beings have killed themselves for as long as there is recorded history. Many persons that kill themselves have a past that includes mental illness. But this is not always the case. Although persons suffering from mental illness commit suicide, not all suicidal persons are mentally ill. History is replete with accounts of persons not considered mentally ill who have intentionally killed or sacrificed themselves for religious beliefs, for comrades, for family, for political purposes, and for other reasons.

Some persons seem committed to killing themselves. If they are knowledgeable and have the opportunity, they will choose a means and method that nearly assures their death.

Recent statistical data shows that over half of all completed suicides involve the use of firearms; this makes firearms instrumental in more completed suicides than all other means combined. The muzzle of a firearm (means) placed over a vital organ of the body (method) in a suicide effort often results in death and leaves little room for resuscitation should the person not immediately die. Because firearms are so lethal, and most impulsive suicidal crises last only a brief period of time, restricting persons known to be even mildly suicidal from access to firearms is a priority.

Suicide is considered a worldwide health emergency. The World Health Organization estimates that in the world, over 700,000 completed suicides occur each year. This is over 1900 each day - about 1 every 40 seconds on average.

Fortunately, most persons that become suicidal are not committed to killing themselves. They are ambivalent about dying. They may think about death, but are undecided about killing themselves. This is the reason that police officers and others are frequently successful at "talking down" persons that are suicidal.

In some cases, persons act out in a suicidal or self-harm way to influence others. This is usually an attempt to compel others to behave in some desired way. In other cases, persons will make a suicidal gesture to send the proverbial cry for help. In both of these circumstances, death is not the underlying goal.

Most suicidal thinking and suicide attempts are not really about dying. They are about stopping emotional pain. Stop or mitigate the pain, and thoughts of self-destruction diminish or disappear.

Persons considering suicide often describe their emotional pain as being close to intolerable. They experience oppressive loneliness, feel abandoned, often think of themselves as worthless, and have no hope for the future. They perceive themselves as an unwanted burden to family and any friends that might still be present. They are tired. They have exhausted their energy to continue the struggle for life. They seek relief through loss of consciousness.

Suicidal thinking and acting out are indications of significant psychological distress. Appropriate intervention is required. When intervention is successful, realistic hope for the present and the future is restored, and thoughts of suicide diminish. This is true even for those who have survived previous suicide attempts.

Incidentally, dying at one's own hand by the failure of a fail-safe device designed for autoerotic purposes is not a suicide. Such deaths are seen when a person engages in a self-induced restriction of oxygen to the brain to achieve or intensify sexual pleasure. This type of self-caused death is unintentional and would be ruled accidental.

Suicide Attempts, Intent, and Means

Suicide attempts and completions must be evaluated in terms of *intent* and *means*. Some people are intent on dying but select a means that proves non-lethal. These survivors remain a significant danger to themselves and require immediate intervention. Conversely, some "suicidal" persons do not intend to die. They wish to accomplish something else with their behavior. But, because they did not recognize that the means selected was lethal, they kill themselves. Both circumstances involve a misunderstanding of the potentially lethal effects of the chosen means. In the first case, the person is very suicidal - even if the suicide attempt appears frivolous (like ingesting four aspirin). In the second case, the completed suicide is more accurately described as an accidental death. However, because the person is dead, this can only be determined upon psychological autopsy. A psychological autopsy is the process whereby investigators and psychologists attempt to determine the state of mind and intention of the deceased.

Suicidal Thinking and Environmental Stressors

Suicidal thinking varies along a continuum. On one end, there are passing suicidal thoughts. On the other end, there are obsessive thoughts of self-inflicted death. Suicidal thinking is more common than might be expected. Many people at some point in their lives have had thoughts of suicide. Suicidal thoughts occur most frequently when persons cannot see a way to resolve a significant problem, cope with a significant loss, or are overwhelmed by negative emotions. Most persons eventually find a way to manage these difficulties and any suicidal thoughts disappear.

In those prone to suicidal thinking, suicidal thoughts often co-vary with environmental stressors. For this group, when things are perceived as going well, suicidal thinking is absent or minimal. As stressors increase or things begin to go badly, suicidal thinking becomes more prominent.

As strange as it may seem, suicidal thoughts can also be triggered by certain medications - even in non-depressed people with no history of suicidal thinking. This speaks to the underlying neurobiological electrochemical basis of all thoughts, including those that are suicidal. In such cases, when the medication is discontinued, suicidal thoughts disappear.

Passive Suicidality

Death is sometimes passively desired. This is known as *passive suicidality*. Passive suicidality may be conscious or unconscious. When persons are passively suicidal, they do not plan or engage in any suicidal behavior. Instead, they wish their death through other means. One passively suicidal person reported praying that the airplane in which she was a passenger would crash. This is an example of *conscious passive suicidality.* There were no thoughts or concerns for the lives of the other passengers. This was not because she was an uncaring person or that she wished others would die. It is because persons in this state of mind cannot see or think past their anguish and despair. The inability to see beyond one's own despair is an example of *tunnel thinking,* a type of thinking that has become so focused that consequences other than that desired simply do not enter conscious awareness.

Another person struggled with thoughts of suicide as part of a major depression. After his depression lifted, he became anorexic and would not eat. This is an example of *unconscious passive suicidality.* Although he reported feeling better and was no longer actively suicidal, he was slowly, unconsciously starving himself to death. In cases of unconscious passive suicidality, the person often consciously fights or resists the unconscious desires, but has little insight into their existence or origin.

All passively suicidal persons retain some energy for life but they are usually apathetic and emotionally exhausted. As they work in therapy to address the prevailing issues, their zest for life frequently returns and they once again experience life's pleasures.

Perspectives, Suicidal Thinking, and Psychological Buffers

There are perspectives that seem to encourage suicidal thinking. Persons that see themselves as inadequate and powerless to change undesirable circumstances are more likely to consider suicide. This is because persons that view themselves as powerless have very little confidence in their ability to make difficult situations better. When they look into the future, they see more of the same, or worse. This projection of doom into the future is the most significant difference between persons who are likely to consider suicide and those who are not.

When most people find themselves at a low point in their lives, they have thoughts like "Well it's bad now, it can't do anything but get better." Thoughts like this are hopeful and optimistic. They act as a buffer against thoughts of suicide. However, optimistic thoughts are not present in persons likely to consider suicide. Instead, they think, "It's so bad now. I don't see how it gets better. I can't bear this anymore. There's nothing I can do about it." Such thoughts encourage further negative thinking and contribute to feelings of despair. With growing feelings of helplessness and a sense of powerlessness to change anything, the person becomes hopeless: "There's no point to living." The situation can worsen. Death can be viewed as relief. Death becomes an escape. It is seen as the only way out. This state of mind can be the result of years of consideration or it can develop rapidly upon a change in life circumstances. When persons reach the "no point to living" stage, the psychological buffers against suicide begin to fail.

There are several predominant psychological buffers against suicide. They include: (1) the ability to experience pleasure and enjoy life - many people that are "tired of living" report that they do not attempt suicide because they continue to experience pleasure and enjoyment in at least some portion of their lives; (2) some meaning in life – there is something to live for or something to look forward to; (3) concerns about family – worry about how their suicide would affect family members; and (4) religious or philosophical beliefs – when suicide is prohibited by personal, religious, or philosophical beliefs.

All of these are excellent buffers against suicide. But when these buffers fail, the person begins to think differently about themselves, family, and their beliefs. Thoughts like:

- Things are bad but at least I still have and enjoy doing X become *I do not enjoy anything anymore.*
- I live because of X become *There is no point to living.*
- I cannot kill myself because it would devastate my family become *My family would be better off without me.*
- I cannot kill myself because it is a sin or against my beliefs become *God has forsaken me or my beliefs are not valid.*

The weakening or failure of any or all psychological buffers increases the probability of suicide. When buffers deteriorate and tunnel thinking becomes focused, suicidal thoughts become prominent. If unabated, these thoughts generate behavior. The end behavior generated by such thoughts is suicide.

Family and Suicide

Survivors often struggle with the suicide of a family member. Common issues include, "Why didn't I see it coming?" "Why didn't he reach out to me?" and "Why couldn't I prevent it?" Sometimes there are reasonable answers to these questions, most times there are not.

Family members can experience a tremendous amount of anguish, guilt, anger, and self-blame over the suicide of a family member. Feeling guilty and blaming oneself, or at least questioning oneself about blame, is more common than might be expected. It is also common to blame others. Sons blaming mothers, mothers blaming daughters, brothers blaming sisters, families blaming employers and so on is often observed following a suicide. Blaming may be expressed explicitly ("It's your fault dad killed himself!") or implicitly ("You and dad never had a good marriage.") as family members struggle to answer the question, "Why?"

Family members must remain aware that there may be little they could have done to prevent the suicide. This is because:

- some persons are committed to dying at the time they decide to suicide. They will not ask for help or seek alternatives.
- some suicides are impulsive. Intoxication increases impulsivity.
- not everyone exhibits suicidal warning signs. Suicidal intentions can be kept secret.
- if warning signs are present, they may be difficult to recognize. For example, a person who says "I'm giving away my stuff because I'm tired of it" may actually be tired of it. Another person might say "I'm giving away my stuff because I'm tired of it" as part of a suicidal plan. The true meaning

of these identical statements and resultant behaviors may be difficult to discern.

- family members may be emotionally numbed by past suicidal threats and behaviors. This can occur even in families that care and have tried their best to help. Emotional numbness is a normal process that can occur following months or years of trying to help a suicidal family member. The development of emotional numbness is facilitated by the difficulty inherent in sustaining a relationship with someone that is consistently pre-occupied with thoughts of suicide (especially prevalent in persons with chronic mood disorders and some personality disorders).

Emotional numbness is characterized by statements like: "He'll either do it or he won't. I can't deal with him anymore. I have no more to give and I'm exhausted from worrying about it. He is responsible for what he does. I have done all I can."

For family members, emotional numbing involves the feeling of not knowing what more can be done. It is sometimes the only remaining way to cope with the consistent suicidal ideation and behaviors of others.

This is not to say that family members or others have no ability to successfully identify and assist a suicidal person. There are observable and knowable suicide risk factors. Many successful suicide interventions are accomplished each year by those that understand the risk factors for suicide.

Suicide, Family, and Cause of Death

As mentioned, many families are in anguish following the suicide of a family member. It is not only the anguish caused by the loss of a loved one, but also the anguish caused by the thought that their loved one would choose to leave them. In an attempt to deny this psychological feature of suicide, family members sometimes beseech the office of the coroner to change the determined cause of death. They insist that the cause of death be changed from "suicide" or "self-inflicted" to "accidental" or even "homicide." This has occurred even in cases where comprehensive investigation can conclude nothing but suicide. Indeed, the idea that a son, daughter, mother, father, or other relative would make the decision to abandon the family by killing themselves is a very difficult thought for many families to accept.

Families must keep in mind that their loved one was not thinking rationally and that their buffers against suicide had likely failed. They may not have "chosen" to leave the family. Instead, they may not have been able to see that other viable options existed.

Suicide and Family Responses

While some persons in a family may be devastated by the suicide of a family member, others family members may not be disturbed by the suicide. Some may be neutral or actually pleased that the person is dead, a fact that Hollywood has incorporated into many of its productions. The expression, observation, or perception of these reactions can create major difficulties within a family system.

A confounding factor in some instances of suicide involves life insurance. Some life insurance policies restrict or deny payment in cases of suicide, at least for a period of time. Others will pay. If there is an insurance payment, what should a family do with the money? Some family members describe the life insurance payoff as "tainted" or "blood money," and are uncomfortable living the good life on the funds provided to them by a loved one's suicide.

For some family members there is embarrassment for the suicide. They may see suicide as "the cowards way out" "a cop out" or a weakness which shames or casts a shadow over the entire family. They feel that the suicide reflects poorly upon them. Therefore, many families maintain the secret of suicide. In such families, no one is permitted to speak of the person or the death, either within or outside the family. If asked about the death, they often create an alternative narrative, "he died of a heart attack." This is especially true for some spouses of the deceased. Often, the primary fear of the surviving spouse is that others will conclude that he or she has driven their spouse to suicide.

Other family members may view the suicide as permission to carry out their own suicidal impulses. There have been several cases wherein the suicide of one family member was followed by the suicide of another. Any or all of this can be present as part of the maelstrom following a suicide.

Suicide Warning Signs and Risk Factors

The National Institute of Mental Health identified the following warning signs and risk factors for suicide.

"Warning signs that someone may be at immediate risk for attempting suicide include:

- Talking about wanting to die or wanting to kill themselves
- Talking about feeling empty or hopeless or having no reason to live
- Talking about feeling trapped or feeling that there are no solutions
- Feeling unbearable emotional or physical pain
- Talking about being a burden to others
- Withdrawing from family and friends
- Giving away important possessions
- Saying goodbye to friends and family
- Putting affairs in order, such as making a will
- Taking great risks that could lead to death, such as driving extremely fast
- Talking or thinking about death often
- Displaying extreme mood swings, suddenly changing from very sad to very calm or happy
- Making a plan or looking for ways to kill themselves, such as searching for lethal methods online, stockpiling pills, or buying a gun
- Talking about feeling great guilt or shame
- Using alcohol or drugs more often
- Acting anxious or agitated
- Changing eating or sleeping habits
- Showing rage or talking about seeking revenge

Risk Factors

Suicide does not discriminate. People of all genders, ages, and ethnicities can be at risk. Suicidal behavior is complex, and there is no single cause. The main risk factors for suicide are:

- Depression, other mental disorders, or substance use disorder
- Chronic pain
- A history of suicide attempts
- Family history of a mental disorder or substance use
- Family history of suicide
- Exposure to family violence, including physical or sexual abuse
- Presence of guns or other firearms in the home
- Having recently been released from prison or jail
- Exposure, either directly or indirectly, to others' suicidal behavior, such as that of family members, peers, or celebrities

Most people who have risk factors will not attempt suicide, and it is difficult to tell who will act on suicidal thoughts. Although risk factors for suicide are important to keep in mind, someone who is showing *warning signs* of suicide may be at higher risk for danger and need immediate attention" (2021).

Behaviors indicative of suicidal thinking range from subtle to apparent. The subtle signs of mounting suicidality include increasingly poor hygiene, greater isolation, less concern with appearance, less verbal communication, less energy and activity, lower standards for house and car maintenance, and behaviors that appear uncharacteristic of the person. These are early signs of depression and may indicate a developing mood disorder.

Those who are the closest to the person are in the best position to assess and evaluate suicidal behaviors. Statements such as, "They'll see something tomorrow" "I can't take this much longer" "I know what I have to do" "Give this to X" "I want you to have . . ." and "When I'm gone . . ." should never go unchallenged. Responses such as "What do you mean . . ." "Tell me more about that . . ." "What are you thinking?" and other exploratory inquiries are appropriate in such instances. Many times, persons considering suicide will readily communicate their thoughts or plans if asked.

Suicide Information: USA

In the United States:

- There are about 125 completed suicides each day. This is one suicide about every 11 minutes on average.
- Suicide rates increased 30% between 2000-2018 and declined in 2019 and 2020.
- In 2021, there were 48,183 reported suicides, 12.3 million adults seriously thought about suicide, 3.5 million people made a suicide plan, 1.2 million attempted suicide.
- The suicide rate among men is about four times that of women.
- Men completed nearly 80% of the suicides.
- Women make about four times as many suicide attempts as men.
- People aged over 85 years have the highest suicide rate.
- After firearms, suffocation and poisoning respectively are the next two most common means used to complete suicide (CDC, 2022).
- The number of annual suicides in the United States have consistently outnumbered homicides by approximately two to one.

Suicide, holidays, and suicide notes

The idea that most suicides occur around the winter holidays is a myth. Although grief for deceased loved ones may intensify and suicides do occur during the holiday season, suicide rates are normally lowest in winter and highest in the spring (Woo et al., 2012).

Some research indicates that suicide notes are left in less than one-third of suicide cases (NIMH, 2010). This seems to differ for police officers. Police officers who complete suicide almost always leave a suicide note. Some police officer suicide notes are lengthy, including desired funeral arrangements, financial information, final thoughts, and final messages. Some are brief. Below is the entire text of an actual police officer suicide note. Unusual for a police officer, the suicide did not involve a firearm.

> *I'm sorry for any pain this may cause anyone. I'm just tired of fighting. I am now at peace.*

It is estimated that about 80% of people that become suicidal give some warning of their thoughts and intentions. This number is not 100 percent because of the human ability to maintain a suicidal secret. Persons considering suicide may look one way, but feel another. In a poem first published in 1923, Maine poet Edwin Arlington Robinson (1869-1935) poetically expressed this component of human experience in his portrayal of *Richard Cory*:

> Whenever Richard Cory went downtown,
> We people on the pavement looked at him:
> He was a gentleman from sole to crown,
> Clean-favored, and imperially slim.
>
> And he was always quietly arrayed,
> And he was always human when he talked;
> But still he fluttered pulses when he said,
> "Good morning," and he glittered when he walked.
>
> And he was rich—yes, richer than a king-
> And admirably schooled in every grace:
> In fine, we thought that he was everything
> To make us wish that we were in his place.
>
> So on we worked, and waited for the light,
> And went without the meat, and cursed the bread;
> And Richard Cory, one calm summer night,
> Went home and put a bullet through his head.

Suicide and Alcohol

Alcohol, like all drugs, is dose dependent. In small body concentrations, alcohol is a thought and behavioral disinhibitor. This is why after a few drinks, you are more likely to have thoughts you would not have when sober, and engage in behavior you would not consider when sober. In larger quantities, alcohol depresses central nervous system activity. This results in the behavioral lethargy and accompanying cognitive impairment seen in alcohol intoxication. If dosing continues, this latter effect will render the person unconsciousness. If enough alcohol has been consumed prior to unconsciousness, death will ensue.

Some persons who are mildly suicidal become more suicidal when intoxicated. This is due to the disinhibiting effect. With greater disinhibition, impulsivity increases - never a good thing for depressed or suicidal persons.

Some suicidal persons will anesthetize themselves with alcohol before attempting suicide. In such cases alcohol functions to increase the ability to act out suicidal thoughts (sometimes called "liquid courage"), to suppress ambivalence, and to provide psychological and physical numbing.

Most persons that become suicidal when intoxicated are not suicidal, or at least not as suicidal, when sober. This makes detoxification the first and primary intervention of intoxicated suicidal persons.

Suicide Plan

Many persons who become suicidal develop a plan for death. Suicide plans may be simple or elaborate. The mere existence of a suicide plan increases the probability of suicide. The more thought out and detailed the plan, the more likely it is that the person will attempt suicide.

While many suicidal persons develop at least a rudimentary plan for their death, suicidal behavior can be impulsive and acted out in the absence of a plan.

Some Types of Suicide

There are various motivations for suicide. Particular motivations correspond with the various types of suicide. Some types of suicide and their motives are:

- blaze of glory—to be remembered or to make a statement
- fate suicide—let another or circumstances decide
- suicide by cop—suicide by provoking a police officer
- protest suicide—political, social, or other cause
- cause suicide—political or military objective
- psychotic suicide—delusion/command hallucination
- medical suicide—terminal illness or health issues
- hopelessness suicide—depression, loss, mood disorder
- revenge suicide—punish someone
- honor suicide—avoid or stop feelings of disgrace
- shame suicide—exposure of secret activity, embarrassment
- guilt suicide—sense of responsibility
- anger suicide—anger at self or others
- hate suicide—self hatred
- life change suicide—overwhelmed by change

There can be combined motivations for suicide. Within the motivation for suicide lies the *rationale*. The rationale for suicide seldom appears *rational* to outside observers.

Suicide by Cop

There are those who seek to be killed by the police. *Suicide by cop (SBC), victim-precipitated suicide,* and *decedent-precipitated suicide* are current terms for this too frequently observed phenomenon. Persons intending to be killed by police officers will act in ways that compel officers to defend themselves. In the majority of cases, persons so disposed will point a firearm at police officers.

Some persons intending to be killed by police officers are armed with functioning, loaded firearms. A proportion of these persons will not hesitate to kill officers or others in their effort to die at the hands of the police.

Other persons use air, pellet, BB, toy, or authentic looking replica firearms to threaten police. Still others draw and point non-firearm objects, like flashlights, wallets, or cell phones in a way that a firearm would be drawn and pointed, in their attempt to get police officers to fire.

There are times when a person indifferent to dying will engage in threatening behavior or point a weapon at an officer and let the officer decide the outcome. This circumstance combines the *fate suicide* with *suicide by cop*. Persons in this frame of mind are incapable of caring whether they live or die, at least at the time. They do not comply with officers' orders, threaten officers, and may compel officers to defend themselves. As might be expected, many of those indifferent to dying or seeking to be killed by the police are suffering from depression or other mental disorders.

The well-publicized Long Island, New York, case of Moshe Pergament and the actions of Matthew Hoffman are illustrative of how far persons might go to be killed by the police. These cases are representative of many tragic intentional suicide-by-cop incidents.

Moshe Pergament

On November 15, 1997, Moshe Pergament, known as Moe to his friends, was intentionally driving recklessly on the Long Island Expressway, planning to be contacted by police. He sideswiped several cars. It was not long before his dangerous driving was reported. A short time after the reports, he was located and stopped by police. Once stopped, Moe exited his car. He pulled out a handgun. Officers ordered him to drop the weapon. He did not comply. He began to walk toward officers with his gun pointed at them. When Moe again failed to comply with the officers' orders, they fired, killing him. During the following investigation, investigators found ten notes in Moe's vehicle. Nine were addressed to family members and friends. One was addressed "To the officer that shot me." It read,

> Officer, It was a plan. I'm sorry to get you involved. I just needed to die. Please remember that this was all my doing. You had no way of knowing. Moe Pergament

The nineteen-year-old Pergament was holding a realistic-looking plastic replica of a silver .38 caliber revolver. He had purchased it earlier the same day. Investigation later determined that Moe owed $6,000 in gambling debts. The *New York Daily News* (News) reported it this way, "A Nassau County teenager with a death wish and $6,000 in World Series gambling debts was gunned down by Long Island police Friday night after he pointed a fake gun at them, authorities said" (November 16, 1997). The next day, The News reported, "The well-off and well-liked 19-year-old college student gunned down by Long Island police in an apparent 'suicide-by-cop,' took his secrets to the grave yesterday" (November 17, 1997).

Apparently the phrase *gunned down* was popular with News staff writers in the 1990s. Sensational terms used in sad and tragic cases are sometimes used to increase newspaper sales. However, this phrase, when used in the context of a forced suicide by cop, demonstrates a general insensitivity on the part of reporters for the officers involved. This type of reporting can have a traumatizing effect on involved officers, and can become a major component of police officer second injury (chapter 4). Unfortunately, this poor standard of news reporting continues today.

Matthew Hoffman

On January 4, 2015, a 32-year-old San Francisco man, Matthew Hoffman, initiated a discussion with San Francisco (SF) police officers working an incident at the intersection of 16th and Mission Streets. He asked the officers what kind of guns SF officers carried, what kind of ammunition they use, and whether they had been involved in officer-involved shootings. The officers did not respond to his questions and Hoffman eventually left. Later that day, about 5:15 p.m., Hoffman was seen loitering inside the Mission District police station parking lot. Although this area was clearly marked "restricted," a gate is kept open for police vehicle access. Three SF police sergeants contacted him and ordered him to leave. He began walking away but stopped. He was again ordered to leave. He began stepping backward out of the parking lot driveway, facing the sergeants. His hands were inside his front-side shirt pockets. The sergeants asked to see his hands. In response, he lifted his sweater to reveal the butt of a handgun. When he reached for and drew the gun, two of the sergeants fired, hitting him three times. He was transported to a local hospital where he died from his wounds. The sergeants were not injured. Subsequent investigation revealed that the gun Hoffman was carrying was an air gun, capable of firing BBs or small pellets.

Hoffman left several suicide notes on his cell phone. One was directed at the police: "Dear officer(s), you did nothing wrong… Please don't blame yourself. I used you. I took advantage of you…I provoked you…You ended the life of a man who was too much of a coward to do it himself…I threatened your life as well as the lives of those around me. You were completely within your legal right to do what you did." He further described himself as "lonely" and "hopeless."

Officer Albie Esparza, spokesman for the department said "I can tell you, some people who read the note were emotional. This is a sad story that this person was disturbed to this point. That they saw no other exit…"

The notes investigators found on Hoffman's cellphone "changes the dynamic" of the incident, Esparza said. "In this case, we didn't know…it was a suicide by cop." Esparza said he wished things had turned out differently for Hoffman. "There's help out there for people," he said. "We wish there was a different outcome."

That Hoffman left a note explaining his intentions to the officers who shot him may actually make it tougher for them, said Gail Wyatt, professor of psychiatry and director of the UCLA Center for Culture, Trauma and Mental Health Disparities. "When you shoot and kill someone you think has a weapon, it may just be easily justifiable," she said. "But if you know this is a person who is unhappy, depressed, and [is allowing] you to do for himself what he probably didn't want to do, it personalizes it" (quoted from article, AP, 2015; Serna, 2015).

Officer-involved Shootings and Suicide

Researchers studied 707 cases of officer involved shootings in North America from 1998 to 2006 (Mohandie et al., 2009). Results revealed that 36 percent of the examined police shootings met the criteria for suicide by cop. This was in contrast to several older studies which estimated the suicide-by-cop rate from 10 percent to 26 percent of all police shootings. The study further found that:

- 95% were male
- the mean age was 35 for men
- 41% of men were Caucasian, 26% Hispanic and 16% African American
- 37% of men were single
- 29% of men had children
- 54% of men were unemployed
- 29% of men did not have housing
- 62% of men had confirmed or probable histories of mental
- health issues
- 80% of men were armed – of these, 60% possessed firearms (of which 86% were loaded) and 26% possessed knives
- 19% feigned or simulated weapon possession
- 87% of individuals made suicidal communications prior to and/or during the incident
- 36% were under the influence of alcohol.

A significant proportion of the men in this study were in possession of functional and loaded firearms. The question arises, why did they not shoot themselves? Why force a police officer to shoot in actual or apparent self-defense? Several factors are suspected in such cases, including:

1. Social concerns. There is still a social taboo against suicide.
2. Suicide by cop allows suicidal persons to die without actually killing themselves.
3. Fear: an inability to follow through with suicide.
4. Religious prohibitions against suicide (SBC as a religion "loophole"?).
5. Concerns over life insurance policies.
6. Wanting to go out in a blaze, make the news.
7. Psychological inability to kill oneself.

Clinton Van Zandt, a former FBI hostage negotiator, commented that persons prone to suicide by cop are those that fear other attempts at death. They are afraid that if they drive into a bridge abutment, cut their wrists, and so forth, they may not die. Provoking a police officer to shoot increases the probability that they will accomplish their goal (1993). This is no less true today.

Suicidal Persons and the Police

Police officers may encounter persons who are suicidal in a number of ways. They can be dispatched to assist a suicidal person, come upon a suicidal person during patrol or other duties, be on a call that starts out as something else and evolves into a suicidal person interaction, and so on. Because police officers may encounter a person who is suicidal at any time and under varied circumstances, it is helpful to consider some basic guidelines for interaction. Of course, what is possible during any contact with a person who is suicidal is determined by the actual circumstances.

Suggestions for Police Officers Interacting with Persons who are Suicidal

Suggestions for police officers interacting with persons who are suicidal necessarily overlap the "Suggestions for Police Officers Interacting with Persons who are Psychotic or Otherwise Mentally Ill" (chapter 9). Several suggestions specified there, which are not repeated here, are equally applicable.

Several of these suggestions are intended to be engaged simultaneously. Some, like officer safety assessment, should be engaged throughout the interaction.

1. *Gather information.* Gather as much information as is practical prior to contacting a suicidal person. This will help you determine your approach. Arrange for additional police units. Do not go it alone. Although in some cases you may be duty-bound to take solo action, it is safer for you and the person to have several officers on-scene.

2. *Determine environment and person variables.* Is the person accessible or barricaded, intoxicated or sober, armed or unarmed, alone or accompanied, angry or cooperative, etc.
3. *Officer safety assessment and contact.* Interacting with a suicidal person requires an immediate and *ongoing* assessment of threat to officers. *Most suicidal persons are not homicidal—but do not bet your life on this probability.* Some suicidal persons are willing to harm others. Utilize all pertinent officer safety procedures. When contact is made, you may have to act rapidly and decisively. More likely, you will have ample time to initiate contact and open discussion. If the situation is chaotic, prioritize your intervention. Try to slow things down. Slowing things down tends to reduce impulsivity, which makes the situation safer.
4. *Remain calm.* Interacting with a suicidal person is stressful. Take a deep breath. Try to relax. Speak in a clear, calm voice. Avoid profanity, excitement, and abusive language. These tend to increase instability. Provide an emotionally stable influence during the interaction. Proceed thoughtfully unless duty-bound to intervene. You will better help the person and increase the probability of a desired outcome if you can remain calm.
5. *Establish rapport.* Obtain and utilize the person's name. You can use first name or title (Mr., Ms., Dr.) as deemed appropriate. Identify yourself by first name if you wish to deemphasize authority. Tell the person that you are there to help. Keep in mind that most people are ambivalent about dying and will readily talk to you.
6. *Obtain or attempt to determine some information quickly.* Ask or otherwise attempt to determine if the person is concealing a weapon, has weapons available, has recently ingested street drugs or medication, has been drinking alcohol, or has just made a suicide attempt (ingested substances cannot be observed and some injuries are not easily seen). This information increases officer safety, allows for appropriate intervention, and contributes to your field assessment.

7. *Remove lethal means.* The priority is to distance the person from any possessed weapon or weapon within reach. If communicative and compliant, direct the person in a step-by-step manner. For example, if the person is pointing a handgun to their head with their right hand, avoid statements like "drop the gun." Instead use statements like "remove your finger from the trigger, point the gun toward the sky, with your left hand grab the barrel of the gun, release the gun from your right hand, move the gun slowly to the floor" and so on. This is much better than watching the gun bounce off the floor in compliance with your order to "drop the gun." It also lowers the probability of an accidental discharge. Additionally, you do not want to be so mentally prepared to see the gun move quickly that your reflexes have to compensate for an unexpected dangerous gun movement. What are your options if the person is not compliant? Remain in a tactical cover position and keep working to establish rapport. As long as the person is not an active threat to you or others, you may continue your efforts for voluntary compliance.

8. *Request additional emergency personnel as needed.* Request specialized police units, paramedics, fire, and so on as necessary. *Tactical considerations.* If you are in contact with the person and feel exposed, threatened, or otherwise unsafe, and immediate apprehension is not possible, withdraw from the environment as rapidly and safely as possible. Once safely out, proceed as outlined in department policy for such circumstances.

9. *Continue conversation.* Keep talking. Ask open-ended questions about recent events in the person's life, such as "What happened today?" "What's happening in your life?" and the always reliable "Tell me more." Ask about how the person arrived at this point. Discuss the person's history to strengthen rapport and gain information for your field assessment.

10. *Acknowledge the person's stated or implied difficulties.* Tell the person that you understand this is a difficult time. Avoid being judgmental - "You're suicidal over that? You're wasting

my time!" is never a good intervention strategy. Watch for *either/or* thinking. This is seen most often in a crisis and is represented by *"either* X must happen *or* I'm going to kill myself"* (a false dichotomy). In cases of either/or, you must present the person with realistic and viable options. For example, "Either my girlfriend has to come here or I'm going to kill myself!" Officer: "Your girlfriend is in the hospital being treated for her injuries. She cannot come here. Here are some things that are possible."

11. *Do not hesitate to bring the issue of suicide into the open.* Ask about the length of time that the person has felt like killing himself, whether there have been previous thoughts of suicide or past suicide attempts (if so, by what means), substance use, and if there is a suicide plan: "Have you thought about how you might kill yourself?"

12. *Avoid deception whenever possible.* Unless necessary or you are directed to provide deceptive information for tactical reasons, avoid deception. Nearly every issue can be discussed honestly and it is often difficult to recall previously made untrue statements. Do not hesitate to say "I don't know" or "I'm uncertain about that" if the person asks a question you cannot answer. What circumstances would justify providing deceptive information? If life is at stake and no other reasonable option exists.

13. *Avoid challenges.* "You don't have the guts to kill yourself!" has never been a very successful intervention when interacting with a suicidal person.

14. *Use authority when appropriate.* An order to "put the gun down now!" may stop a person from following through on a suicidal intention and engaging behavior (like pulling the trigger) when rapport has failed. Consider using a *short order* when appropriate (chapter 9).

15. *Personal inquiries and self-disclosure.* If the person begins to ask you questions that become too personal, such as *where do you live* and *where do your kids go to school,* advise the person that you are interested in them. Redirect the conversation. Ask the person to tell you more about what is happening in their life. Is it ever appropriate to

discuss your experiences? Yes, but keep it limited, then refocus on the person. For example, a person who is suicidal because his business failed may respond well to you sharing information that your father once had a business that failed. You can inform the person that your dad struggled for a time, but things improved. Follow-up with something like "Let's talk about how this might happen for you." Build upon the discussion.

16. *Provide realistic hope.* Throughout your discussion, talk about the person's issues, views, and when appropriate, introduce alternatives, "I'm wondering if you've thought about . . ." Inform the person that you can arrange a meeting with professional people that can help address current difficulties. Assure the person that you have done this before with positive results. Keep in mind that realistic hope involves helping the person see beyond present circumstances. It explores the *possible* and the *potential*. Inform the person that (1) even if it looks like there is no way out, others can help, (2) specially trained people may be able to help in ways not yet imagined, and (3) the future could be very different from the present.

17. *Avoid arguing.* Arguing is seldom helpful and it can lead to angry exchanges and impulsive behavior. It is frequently better to ameliorate any disagreements, maintain rapport, and provide realistic hope.

18. *Maintain your psychological boundary.* Do not allow yourself to become angry. It's easy to become tired, tense, and frustrated, especially if the interaction endures for a lengthy period of time. If you begin to have thoughts like "either accept help or kill yourself, I just want this over" it is time to take a deep breath and try to relax. If successful, reengage the person. If this does not work, bring another person into the interaction and take a break. Inform the person that you need a little time to refresh yourself, check on some things, or go to the restroom. Take the time to appropriately introduce the person taking over for you. You can return to the interaction when ready.

19. *Psychological boundary.* Human beings have killed themselves for as long as there is recorded history, and probably long before that. When interacting with persons who are suicidal, keep in mind that all you can do is to support them and help them explore options. You cannot read minds or control behaviors. Persons who are suicidal will eventually decide their course of action. This is because by the time persons who are suicidal come to the attention of the police, officers may have no or little ability to control the situation. Instead, officers can only attempt to influence the person and thereby hope to increase the probability of a positive outcome. There are no guarantees. You cannot assume responsibility for the life of the person, even though the rescuer part of you might like to. What is your responsibility to a suicidal person?...to do your best.

20. *Resolution.* By far, most police interactions with persons who are suicidal end in a desirable way, with the person cooperating and receiving treatment by mental health professionals. Many persons that are feeling suicidal readily accept the help of police officers. Some do not. Some will be taken into custody by forceful action. Most times the force needed is minimal. Other times it may involve the use of less than lethal weapons and the SWAT team. Some will compel suicide by cop. Others will, in spite of your best efforts, attempt or complete suicide during your interaction and in your presence.

For police officers, interacting with persons who are suicidal is an unavoidable occupational stressor. Officers should think about the likely psychological issues that can arise after a suicidal person call. How would you cope with the aftermath of a person who completes suicide in your presence? What are the possible short and long-term effects of witnessing a suicide? These are questions that should be considered by all officers.

Suicidal-Person Call Resolution

In cases where the person is at least somewhat cooperative, there are a number of resolutions possible. After your interaction and field assessment:

1. if you determine that no imminent threat of suicide exists, you may leave the person, contact family or friends, provide referrals, transport to a support or mental health agency, or arrange for another appropriate disposition;
2. if you are uncertain whether an imminent threat of suicide exists, you should contact someone who can assist you, such as an officer specially trained in suicide crisis intervention, a member of your first-response mental health team, or your supervisor;
3. if you conclude that an imminent threat of suicide exists, ask the person to cooperate with your assistance efforts. If yes, follow your department policy for transport to an appropriate facility. In such cases, even though the person represents an imminent threat for suicide, you do not need to take the person into *involuntary* custody;
4. if you conclude that an imminent threat of suicide exists and the person will not accept assistance, you must engage the emergency procedure.

Emergency detention and treatment

Every state has a statutory provision for the involuntary emergency detention and treatment of persons that are mentally ill and suicidal. Most of these statutes authorize a detention of 72-hours, and include the emergency detention of those that are mentally ill and present a danger to others or are gravely disabled. When a person is taken into custody under an emergency detention statute, officers must follow agency policy for proper implementation. If your agency does not have an emergency detention policy, advocate for one. A policy is necessary because most statutes that provide police officers with the authority to initiate emergency detention do not specify agency-specific procedures detailing what is to be done once a person is in police custody.

The emergency detention is sometimes erroneously thought of as a *seventy-two-hour hold*. It is erroneous because, while those detained under such a statute may be held for up to seventy-hours, they may be released earlier. Persons detained as suicidal under the emergency procedure will be released prior to seventy-two hours if within this time period they are assessed to no longer present an imminent danger to themselves. Often, prior to release from involuntary detention, persons consent to voluntary intervention and follow up treatment. Release prior to seventy-two-hours authorized under the emergency procedure corresponds with the reigning treatment ethic in the field of mental health: *least amount of medication* in the *least restrictive environment*.

Short and Long-Term Involuntary Treatment

What happens when a person who is imminently suicidal remains suicidal after the period of time authorized under emergency detention? If the person refuses voluntary treatment, involuntary detention may be extended. The legal procedure for extension depends upon the laws of each state. However, every state has provisions for extended involuntary short and long-term care of persons who remain a danger to themselves or others or are gravely disabled due to mental illness.

Police Officer Suicide

Some police officers kill themselves. They kill themselves mostly by firearms. This is no surprise as police officers have ready access to firearms.

Police suicide rates in America have traditionally been reported as being two to three times that of the general population. This estimate was based upon the belief that between 400 to 450 police officers completed suicide each year. These numbers have never been confirmed and they are not supported by recent research. Specialized studies conducted from 2008 through 2012 concluded that there were 141 police officer suicides in 2008, 143 in 2009,

147 in 2010, 146 in 2011, and 126 in 2012 (O'Hara & Violanti, 2013). Although every suicide is a tragedy, and a police officer suicide is especially painful to those in policing, these numbers are significantly lower than some earlier estimates.

Some research suggests that when certain variables such as the state of residence, age, gender, race, and marital status are taken into consideration, suicide rates for police officers may be as much as 26 percent lower than that of the general population (Aamodt & Werlick, 2001). If this is accurate, the fact that most police officer candidates are psychologically assessed for emotional stability prior to being hired may prove to be a factor. Other research suggests that the police officer suicide rate is higher than that of the general population (Violanti & Steege, 2020).

The diverse conclusions of past police-suicide research highlight the difficulty inherent in conducting research on suicide. A major problem is data collection. Historically, there was no governmental agency or private organization responsible for recording the number of police suicides. Therefore, researchers had to rely upon various sources for data, including police organization websites, news reports, social media systems, individual police agencies, and police officers themselves. To address this issue, Congress passed the *Law Enforcement Suicide Data Collection Act* (LESDCA), signed into law on June 16, 2020. The LESDCA established a data collection program for law enforcement agencies to report officer-suicides and officer-suicide attempts. "According to the LESDCA, the FBI must collect, at minimum, the following information for each officer who died by or attempted to commit suicide:

- The circumstances and events that occurred before the act or attempt
- The general location where the act occurred
- The demographic information of the officer
- The occupational category of the officer
- The method used in each suicide instance or attempt" (Perine, 2021, 1)

The LESDCA further allows for the submission of information relating to the officer's employment status, known contributing stressors, whether mental health services were available through the agency, and whether the officer reported or the agency observed any mental health-related warning signs prior to the incident (ibid). While submission of data to the LESDCA database is voluntary, it represents a significant step forward in the effort to better understand police officer suicide.

Cops Helping Cops

Police officers should not avoid other officers that they think might be suicidal. If officers feel another officer may be suicidal, it is best to initiate contact. During the contact, discuss your observations and concerns. *Do not hesitate to bring the subject of suicide into the open.* Conduct a field assessment and follow through on your observations. If you feel that the officer is imminently suicidal, do not leave the officer alone. Arrange for professional help, including involuntary treatment and evaluation if necessary. If the officer is not imminently suicidal, spend some time together. Listen and provide emotional support. Contact or encourage the officer to contact the police psychologist, the peer support team, the employee assistance program, clergy, or a family member. The point is, *do not hesitate to do something.* You may save a life.

Recent technological developments have increased the ability of cops to help cops. Several states have created statewide law enforcement support programs that operate through the internet or device apps. One such program is the Texas Law Enforcement Peer Network (TLEPN). The TLEPN was launched in the spring of 2022 and is the first of its kind in Texas. It uses an app to connect officers in distress with officers who have completed state-approved training in peer support. The Texas legislature approved funding for the Network after recognizing that a mental health crisis exists for those in law enforcement. As Dustin Schellenger, state director of the program, stated in a recent interview, in Texas during the period of 2017 to 2021, 98% of first responder suicides were police officers. The Network is available to assist officers dealing with work and non-work-related stressors. It hopes to reduce the number of police officer suicides and other self-harm behaviors by making anonymous and confidential support available 24/7 (as reported by Smith, 2022).

Police Officer Suicide Risk Factors

There are certain factors that increase the probability that a police officer will suicide. Most of these factors have been specified previously and apply to all persons, but some are particularly applicable to police officers. The greater the number of risk factors present, the greater the risk of suicide. Police officer suicide risk factors include:

- A diagnosis of depression, bipolar, anxiety, or psychotic disorder
- Veiled or outright threats of suicide.
- Development of a suicidal plan.
- Marital, money, and/or family problems.
- Recent or pending discipline, including possible termination.
- Over-developed sense of responsibility. Responsibility absorption.
- Frustration or embarrassment by some work-related event.
- Internal or criminal investigations against the officer.
- Allegations of wrongdoing; criminal charges.
- Assaults on an officer's integrity, reputation, or professionalism.
- Recent loss, such as divorce, relationship breakup, financial, etc.
- Little or no social support system.
- Uncharacteristic dramatic mood changes. Always angry.
- Feeling "down" or "trapped" with no way out.
- Feelings of hopelessness and helplessness.
- Feeling anxious, unable to sleep or sleeping all the time.
- History of problems with work, supervisors, or family stress.
- Making permanent alternative arrangements for pets or livestock.
- Increased alcohol use or other substance abuse/addiction.
- Family history of suicide and/or childhood maltreatment.
- Uncharacteristic aggression; increased citizen complaints.
- Diagnosis of physical illness or long-term effects of physical illness.

- Recent injury which causes chronic pain; overuse of medications.
- Career ending injury or disability.
- Disability that forces retirement or leaving the job.
- The suicide of another officer, coworker, friend, or family member
- Self-isolation: withdrawing from family, friends, and social events.
- Giving away treasured items.
- Saying "goodbye" in unusual manner.
- Easy access to firearms (a constant for police officers).
- Sudden sense of calm while circumstances have not changed.
- Unwillingness to seek help because of perceived stigma.

By knowing some of the risk factors involved in police officer suicide, you can help other officers, and help other officers to help themselves. You can also help yourself. Keep in mind that if you become suicidal, it is more likely that you are already acquainted with those most likely to assist you.

If you are thinking about suicide or feeling suicidal, whether this is a new feeling for you or you have been struggling with these thoughts and feelings for some time, help yourself - *reach out now!* There are people who care and people that can help.

Police Officer Suicide: Physical/Psychological Primary Danger and Secondary Danger

The primary danger of policing has two components: (1) physical primary danger and (2) psychological primary danger. The *physical primary danger* of policing is comprised of the inherent, potentially life-threatening risks of the job, such as working in motor vehicle traffic, emergency vehicle operation, representing a target for disgruntled persons, and confronting armed and violent individuals. One needs only to read a newspaper or watch a news program to understand the physical primary danger of policing.

The *psychological primary danger* of policing is related to, but distinguishable from the physical primary danger of policing. The psychological primary danger of policing is represented in the increased probability that, due to the physical primary danger of policing, officers will be exposed to critical incidents, work-related cumulative stress, and human tragedy. The increased probability of such exposure results in a greater likelihood that officers will suffer psychological traumatization and stressor-related disorders. Another way of saying this is that the physical primary danger of policing constitutes a work environment that generates the psychological primary danger of policing.

There is also an insidious and lesser-known *secondary danger* of policing. The secondary danger of policing is often unspecified and seldom discussed. It is an artifact of the police culture and is frequently reinforced by police officers themselves. It is the idea that equates "asking for help" with "personal and professional weakness." Secondary danger has been implicated in perhaps the most startling of all police fatality statistics, the frequency of police officer suicide.

How serious is police secondary danger? So serious that some officers will choose suicide over asking for help.

For the years in which there is reasonably reliable data, the number of police officer suicides has consistently exceeded the number of officers killed by felonious assault or by accident. In most of these years, the number of police officer suicides has exceeded the number of officer deaths from felonious assault and accidents *combined*. This makes secondary danger and the accompanying propensity for suicide the number one killer of police officers.

The Public Safety Officer Support Act of 2022

As part of increased awareness of the psychological toll of traumatic events on first responders, the U.S. Congress passed the *Public Safety Officer Support Act*. The Act was signed into law on August 18, 2022. It expanded eligibility for death and disability benefits to public safety officers and their beneficiaries.

The Public Safety Officer Support Act:

- Allows public safety officers to seek disability benefits for PTSD linked to severe trauma by directing the Public Safety Officers' Benefits Program (PSOB) to designate work-related PTSD and acute stress disorders as a line of duty injury for eligible officers, as well as those who are permanently disabled as a result of attempted suicide.
- Allows families of public safety officers who die by trauma-linked suicide to apply for death benefits by directing the PSOB to presume that suicides are a result of job duties in certain traumatic circumstances where there is evidence that PTSD or acute stress disorder would be the cause of the injury (Reschenthaler, 2022).

Within the Act, Congress recognized the *physical and psychological primary dangers* of policing, "Every day, public safety officers, including police officers, firefighters, emergency medical technicians, and others, work to maintain the safety, health, and well-being of the communities they serve...This work not only puts public safety officers at-risk for experiencing harm, serious injury, and cumulative and acute trauma, but also places them at up to 25.6 times higher risk for developing post-traumatic stress disorder when compared to individuals without such experiences... Psychological evidence indicates that law enforcement officers experience significant job- related stressors and exposures that may confer increased risk for mental health morbidities (such as post-traumatic stress disorder and suicidal thoughts, ideation, intents, and behaviors) and hastened mortality" (ibid).

While the Act is a major step forward, there are concerns. The primary concern is related to suicide buffer #3 - *worry about how their suicide would affect family members*. This buffer fails when thoughts change from "I cannot kill myself because it would devastate my family" to "My family would be better off without me." Within the midst of depression, will family compensation become a factor for some suicidal officers? Will the number of officer suicides increase due to the knowledge that their family will be compensated and thereby "better off" by their suicide? Time will tell.

Officers must come to understand that their families would *never be better off without them*. The thought that it would is based upon a false premise – the premise that monetary compensation could ever take the officer's place. Officer suicide, in fact most every suicide, truly devastates the family. So much so that the effects are often experienced beyond the generation within which it occurs.

The "Make it Safe" Police Officer Initiative

The "Make it Safe" Police Officer Initiative was developed in 2013. It is comprised of 12 elements designed to reduce secondary danger and thereby lower the frequency of police officer suicide.

Officers must be able to ask for help without fear of negative career consequences, being belittled by peers, and feeling that asking for help is a personal and professional weakness.

Law enforcement personnel need to re-think what it means to be a police officer. Being a police officer does not mean that you have to suffer in silence. It is easy enough to ask for help with physical illnesses and injuries. Why should it be any different with psychological difficulties?

Help reduce secondary danger by making it safe to seek psychological support when needed. Take a positive step forward. Become part of the "Make it Safe" Police Officer Initiative.

The "Make it Safe" Police Officer Initiative encourages:

(1) every officer to "self-monitor" and to take personal responsibility for mental wellness.
(2) every officer to seek psychological support when confronting potentially overwhelming difficulties (officers do not have to "go it alone").
(3) every officer to diminish the sometime deadly effects of secondary danger by reaching out to other officers known to be facing difficult circumstances.

(4) veteran and ranking officers to use their status to help reduce secondary danger - veteran and ranking officers can reduce secondary danger by openly discussing it, appropriately sharing selected personal experiences, avoiding the use of pejorative terms to describe officers seeking or engaging psychological support, and talking about the acceptability of seeking psychological support when confronting stressful circumstances.

(5) law enforcement administrators to better educate themselves about the nature of secondary danger and to take the lead in secondary danger reduction.

(6) law enforcement administrators to issue a departmental memo encouraging officers to engage psychological support services when confronting potentially overwhelming stress - the memo should include information about confidentiality and available support resources.

(7) basic training in stress management, stress inoculation, critical incidents, post-traumatic stress, police family dynamics, substance use and addiction, and the warning signs of depression and suicide.

(8) the development of programs that engage preemptive, early-warning, and periodic department-wide officer support interventions - for example, proactive annual check in, "early warning" policies designed to support officers displaying signs of stress, and regularly scheduled stress inoculation and critical incident stressor management training.

(9) law enforcement agencies to initiate incident-specific protocols to support officers and their families when officers are involved in critical incidents.

(10) law enforcement agencies to create appropriately structured, properly trained, and clinically supervised peer support teams.

(11) law enforcement agencies to provide easy and confidential access to counseling and specialized police psychological support services.

(12) police officers at all levels of the organization to enhance the agency climate so that others are encouraged to ask

for help when experiencing psychological or emotional difficulties instead of keeping and acting out a deadly secret (Digliani, 2013).

If law enforcement officers wish to do the best for themselves and other officers, it's time to make a change. It's time to make a difference.

National Suicide Prevention Lifeline
Suicide and Crisis Lifeline – call or text 988
or call 1-800-273-8255, available 24/7
www.https://988lifeline.org

Chapter 11

Life After a Police Career

For the police officer, retirement is far from the end. Eligible for retirement at mid-life, police officers are faced with the difficult decision of staying in police work or returning to civilian life.
-John M. Violanti, 1992, retired NY state trooper,
professor University of Buffalo

Unless officers die during their police career, they will again become civilians. Like entering policing, leaving policing involves a psychological transition. The psychological transition from police officer to civilian involves leaving police authority, the police family, and any status associated with being a police officer, behind.

Police officers make the transition to civilian life either voluntarily or involuntarily.

Voluntary Departure

Voluntary departure from policing, unless an officer is leaving to avoid termination, involves leaving on one's own terms. There are many reasons that officers choose to leave policing, including the pursuit of other interests and planned retirement. Whatever the circumstance, officers must consider the future. Nearly everyone has heard the adage, "You should retire *to* something, not *from* something." This is good advice.

Many officers successfully move beyond policing careers. Yes, there is life after policing. Whether after just a few years or decades of service, these officers anticipate and accept their retirement from policing. They often start preparing long before their planned departure. They attend professional training classes, complete university studies, and otherwise take steps necessary to achieve their retirement goals. Following retirement, they transition into their new life, often becoming educators, politicians, lawyers, real estate agents, business owners, and even psychologists. It is career life-by-design at its best.

Some officers retire from their agency and accept civilian positions within their department. These officers-turned-civilian ease their transition out of policing by remaining employees of their agency. They often become lab techs, evidence custodians, background investigators, and so on. While this supports officers in their transition, the agency benefits as well. It retains the officer's years of training and experience. A pretty good deal for all involved.

Other officers continue their policing career by retiring from one agency and joining another. This is most often seen in agencies that have a fixed-period retirement system (see *Timing of retirement*). Still others take advantage of their police training and become civilian security consultants, bodyguards, and private operators.

Some officers transition into full retirement. These officers are not interested in launching new or second careers. Instead, they find fulfillment in family, friends, travel, community service, and other endeavors. The important thing in full retirement is to do something. Ideally, it is something that is personally fulfilling and meaningful. For many former officers, volunteering for favorite charities, organizations, or worthy causes fills the bill.

Of course, whether an officer continues to work or enters full retirement after a policing career depends upon many factors, not the least of which is the officer. And even fully retired officers often pick up various "retirement gigs" to keep themselves busy and to earn some pocket money. Such gigs are normally, but not necessarily, far removed from policing. In the end, it seems that life after policing is limited only by one's goals and imagination.

Involuntary Departure

Involuntary departure includes leaving to avoid being fired, being terminated, and separating due to disability. When officers leave to avoid being fired it frequently involves an internal investigation that would likely result in the officer being terminated.

When officers are terminated, it is usually for cause and involves *due process*. Due process allows officers to challenge the reason(s) for termination and the imposed discipline. It also allows an appeal in the event the challenge is unsuccessful. Some police agencies are not subject to the rules of due process. In these agencies, officers serve at the discretion of the chief, sheriff, or other authority. As at-will employees, they can be terminated without cause.

Some police careers end through disability. Disability can result from illness or injury, including psychological injury caused by traumatic exposure. If the disability is job-related, there may be benefits that are not available otherwise. These benefits may make a significant difference in how the disability affects disabled officers. Regardless of the circumstances, in many cases of disability, officers struggle with the premature ending of their police career.

Grief and sometimes depression are observed when disability ends an officer's career. The grief experienced in such cases is twofold: grief for the loss of career and all that goes with it (status, income, benefits, comradeship) and grief for the loss of the "healthy self."

The experience of grief in response to a lost career can be significant and include practical and existential concerns. Former officers that find themselves coping with career loss due to disability often express these concerns by asking "how do I support my family?" "who am I without this job?" and "what do I do now?"

For most officers, the grief for the loss of the healthy self or the loss of an ability is personal and often unique. Much depends upon the actual loss and the officer's ability to compensate for it or cope with it.

Separately, the loss of a career or the loss of health/ability can cause significant psychological distress. The loss of both simultaneously can be devastating.

Role Transition

Regardless of the type of departure from policing, successfully managing the transition means dealing with the loss of the police role. For some officers, leaving policing is a welcomed change. For most, it is a challenge. Even officers that have planned for and welcome the transition to civilian life will acknowledge missing at least some parts of the job - the most often cited is "the camaraderie."

Many officers have lived the "cop life" for so long that they do not know how to live any other way. This is reflected in their continued practice of carrying a firearm, meeting with the "boys" and "sisters," and hanging around the police station. However, it is not long before they notice that something has changed. As one officer explained it, "It's like I belonged to a big club. I made my mark, I was one of the guys, I did my job. Everyone in the station respects you. Suddenly, all of that is gone and you are on the outside looking in. I felt so different. I called the guys almost every day to see if they still related to me the same way. I visited the station, wondering what was going on and wanting to be part of the action. Somehow, it wasn't the same. I wasn't one of them anymore. It's hard to explain. I left, but I couldn't let go of this strong attachment" (Violanti, 1992, 41). Not much has changed since 1992.

Normally, as the length of time increases from the date of departure, such behaviors decrease. Slowly, for most officers, the "ownership" of the police agency is given over to the next generation of officers and the attachment to the police role diminishes.

The loss of the officer's role can also affect spouses. Some wives of retired police officers talk about their husbands as if they were still police officers. There seems to be a vicarious social status enjoyed by these women and many find the status difficult to relinquish. For example, one wife consistently referred to her retired officer husband as "the lieutenant." This was interesting because she would do so only in public. Another wife of a former police officer, upon his transition to new car salesman, complained, "I used to be somebody. I was the wife of a police officer." Evidently, she did not derive similar satisfaction from being the wife of a car salesman. Although the husband's job-change was not the only factor, this couple divorced about a year after he left the police department. Clearly, wives, like officers, sometimes struggle with the idea that relinquishment of the police role is tantamount to not being a "big shot" (as one officer put it) any longer.

Children of police officers can have similar experiences. Of course, this pattern may also be observed when wives are the former police officers, and within any other interpersonal relationship.

Timing of retirement

Many officers struggle with the timing of their retirement. Although there are no strict rules for when an officer should retire, the retirement system of an officer's agency often influences this decision. There are still some police departments with a fixed-benefit retirement system. In these agencies, if officers work for a specified number of years (usually twenty or twenty-five), they receive a percentage of their active-duty salary upon retirement. For most, this is collectable immediately upon retirement and is paid for life. Although it happens, it is unusual to see officers work much beyond their fixed retirement period. This is because after reaching the required years of service, officers are effectively working for a portion of their salary (the amount difference between their salary and what they would receive in retirement). As one officer put it, "I'm not working for half-pay. I'm outta here."

In agencies that provide an employer sponsored, defined contribution personal pension retirement, such as the 401K program, it is not unusual to see officers with more than thirty-five years of service. This system encourages longevity because the longer that officers work, the more money is accumulated. Unlike a fixed benefit retirement, when 401K money is exhausted, there is no further benefit. Add this to the fact that most police officers do not pay into social security, so that benefit may be lacking, and it is easy to see why some officers will work for many years in the same agency with 401K retirement plans.

Some officers working under a 401K or similar retirement benefit system have difficulty thinking they ever have enough money in their account to retire. The sad result of this is that some officers stay well beyond the time that they should have left. They become disinterested ROD (retired on duty) or ROAD (retired on active duty) officers. ROD/ROAD officers are just marking time, stacking money. They have "quietly quit" and do only what is necessary to get by. This becomes evident in their attitude and performance. They eventually end their police careers with a history of less-than-desirable performance and a poor work reputation.

Successful Retirement

For successful retirement from policing, officers need to prepare. Although having sufficient funds is important, this preparation should go beyond finance. Officers should think through the Retirement Checklist:

Retirement Checklist

1. Have you planned your retirement income to meet your needs? Is the income sufficient to support your anticipated retirement lifestyle?
2. Have you talked to your family about your retirement? How might it affect their lives? Discuss the fact that you may be around much more of the time.
3. Have you arranged for affordable medical and other insurance benefits?
4. Is it time for a change? Have you given all that you reasonably can to policing? Are you ready for a change?
5. Are you satisfied with your police career? Are there still things you wish to accomplish as a police officer?
6. Are you still connected to policing or have you mentally checked out? If you are still connected and it is not time for a change, continue your career. You are not ready to retire. If you have mentally checked out and it is not time for a change, reclaim your career. If it is time for a change, consider retirement. *Do not end your successful police career as a ROD or ROAD officer.*
7. How will you occupy the time formerly spent at work? Hopefully, not with food, alcohol, or computer games. Some officers that have never had a serious problem with overeating, drinking too much, and spending unproductive days in front of a computer, develop these behaviors following retirement.
8. Are you ready for a change of pace? Have you thought about the possibility of not having enough to do or feeling overwhelmed with too much to do? When retired, there may be times that you feel a bit bored. This is not unusual, as occasionally

feeling bored is a part of life for most everyone. The same goes with feeling overwhelmed. The important thing to avoid in retirement is a bored or overwhelmed lifestyle. For most officers, this means actively pursuing balance, a balance that may not have been available when working.

9. Are you prepared for a change in perceived stress? The stress reduction experienced by most officers upon retirement is often remarkable. This is often unanticipated and can lead to a collision of emotions – a simultaneous sense of relief from job stress and a feeling of sadness due to no longer being part of the police department.

10. What will you do? Do you have a plan? Will you begin another career, pursue a hobby, or take a retirement break before deciding? It can be beneficial to simply enjoy some time off after years of a police career. Whatever you are considering, write it down. You might surprise yourself with what you can discover when you write out what you are thinking.

Time structuring and time management are important in retirement. Even the pleasure of travel, sports, activities, and not having to work may eventually wear off. This is especially true if many of the officer's closest friends are still working and frequently unavailable for social activities.

Managing time and making it meaningful is a major challenge of retirement. Remember that retirement is a transition. Transitions take time. Once retired, be patient. It may take some time to find your retirement rhythm.

Retirement and Emotional Abandonment

Upon retirement, some officers report feeling emotionally abandoned by the department and former coworkers. They express these feelings in statements such as "My department has forgotten me" and "I guess when you're gone, you're gone!" For these retired officers, it seems that once the retirement ceremony ended, so did the years of work-group camaraderie. This can be especially distressing for officers who feel that they have given decades of honorable service to the agency, only to be swiftly forgotten.

To address this issue, some police agencies have developed programs which actively involve retired officers. These programs include volunteer services and assignments, periodic retired-officer social events or meetings, invitations to attend regular department events, and alumni associations. Additionally, many agencies support retired officers by offering periodic firearms qualification courses for those that wish to carry a concealed weapon as authorized under the *Law Enforcement Officers Safety Act* (LEOSA)(2004). However, as desirable as these programs have proven to be, many departments lack them.

Retired officers that feel emotionally abandoned and have a desire to reconnect with former coworkers have at least two options: (1) wait for someone to reach out or (2) initiate behavior to maintain or reestablish former relationships. As you might guess, pursuing option two significantly increases the probability of success.

The behaviors initiated under option (2) would depend upon the desired outcome. Therefore, a desire to stay in contact with specific former coworkers might involve arranging a coffee meeting. Maybe this coffee meeting evolves into a periodic breakfast gathering - an excellent way to stay connected to friends. Planning and inviting others to common interest activities is another great way to keep in touch. The point is, as a retired officer, if you feel emotionally abandoned, you do not have to wait for others to remedy the situation. Instead, take the initiative. Your efforts may not result in exactly the outcome you want, but it is likely that it will be good. Remember, the outcome does not have to be perfect to be ok. Try again if things do not first turn out as you hoped.

If you are a working officer and have had close ties with a now retired officer, consider reaching out. The reach out does not have to be anything elaborate, an occasional telephone conversation or invitation for coffee will do. Even if the retired officer does not feel emotionally abandoned, your efforts will almost certainly be appreciated. Keep in mind that when you reach out, you honor the service and contributions of a retired officer who made some difference in your life and police career. Reaching out to a retired officer that meant something special to you is a very good thing to do, for both of you. Of course, retired officers can also reach out to other retired officers.

Retirement and Marriage

If married, retirement will often bring the couple back to the beginning. The kids, if any, are usually out of the house. The couple, as when first married, is back to living as a couple. The difference this time is that there is no job to go to. This means a lot of unprecedented time together. In 1984, psychologist John Stratton said that for police marriages, retirement can be a "time of friction or a time of rediscovery" (284). This is as true today as it was then. As Stratton reported, one police wife put it this way when asked how it felt to have her husband home. She answered, "Great, I went out and got a job." Another said, "I took him for better or for worse, but not for lunch" (284).

Following retirement, couples can expect an adjustment period. During adjustment, couples can re-discover one another in a way not previously possible. They can also drift apart. Find what works to strengthen your bond. Do not allow the golden years of retirement to distance the intimacy in your relationship. Keep in mind that with a little planning and some patience, retirement can bring everything that you hoped it would. With a little planning and some patience, most officers go on to live rewarding, fulfilling, and enjoyable lives with their spouse after a career in policing.

Retirement and the Police Officer Bond

While nearly every retired officer would agree that their place in the police family has changed, few would deny that there remains a lifetime emotional bond among police officers that have served honorably. This bond goes beyond that developed with other officers while on the job. It is forged by the common experiences, risks, and dangers confronted by police officers, no matter what country or time period within which they served. This bond is felt and expressed by officers throughout the world.

Once a police officer, always a police officer

The police officer bond is expressed in sociable conversations with previously unknown officers, exchange of small gifts and uniform arm patches when in other jurisdictions and foreign countries, tours of police facilities, and so on. It is the enduring emotional connection that active and retired police officers share with every other police officer. In this sense, for most officers, *once a police officer, always a police officer.*

Graffiti on a wall in Vittoria, Sicily (Italy) expressing an attitude toward the police.

Graffiti in Regensburg, Germany.
Common stressors and experiences bond police officers worldwide.

The Poetry of Retirement

Police Retirement: The Uniform

The uniform is put away,
In the closet, there to stay,
Never more to take a seat,
Never more to walk a beat.

It has worked, day and night,
In full sight, through calm and fight,
Through the sun and through the snow,
Through each shift, busy or slow.

It has faced danger, served and protected,
Taken the best and the worst, as expected.

No longer a witness to a report,
No longer needed to stand up in court,
Now it has taken its last dispatched call,
It has served honorably once and for all.
- Jack A. Digliani, 2022

Stopping by Woods on a Snowy Evening

Perhaps renown American poet Robert Frost (1874-1963) best expressed one way to view life after retirement. In his celebrated poem published in 1923, *Stopping by Woods on a Snowy Evening*, he closed with these words:

The woods are lovely, dark and deep,
But I have promises to keep,
And miles to go before I sleep,
And miles to go before I sleep.

Like the person in Frost's poem, retired police officers have promises to keep and miles to go before they sleep.

Chapter 12

Reflections of a Police Psychologist
Things That Every Police Officer Should Know

...in the future the psychologist...will be less of a rare
bird in the police profession.
-Martin Reiser (1927-2015), LAPD psychologist,1972

The following reflections are the result of working within the professions of policing and psychology. They are not presented in any particular order. They are a collection of thoughts that bear some significance to those in policing. Many are also relevant to those outside of policing.

Police Officer and Husband Modes of Transaction: The Mode Zone

- you should have come with a warning label
Lorie Digliani

Have you ever tried to assist your wife with a problem that *she* brought to you, only to have her become upset when you provided a solution? Did it seem like she became more frustrated each time you told her how to solve the problem? If you answered "yes" to either of these questions, it is most likely that you have unwittingly violated the *mode zone.*

Police officer-husbands have at least two marital transactional modes: *cop mode* and *husband mode.* In the cop mode, the husband transacts with his wife in a work-like manner, similar to that involving any person he might encounter while on the job. So, when his wife has a problem, the "cop" husband fixes it, tells her how to fix it, or informs her that he cannot help. This communication is usually cold and matter of fact. Frequently and secretly, he often wonders why she could not see these "obvious" fixes for herself.

In cop mode, husbands often become irate if wives do not take their advice, "I told you what to do, just do it." The officer's unsaid (although sometimes said) thoughts are "I already told you what to do. Do it, don't do it, I don't care. Your problem is not a big a deal."

Things are different in the husband mode. In the husband mode, the husband listens patiently as his wife describes the problem. He tries to understand it from her point of view and supports her efforts to explore, discuss, and address the problem. He is fully attentive and listens carefully. He does not try to fix things. He avoids "mansplaining" and helps her to work through it in her own way. He responds to any questions calmly. He chooses his words thoughtfully, careful to avoid any hint of minimizing the issue or belittling her for bringing the problem to him. He makes it safe (chapter 7).

Husband mode - positive outcome

For the most part when wives bring up a problem for discussion, they are seeking their husbands and not a police officer - this is a very good thing to remember.

When your wife is looking for her husband and finds only the cop, you can rest assured that she will leave the conversation feeling frustrated, discouraged, and maybe angry. Too frequently, wives of police officers have reported feeling minimized and "treated like a child" when spoken to by their husbands in cop mode. To wives dismay, instead of a supportive and empathetic husband, they find a somewhat emotionally uninvolved, sometimes annoyed, police officer ready to provide direction and eager to move on.

To avoid an unintentional excursion into cop mode, keep in mind that most wives want and need a *husband*, not a cop, when they are confronting difficulties. In such circumstances, a response from cop mode will fall short and produce less than desirable results.

The next time your wife comes to you with a problem, no matter how small it seems to you, turn the transaction into something positive. Be a husband. You can strengthen your marriage, enhance intimacy, and contribute to your wife's happiness by doing so.

Cop mode, relationships, and emotional insulation

The characteristics of the "cop" and the "husband" transactional modes apply equally to unmarried police couples, female officers and their husbands, gay and lesbian police couples, and all other partner relationships. These modes of interaction can also be seen in other personal relationships, such as parent-child and friendships.

The development of cop mode is related to the psychological defense mechanism *emotional insulation* (chapter 7) and appears to be an occupational hazard for police officers.

Counseling and Change

Little is guaranteed in life. The same is true of counseling. In counseling, a psychologist can guarantee only effort. Effort is not result. The result of counseling is dependent upon several things, not the least of which is the person seeking help.

Accepting responsibility for oneself and for any desired change is one of the primary challenges for persons entering counseling. It is a primary challenge because it is common and easy to blame others for our difficulties. When confronting a problem or seeking change, persons must ask themselves, "What role am I playing in the maintenance of this problem?" and "What do I need to do differently to help bring about the life changes I want?" The path for improvement becomes clearer when these questions are honestly addressed.

Counseling is founded upon the premise that people can do something other than what they have done. Without this premise, there would be no reason to enter counseling - there would be no hope for change.

Change can be difficult. Although change can be difficult, change is possible. The difficulty of change should not be confused with the possibility of change. A simple way to think about this is, *change may be difficult but it is not impossible.* Even the remnants of an undesirable childhood can be altered. This is also true for the seeming enduring effects of traumatic life experiences.

Perception, Insight, and Other People

Many of us can readily perceive the changes needed in the lives of our friends, family members, and others. It is easy to see that others should stop drinking, stop bullying, be more assertive, start treating others kinder, and so on. So why do we have such a difficult time seeing these things in ourselves? There are many reasons. The self-centered perspective is one of the most important. The self-centered perspective is characterized by seeing things only from your point of view. Why is this so important? It is important because our perspective drives our behavior.

While it is normal to see things from a personal point of view, most of us have a degree of self-insight and at least some ability to see things from the view of others. These abilities help us to see and understand the effects of our behavior. They allow us to continually assess ourselves and change things when necessary to make desired improvements. In this way, we learn from our experiences and develop wisdom as we move through life.

But this is not true of everyone. Some people lack insight and an ability to see things from other points of view. They consistently repeat behaviors that are harmful to themselves and others. They do not seem to learn from experience. They gain little wisdom. They are blinded by internalized dysfunctional principles such as, "A real man wins every argument" "Children should be seen and not heard," and "What kind of man (or woman) would I be if I did (or didn't do) X."

Confronting and evaluating internalized principles and the behaviors founded upon them is a primary task of self-examination and personal growth. It is a fundamental goal of most counseling and self-help programs. The bottom line is, *avoid being blinded by a dysfunctional principle.* Blindly following some principle learned early in life that does little but cause trouble will make your adult life more difficult. It is much better to think about what is possible, instead of being locked into what has always been.

Other People Are Not You

Related to a self-centered perspective is the realization that other people are not you. Who would argue with the validity of this statement? Realizing that "other people are not you" appears intuitive, self-evident, a component of human consciousness, and something that everyone knows. But *knowing* that other people are not you is insufficient to make much difference in your life. To really benefit from this potentially profound insight, you must come to *understand* that other people are not you. This understanding will help you to maintain better personal boundaries, avoid frustration, become more tolerate of others, and better manage your life.

Other people are not you - this means that at times, others will wait when you would act. They will act when you would wait. They might remain in circumstances that you would abandon, and abandon circumstances in which you would remain.

Why do others not see things in the way you see them? Why do they not act as you would act? (or believe you would - *you might not act as you think you would if you were actually facing their circumstances!*) And why is it so easy for you to see (know) what they should do in circumstances that create great ambivalence for them?

The answers to these questions are psychologically and sociologically complex. For current purposes, suffice it to say that there are five primary factors that make it possible for you to "know" what other persons should do in circumstances that create ambivalence and indecision for them:

1. Different personal histories
2. Differences in actual or perceived abilities
3. Differences in personal values, beliefs, and personality
4. You do not have the emotional investment or attachments that exist for them
5. You will not experience the real-life consequences that they will experience upon making a decision

Therefore, the personal process of making any significant decision is fundamentally different for the involved person than it is for any outside observer. This is how you can know what another person should do, even when they don't. (adapted from: Digliani, J.A. (2015). *Contemporary Issues in Police Psychology*).

Confronting What You Fear

There is an old saying, "If you see a ghost and run, it will chase you. If you stop and look at it, it will disappear." This adage captures the essence of *confronting what you fear*. Although fear is normal and serves as a warning of impending danger, unreasonable fears limit and diminish life experiences. If you hope to overcome a fear and any associated anxiety, you must confront it (like our swimmer in chapter 2). To do otherwise allows the fear to continue.

In situations that produce fear, we have three fundamental choices: avoidance (stay away from what we fear), withdrawal (get away from what we fear), and confrontation (engage what we fear).

Avoidance and Withdrawal

Most of us deal with fear by avoidance or withdrawal. Avoidance or withdrawal are functional options and are excellent choices in many situations - avoiding a dark alley in a crime ridden neighborhood or withdrawing from a burning building are certainly wise choices. However, there are circumstances in which avoidance or withdrawal might not work as well. Consider an office worker whose cubicle is located on the 35th floor of a high-rise building. Avoiding the elevator due to a fear of confined spaces would undoubtedly prevent the experience of anxiety, but it would also make going to work much more difficult. Hence, when we avoid, we do not experience fear, but the consequences of avoidance can be less than desirable. Additionally, when we avoid, the underlying fear remains.

When we withdraw, we remove ourselves from a fearful situation. Our fear terminates for the present but, like with avoidance, the underlying fear remains. Because fear terminates following withdrawal, the act of withdrawal is *negatively reinforced*. Negative reinforcement occurs whenever an uncomfortable experience is terminated by some action. Therefore, in the example of our office worker, if she enters the building elevator, becomes overwhelmed by fear, hurriedly walks out of it and feels relieved, the act of walking out of the elevator is reinforced.

The reinforced behavior of walking out of *this* elevator will extend to all elevators, and likely be generalized to all confined spaces. Reinforced withdrawal often leads to thoughts like, "I've tried to deal with this fear and failed. I'm not trying again." Such thoughts then work to drive future avoidance behavior. In simple terms, avoidance and withdrawal work in tandem to maintain the fear.

Incidentally, negative reinforcement should not be confused with punishment. Punishment is the presentation of an aversive stimulus, such as spanking (*positive* punishment) or the removal of something desirable, like a favorite toy (*negative* punishment). When applied immediately following a behavior, punishment tends to suppress that behavior. When applied later, as in the popularized maternal admonishment to a child behaving badly, "Just wait until your father gets home!" the mom is relying upon the fact that the child will make the connection between the punishment and the act being punished. As punishment does not increase the likelihood of any particular behavior, it is not considered a reinforcer.

One last word on negative reinforcement and punishment: as a parent, if you spank a child that is behaving badly and the child's undesirable behavior stops, you have been negatively reinforced for spanking. Therefore, *spanking is punishment for the child* and *negatively reinforcing for the spanker.* You may have to think about this for a while. However, it helps to explain why parents that spank are more likely to continue spanking. For reasons too complex to be specified here, spanking or any form of corporal punishment for child discipline is strongly discouraged.

Confrontation

If we confront what we fear in a manner that enhances our ability to overcome it, the fear subsides.

There are several ways to positively confront what you fear. The exposure therapies of *systematic desensitization, flooding,* and *response prevention* are strategies designed to assist persons confront what they fear.

Systematic desensitization (Wolpe, 1969) involves incremental exposure to the feared object or circumstance. It utilizes relaxation training and a stressor hierarchy. Briefly, it works like this. Persons wishing to confront their fears construct a fear hierarchy. At bottom of the list is the item least problematic; at the top, the most problematic. They learn relaxation techniques. In a relaxed state, they confront the items listed on the hierarchy from least to most problematic. When the least problematic item no longer produces fear or any associated anxiety, the next item is addressed. This continues until the top item is addressed and no longer produces fear. Systematic desensitization is based upon the theory that a person can overcome fear by mastering incremental exposure to that which is feared. This is accomplished through the principle of reciprocal inhibition, the idea that a person cannot be relaxed and fearful simultaneously (relaxation inhibits the experience of fear and vice versa). An actual hierarchy might start with imagining the feared object or situation, then looking at pictures, and finally moving on to real-world exposures. Recently, and with great promise, virtual reality devices have been employed in systematic desensitization.

Another way to confront what you fear is by flooding. Flooding involves intense exposure to what is feared. The exposure is maintained until the fear subsides. Keeping persons fearful of tight spaces in an elevator until their fear subsides is an example of flooding. Flooding is more traumatic than systematic desensitization and is not always the best way to confront fear. Flooding may be more appropriate in cases of mild fear and anxiety.

Flooding and systematic desensitization have had some success in the treatment of phobias, conditioned fear and anxiety responses, acute stress disorder, posttraumatic stress disorder, generalized anxiety, and other anxiety-related psychological disorders.

Like flooding and systematic desensitization, response prevention has demonstrated efficacy in the treatment of anxiety. Response prevention has a primary application in the treatment of obsessive-compulsive disorder (OCD). Obsessive-compulsive disorder is comprised of two basic elements; obsession (thought) and compulsion (behavior). In OCD, irrational thoughts create anxiety, while directed behaviors reduce it. For example, persons who cannot stop thinking of germs, are driven by these thoughts to wash excessively (directed behavior). In this example of OCD, the thoughts of germs are the obsession, while the washing is the compulsion. A complicating factor in OCD is that the compulsion is negatively reinforced by the reduction of anxiety associated with the obsession.

In response prevention, the person is prevented from engaging the compulsive behavior. Therefore, the person is compelled to cope with the obsession without the compulsion. Eventually, the person comes to understand that the obsession represents no real danger. This often results in a reduction of obsessional thoughts and a realization that the compulsive behavior is unnecessary.

You can think of it this way: if obsessional anxiety is relieved by engaging the compulsion, the compulsive behavior gains strength (it is negatively reinforced). If obsessional anxiety is successfully confronted, the person gains strength. As the person becomes stronger, the intensity of the obsession diminishes. The power of the obsession to drive the compulsion is weakened, and neither the obsession nor the compulsion remains dominant in the person's life.

It is possible to experience obsessions without overt compulsions. In such cases, the obsession may drive mental exercises or mental rituals (like mentally reciting a secret incantation) which function to reduce the anxiety produced by the obsession (Null, 2006).

Police Officers, Fear, and Behavior

Fear has an interesting relationship with behavior. We can act out of fear and we can act in spite of fear. This is as true for police officers as it is for anyone else.

Some police officers struggle with the emotion of fear. They have an idea that once they become police officers, they should never experience fear. This is irrational. There is no badge that will keep anyone from ever experiencing fear. For officers, being fearful at times is normal. Experienced officers cope with fear by learning to manage it. This allows officers to act, even when fearful. If the actions are reasonable and appropriate, officers should not punish themselves for sometimes feeling afraid. No one is immune from fear. Even seemingly fearless persons will experience fear in certain circumstances. Police officers should accept this fact and move forward with their careers.

Don't Have to Like It, Just Have to Do It

In life there are many things that are easy to dislike. Consider the colonoscopy. This procedure is not something most people look forward to. So why do we do it? We do it because we value the outcome. We do it, but we don't like it. Flu shots, same thing. We do it because we value the outcome. Imagine if we had to like having a colonoscopy or getting a flu shot before consenting to one. It seems a bit too much to ask.

The same is true for other things. For example, we don't have to like all the classes required to obtain a college degree but if we wish to graduate, we have to take them. We don't have to like vegetables but if we desire their nutritional benefits, we have to consume them.

People sometimes get confused about having to *like* something in order to *do* something. They think that in order to bring about positive change, they have to learn to like something they dislike. This is not true. We can do things solely because we desire the outcome; we can work through something we dislike in order to achieve something we like. Understanding this makes doing things once thought impossible, possible - like quitting smoking.

When tempered with positive values and a sense of social responsibility, doing something you dislike to achieve something desirable can produce very good outcomes. To reap the benefits of doing something for a desirable outcome, remember- *you don't have to like it; you just have to do it.*

Contingency, Possibility, Probability, and Relativity

Have you ever walked down a country lane in autumn and looked up just in time to see a leaf falling gently to the ground? Or walked outside in the winter and noticed one specific snowflake on your hand, mitten, or glove? Have you ever wondered about all the things that had to happen to make that particular experience possible?

We live in a world of contingency. The contingencies of everyday life are comprised of the possibilities and probabilities that have existed since the dawn of time. Some probabilities are so high that they become "normal" and expected, like an uneventful drive to work. This means that while the possibility of something extraordinary happening while driving to work on any given day is not zero, the probability of such an occurrence is quite low. In other words, there are many ways in which today will be similar to yesterday, but only a small number of ways for today to be extraordinary. The probability of today being similar to yesterday is so high that we sometimes complain about "nothing ever happening" or being "stuck in the same ol' routine." And what police officer is unfamiliar with the phrase, "same shit, different day"? There is such a high probability that today will be like most others that we come to rely on and expect that which has become our everyday normal.

It is only under unusual circumstances that we get to see and come to appreciate the contingent nature of the world. When this happens, we say things like "Who would have ever thought this was possible!" and "What are the odds!"

Take the case of Ann Elizabeth Hodges (1923-1972). Ann was napping inside her home in Sylacauga (Oak Grove), Alabama, on November 30, 1954. Around 6:46 p.m., she was awakened by a loud noise and shortly thereafter felt a pain on her left side. It took a while, but she soon realized that a meteorite fragment had crashed through the roof of her home. It bounced off a wooden radio in the living room and struck her in the left hip. The fragment weighted about 8.5 pounds. Ann's case was the first well-authenticated injury to a person caused by an extraterrestrial object (Povenmire, 1995). As far as contingencies go, can you imagine all that had to happen for Ann to be struck by this particular fragment of meteorite? The contingencies involved in observing a leaf falling from a tree seem to pale in comparison (although the falling leaf is no less contingent). Considering that the Hodges meteorite, as it came to be known, is *billions* of years old (Taylor, 2001) and that it had been zooming around the universe for all that time, makes the odds of it striking Ann incalculable. Still, it happened.

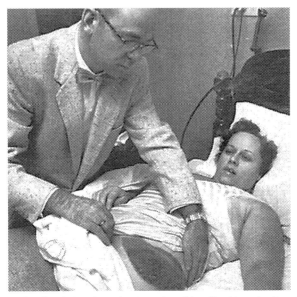

Ann Elizabeth Hodges is examined by Dr. Moody Jacobs
after being struck by a fragment of meteorite in 1954.

Understanding contingencies helps to answer the question, "Why me?" The answer to this question becomes clearer as our understanding of the universe deepens. The answer to "why me?" is that we live in a contingent universe. In a contingent universe, it makes just as much sense to ask, "Why not me?" It is simply a matter of probability. In a contingent universe, things do not always happen to the other guy, sometimes things happen to us – and consider, it's never the "other guy" to the other guy. Things are always happening to *someone,* no matter how low the probability.

The human perception of, and emotional responses to, life's probability is relative. This is sometimes called the *relativity principle.* To better understand this, imagine that ten thousand people are gathered in an arena. Each person holds a piece of paper. On the paper is a number ranging from one to ten thousand. A person not included in the group has a bin that contains ten thousand pieces of paper. Each piece of paper in the bin is numbered from one to ten thousand. The person not included in the group will draw a single piece of paper from the bin. The person in the group holding the number indicated on the piece of paper drawn from the bin will win one million dollars. This seems simple enough. It is nothing more than a raffle with the odds of winning being one in ten thousand. Now think of the experience of the person who will draw the number. For the person drawing, it is "Well, someone has to win. It will be one of these ten thousand people. No surprise there." He knows that the probability of someone winning the one million dollars is 100 percent, a sure thing. Contrast this to the experience of the person whose number is drawn. For that person, winning one million dollars can be life changing. Their experience may be expressed in words similar to "Wow, me?" "I don't believe it!" and "Why me!?" In fact, the odds of winning this raffle were so small that the winner will likely need to answer the "why me" question.

Depending upon personal beliefs, the winner's answer to the "why me" will range from *pure chance* or *dumb luck* (after all, someone had to win) to divine intervention. For those who did not win, the question "why not me?" will likely be answered in terms of the probability; "Well, look at the odds. What chance did I have?" Regardless of the outcome, each of the ten thousand and one people involved in the drawing will have had some personal experience. Their experience is relative to the outcome and circumstance. The point is this: life's experiences look and feel different depending upon probability and one's beliefs, perspective, position, and involvement...*relativity*.

Contingency, Relativity, and Human Values

To the universe, all events are neutral. It is only how events relate to human endeavors that values are assigned. This is why we can have *good* weather and *bad* weather. Really, isn't weather just weather? Weather is perceived as good or bad depending upon how it directly or indirectly affects humans. And how it effects humans is relative. So, the same rainstorm that is good for the farmer can be bad for the camper; but in the universal scheme of things, it is just a rainstorm.

Many persons unwittingly recognize contingent events by saying things like "I guess I was just in the right place at the right time." Interestingly, and dependent upon whether the outcome is viewed as desirable, events seem to be equally well explained by any combination of the right-wrong and place-time dichotomies: *the right place at the right time, the wrong place at the right time, the right place at the wrong time,* and *the wrong place at the wrong time.*

Sometimes contingencies come together to create catastrophe. When this happens, the result can be tragic.

<u>Case in point</u>: The Riverhouse incident occurred in Loveland, Colorado, on January 3, 1989. This incident, so called because it ended at the Riverhouse Restaurant, involved Larimer County sheriff's deputies as well as Loveland police officers. Brief synopsis: It began when officers responded to a domestic disturbance call. A deputy sheriff and a police officer met alongside the roadway leading to the address to discuss their approach. The suspect, later determined to be a 35-year-old military veteran armed with a 9mm handgun, confronted them. He shot at the deputy, hitting him in the arm, then sped away in his vehicle. He drove to the Riverhouse Restaurant. There he confronted staff and customers. Several customers escaped through various exits. He allowed others to leave, eventually taking control of about 15 persons whom he held as hostages. There was initial telephone contact with police. The suspect demanded a plane or helicopter to take him to Libya. He said he had contacts there. He later destroyed the telephone, limiting his communication with police to periodic appearances at the front doorway. During these appearances, he used a waitress as a shield. He informed police and hostages that any police assault would result in the killing of hostages. At one of his doorway appearances he fired at police, hitting a police officer. After some time and following a series of events including one in which the suspect fired several rounds inside the restaurant, he announced that if his demands were not met by 9 p.m. he would kill hostages and burn the restaurant. As 9 p.m. approached, a police sniper was provided authorization to shoot. The sniper shot the suspect through the front door window, the bullet striking him in the left torso. He was not killed. As the suspect fell backward, he fired three rounds, killing the 40-year-old waitress he had previously used as a shield. Immediately after, he fired a bullet into his head, killing himself.

During the confusion that followed, one of the hostages, a forty-five-year-old man, attempted an escape through a front-facing bathroom window. The window was dressed with a curtain similar in color to the suspect's jacket. A police officer on the restaurant perimeter, seeing a flash of the curtain color and believing the escaping man to be the suspect, shouted commands for him to stop. When the commands were not followed, in a split-second decision, the officer fired five rounds. The man was killed. It was later reported that the man attempting escape may have been hearing impaired.

When it was over, a deputy sheriff and police officer had been shot. Both survived their wounds. Three persons were dead, the waitress, the suspect, and a hostage mistakenly shot by a police officer.

Recognizing risk

Despite our best efforts, contingencies cannot be entirely anticipated or controlled. Even with advanced science, prediction models, weighing of probabilities, and near complete life-by-design, the unanticipated can occur. This means that life involves unavoidable risk. *Risk* is as good as it gets for living organisms.

Decision Making

Most persons find it difficult to decide some things some of the time. This is normal and part of everyday life. Some persons find it difficult to decide most things most of the time. For persons like this, every choice is a challenge.

Difficulty in making decisions is frequently correlated with anxiety - the greater the anxiety, the more difficult the decision making. As journalist Daniel Smith, a long-time sufferer of elevated anxiety put it, "(anxiety) is a petty monster able to work such humdrum tricks as paralyzing you over salad, convincing you that a choice between blue cheese and vinaigrette is as dire as that between life and death" (2012).

Even in cases where elevated anxiety is not an issue, some persons have difficulty making decisions. Reasons for this include: (1) the experience of *some* level of anxiety, (2) a desire to avoid responsibility for decision consequences, (3) some or all other options may be lost once a decision is made, and (4) the competing attractiveness of available options. Any of these factors, as well as a combination of them, makes choosing from available options difficult, and for some persons, nearly impossible.

The competing attractiveness of available options can literally paralyze decision making, but it is not the only factor. Frequently, the attractiveness of any available option is offset by some real or imagined undesirable component that accompanies it. For example, the attractiveness of an evening out with friends may be accompanied by an undesirable monetary expense. Most attractive options are like this. They come with the good and the not so good. This makes most options imperfect. It is the reason why most decisions involve *selecting from imperfect options*.

Decision-making and conflict

If a person has to select from two equally attractive options, an *approach-approach* conflict exists. In an approach-approach conflict, decision making is difficult because selecting one desirable option often locks out the other.

If a single option includes desirable and undesirable components, an *approach-avoidance* conflict ensues. In this type of conflict, a person might consider selecting (approach) the option due to its attractiveness, only to be repulsed by its undesirable aspects (avoidance). Approach-approach and approach-avoidance conflicts exist in nearly all aspects of life.

It is also possible to experience an *avoidance-avoidance* conflict and a *double approach-avoidance* conflict. Avoidance-avoidance conflicts are characterized by having to select from two undesirable options, like unemployment or working for an autocratic boss. A double approach-avoidance conflict is present when a person is confronted with two attractive options, but the selection of either would also bring about something undesirable (Lewin, 1935). All variations of approach and avoidance conflicts frequently result in a state of decision deadlock.

The right decision

Searching for the "right decision" is often frustrating and sometimes stifling. This is because in most cases, *there is no one right decision*. There are only decisions that lead to various outcomes; and the outcomes may include undesirable and unanticipated consequences.

In major life decisions, no matter what is decided, persons often question their decision at some future time. Self-questioning a major decision does not always happen, but it should not be a surprise if it does. For example, a person who spends an entire career in an unsatisfying job, might, upon retirement, question the decision to remain in the job for so many years. Correspondingly, persons that quit a job early in a career might wonder what life would have been like had they decided to stay. The same is true for marriages. Some persons that have stayed in marginally satisfying marriages live with the idea that "I should have left years ago" while many divorced persons wonder if "maybe I should have tried harder to make my marriage work." Interestingly, the degree of self-questioning seems to be negatively correlated with the perceived desirability of the results of the decision; the more desirable the actual outcome, the less degree of self-questioning.

It is normal to wonder about the probable results of the roads not taken. But be careful, such speculation frequently takes on a hue of fantasy - it is often imagined that the road not taken would have been much better than it likely would have been if actually chosen.

Not Perfect - But Ok

The outcome of most decisions will not be "perfect," but is it ok? If it is ok, we can move forward. Sometimes, regardless of effort, *ok* is the best we can achieve. For some things, *not perfect-but ok* may be as good as it gets. Life-by-design involves not getting stalled or stuck by an unreasonable expectation or pursuit of self-defined perfection.

What Should I Do?

When confronting difficult circumstances, many persons ask others "What should I do?" Nearly everyone has people in their life that would be happy to provide an answer. While blindly following the direction of others may be helpful for some persons, especially those with a dependent personality, it is not helpful for many. Most of us cannot simply follow advice that usually comes in the form of "Well, you should..." or "If I were you, I would...." In reality, most of us like to decide for ourselves. We like to decide for ourselves because there is something inherently gratifying in making our own decisions. When confronting a situation that requires a decision, most persons will *decide-to-decide* for themselves.

When uncertain about what to do, it often helps to think backward until something becomes certain. This "certainty" is the point from which you can reliably move forward. For example, if you are uncertain about whether you wish to remain married, think backward to when your doubts first arose. If your marriage has progressed from the *difficult* to the *intolerable*, the one thing of which you can be certain is that something has to change. With this insight, all options for change can be explored.

Mandated Counseling and Fitness-for-duty Evaluations

At times, it becomes necessary to mandate officers into counseling. Mandating officers to counseling is appropriate when significant concerns for their mental health arise. Ordering officers to counseling is different from ordering officers to undergo a psychological fitness-for-duty evaluation (FFDE).

Mandated counseling

Officers may be ordered to counseling for a variety of reasons, including poor performance, poor attitude, stress-related difficulties, and so on. Authorized supervisors should consider ordering a subordinate into counseling only after attempts to encourage voluntary participation have failed. This is because voluntary participation in counseling normally increases the probability of a successful outcome. If an order becomes necessary, a written document must be provided to the officer and the psychologist. In the document:

1. *Avoid referring to mandated counseling as discipline.* Although ordering an officer to meet with a psychologist may be the result of a corrective action which includes discipline, describing a psychological counseling program as a component of discipline characterizes it as punishment. This places the psychologist in an untenable position and makes successful intervention more difficult. If the program is thought of as an element of punishment by the officer being ordered, this mindset becomes the first obstacle to overcome in the psychologist's therapeutic effort. Supervisors can assist the goals of the agency and the psychologist by keeping identified discipline separate from the mandated counseling program.

2. *Identify the reason(s) for the mandated counseling program.* When supervisors order officers to counseling it is usually because they have observed or learned of difficulties which concern them enough to conclude that psychological counseling may be beneficial. Identifying the reasons for mandated counseling is necessary as it helps the psychologist to focus the therapeutic effort. Without this information, psychologists must rely upon officers' perceptions of why they were ordered into counseling. To best serve the agency and the officer, identify the reasons for the mandated counseling.

3. *Specify how you have tried to address the problem.* This information assists the psychologist in assessment and counseling program design. Advise if a performance improvement plan has been initiated. If so, include a copy.

4. *State your order in a manner that facilitates motivation.* For example, "In an effort to assist you to better manage your anger, you are ordered (directed, mandated, required) to contact psychologist Dr. (name) prior to (date) and to participate in a counseling program. The design and duration of the program will be determined by Dr. (name)." *Note*:

Avoid designing intervention programs. Do not specify "You will meet with the police psychologist weekly for a period of six weeks" or something similar. This was once included in a Chief's order. It was the first item impeached by the officer's attorney who successfully argued that police chiefs were not qualified to design psychological counseling programs.

5. *Clearly specify the privilege of confidentiality.* When an officer voluntarily becomes a client of a psychologist, the privilege of confidentiality rests with the officer. However, when an officer is ordered to counseling, the confidentiality privilege rests with the agency. Like individuals, law enforcement agencies have the option of waiving their confidentiality privilege:

(A) If the department is interested in having an officer engage a counseling program and is not interested in receiving any information about it, supervisors may order the person into counseling and specify "As you are being ordered to counseling, the department has the privilege of confidentiality. The department waives this privilege to the extent specified: the counseling program and any communication, oral or in writing, between you and Dr. (name) shall remain confidential as prescribed by law. Dr. (name) will only be required to confirm your compliance with this order and your continued participation in the program." *Note:* To confirm the officer's compliance with the order and continued participation, the ordering supervisor must contact the psychologist. Determining the officer's compliance is the responsibility of supervisors. The psychologist should never be placed in the role of "snitch" by being asked to periodically inform the department of the officer's compliance. This is especially true in cases where the officer does not comply with the order or fails to continue in the program.

(B) In the event that the department wishes to receive information regarding the officer's program and progress, it is best if supervisors include something similar to "As you are being ordered to meet with Dr. (name) you have no privilege of confidentiality. Dr. (name) will be required to report on your program design, your program compliance, and your progress within the program. Dr (name) will also be required to provide to staff any other pertinent data, including but not limited to information relating to assessment, opinion, prognosis, and outcome."

6. *Specify off-duty compensation.* It is not always possible or feasible for the officer and psychologist to meet during the officer's duty hours (assuming the employee remains in some work capacity). When an officer is ordered to counseling, like any mandated activity, most agencies must compensate the officer. The ordering document should clearly state the agency's off-duty compensation policy.

Supervisors must not casually order a person to meet with the psychologist or with a member of the Peer Support Team. Such "orders" are ethically unsustainable, primarily because the privilege of confidentiality is unspecified. For this reason and others, casual orders must be avoided.

If supervisors are concerned about a subordinate and justification for a mandated counseling program is lacking, they are encouraged to contact the psychologist or a member of the PST and relay their concerns. A psychologist or PST *reach out* or other appropriate support intervention will be initiated.

Supervisory suggestions or recommendations to subordinates to contact the psychologist or the PST are acceptable and encouraged. Be careful not to turn supervisory *suggestions* into unofficial casual *orders*.

Psychological fitness for duty evaluation

A psychological fitness for duty evaluation (FFDE) is ordered in cases where the agency has a genuine concern pertaining to officers' ability to appropriately perform their duties due to their current state of mental health. In mandated psychological FFDEs, the privilege of confidentiality is held by the agency. The evaluating psychologist completes the evaluation and reports the findings to the department. Three determinations are possible: (1) the officer is fit for duty, (2) the officer is not fit for duty, or (3) the officer is not fit for full duty but capable of modified duty. If officers are found fit for duty, they return to work. This finding, and that of "fit for modified duty," may include a recommendation for ongoing counseling.

If officers are found unfit for duty, they are placed on leave and a psychological counseling program is normally initiated. Following completion, they are reevaluated. If found fit for duty on reevaluation, they return to work. If reevaluated as unfit for duty, other options must be considered. Other options include additional therapy and subsequent reevaluation, additional therapy with modified duty and reevaluation, and occupational or total disability.

Fitness for duty evaluations can become complex as they may spark numerous legal issues. This is to be expected when an officer's career is on the line. The same is true if officers are found unfit for full duty but capable of working modified duty.

Psychological fitness for duty evaluation and mandated counseling

It is possible for officers to be mandated into counseling *and* ordered to undergo a FFDE. Most times when an officer is ordered to counseling there are no questions regarding fitness for duty. Other times, this is not the case. FFDEs, if needed within mandated counseling:

(A) Must be independent of the mandated counseling program. The FFDE must be completed by a clinician other than the psychologist providing counseling.
(B) Must be appropriately sequenced within the mandatory counseling program. The placement of a FFDE associated with a mandatory counseling program will depend upon actual circumstances and the assessment of the primary counseling clinician.

Police Psychologists and Training

The training role of the police psychologist has been widely accepted in policing. As early as the 1960s, police administrators recognized the value of having psychologists involved in officer training. Traditionally, psychologists have provided training on topics ranging from human relations to critical incident management.

One of the most important psychologist presentations is stress inoculation training (SIT) (Meichenbaum, 1993). SIT, or similar stressor management programs, are ideally presented during the police pre-service skills academy. Such programs are comprised of specialized training in the characteristics, effects, and management of everyday stressors, traumatic stressors, and critical incidents. They are normally the first exposure of new officers to the complexities of unavoidable police stressors.

The Trauma Intervention Program (TIP) (chapter 4) is constructed to incorporate the advantages of pre-service stressor management training. Because stress management programs are designed to provide officers with a psychological buffer (inoculation) against the negative effects of occupational stress, they comprise the first element of the TIP. The remainder of the TIP enhances the original goal of stressor management programs—the continued psychological health of police officers exposed to the stressors of policing.

Other common psychologist-presented programs include: interpersonal communication, police marriage and family dynamics, alcohol use and disorder, suicide and depression, and interacting with persons that are mentally ill.

Psychologists and Lawyers

"The first thing we do, let's kill all the lawyers" (Shakespeare, 1591). Although historically there is no love lost between defense attorneys and police officers, police officers and police psychologists would never seriously agree with this line from Shakespeare's *King Henry the Sixth*. Lawyers serve a vital role in complex modern societies. Without their expertise, many issues would not be resolved and many injustices would go without redress.

There are two interesting circumstances that can arise among officers, their attorneys, and police psychologists: *therapeutic outcome versus claim standing* and *stress inherent in litigation*.

Therapeutic outcome versus claim standing

Therapeutic outcome versus claim standing involves situations wherein a psychologist and an attorney have the same client. Both the psychologist and the attorney are professionally obligated to act in the client's best interest. At times these goals clash, especially if the client is involved in an injury claim for enduring psychological difficulties. The psychologist and the client work to eliminate psychological symptoms. The attorney and the client have a stronger case if psychological symptoms persist. This is because in most injury litigation, the more disabling the symptoms, the greater the monetary reward. This circumstance was once summed up by an officer who reported, "The better my symptoms get, the more money I lose." In situations like this, clients have to set a priority. Most choose good mental health. Regardless, consciously or unconsciously, pending litigation supports the experience and reporting of ongoing psychological difficulties...some undoubtedly due to the stress inherent in litigation.

Stress inherent in litigation

Whatever the reason for attorney involvement, confronting legal issues is stressful. By their very nature, legal issues draw energy, generate anxiety, and almost always complicate psychological intervention. Once any existing legal issues are resolved, psychological conditions generally improve, sometimes remarkably. This is because the stressor of pending litigation is eliminated, resulting in an overall reduction of experienced stress and symptomology related to claim standing.

Similar to psychological symptoms, improvement in reported stress-related physical symptoms such as gastrointestinal problems, headache, and fatigue have been reported upon conclusion of legal matters.

Therapeutic outcome versus claim standing and stress inherent in litigation is not *malingering*. Malingering is the intentional feigning of psychological and/or physical symptoms in an effort to obtain monetary or other rewards.

Alcohol and the Police Officer

The consumption of alcoholic beverages is common throughout the world. In moderation, alcohol seems to represent no significant health or career risk. In higher quantities and long-term consumption, alcohol can lead to relationship difficulties, loss of career, serious disease, and death.

Some police officers experience difficulties with alcohol. Even one night of abusive drinking can lead to behaviors that are *unbecoming a police officer*. Getting drunk, getting into a fight, and getting arrested might not result in an internal investigation and discipline for those in some jobs, but such investigations and discipline are nearly guaranteed for police officers. Why? Police officers are held to a higher standard of conduct, even off duty, than many other workers. This standard is made explicit in the IACP Law Enforcement Code of Ethics (www. theiacp.org) and in the values statement of most police agencies.

Alcohol use disorder and alcohol use spectrum

Some police officers develop an *alcohol use disorder*. If their alcohol use is addressed in a timely manner and the officer has been fortunate enough to have avoided behavior resulting in termination, police officers can salvage their careers. To accomplish this, officers must accept and confront their problematic use of alcohol. If this is done, a plan for change can be developed. Such plans often include peer support and/or professional treatment.

While officers can be terminated for alcohol use and related behavior, seeking treatment for alcohol use disorder is protected under the American with Disabilities Act (ADA) (1990) (42 U.S.C. § 12101). As chemical dependency is viewed as a disability under the ADA, an officer cannot be fired for seeking and receiving treatment for an alcohol use disorder.

Unfortunately for some officers, they do not recognize their problem with alcohol, deny the problem when confronted about it, and fail to engage support interventions when offered. If their drinking is serious enough, it may eventually destroy their career. This can occur over a period of time or as the result of a single alcohol-fueled event - in spite of the best efforts of family members, peers, police administrators, treatment specialists, and mental health professionals to prevent it.

Historically, a distinction was made between *alcohol abuse* and *alcohol dependence.* Alcohol abuse was described as a maladaptive pattern of drinking that caused a multitude of difficulties including (1) failure to meet primary obligations, (2) drinking or intoxicated in situations where it can be hazardous, (3) legal difficulties arising out of intoxication, and (4) social problems arising from drinking.

Alcohol dependence was associated with (1) tolerance - greater amounts needed to achieve the desired effect or lessened effect at same amount, (2) withdrawal - symptoms appear if alcohol is not consumed or is discontinued, (3) lack of control over the amount of alcohol consumed, (4) unsuccessful efforts to drink less, (5) spending a significant amount of time obtaining alcohol or recovering from its effects, (6) missing important events so that alcohol can be consumed, and (7) drinking in spite of the fact that it is creating or exacerbating psychological or physical problems (APA, 2000).

Today, the conceptions of alcohol abuse and dependence have evolved into an *alcohol use spectrum.* The spectrum is characterized as a "problematic pattern of alcohol use leading to clinically significant impairment or distress" and is diagnosed as Alcohol Use Disorder (AUD) (APA, 2022, 553). Alcohol Use Disorder may be mild, moderate, or severe depending upon the number of symptoms present. Each may be further specified as "in early remission" or "in sustained remission." Tolerance and withdrawal remain components of AUD.

What about alcohol addiction? The term *addiction* is not used in the diagnosis of AUD. In fact, it is not used in any of the diagnoses included in the "Substance-Related and Addictive Disorders" section of the DSM-5-TR. This is because of the difficulty in appropriately defining its meaning and use.

Alcohol use and police officers

According to a 2002-2004 study by the U.S. Department of Health and Human Services (USDHHS), there is an average 9 percent prevalence of what is now considered alcohol use disorder among police officers. This is lower than the rate found in at least eight other occupations. The idea that 25 to 30 percent of police officers regularly misuse alcohol, first presented during the 1980s, is a modern-day myth according to psychologist Audrey Honig, former director of the Employee Support Services Bureau at the Los Angeles County Sheriff's Department (2007). Since the 2002-2004 USDHHS study, further research into the use of alcohol by police officers has produced various and sometimes conflicting results.

As might be expected, the actual police officer alcohol use disorder prevalence rate is difficult to determine and likely to vary widely across various police agencies and jurisdictions.

Settings for alcohol and substance use treatment

There are three primary settings for alcohol and substance use treatment: non-residential treatment, residential treatment, and partial residential treatment.

(1) Non-residential treatments include individual and support group programs such as Alcoholics Anonymous that take place outside of a residential facility.

(2) Residential alcohol treatment programs involve living within a facility. They provide twenty-four-hour care and can be short-term or long-term. Many of the short-term interventions were previously called twenty-eight-day programs; however, most are now shorter in duration. Long-term residential programs serve those who wish to be treated residentially and those with a history of multiple non-residential treatment relapses. They normally range from four to twelve months and may include individual and group therapy, health education, life management, holistic approaches, and family counseling.

(3) Partial residential programs allow persons to remain in a treatment facility for six to eight hours during the day and return home at night. In partial residential programs, treatment and structure is provided for those persons who are less likely to succeed in non-residential programs, but do not require a residential setting.

Some alcohol treatment programs include the use of medications. Medications can be used to discourage alcohol consumption (disulfiram), treat or reduce withdrawal symptoms (chlordiazepoxide), and reduce the craving for alcohol (naltrexone). Other medications that have demonstrated some efficacy in treating problematic alcohol use include gabapentin, varenicline, and topiramate.

Even with the best treatment, quitting alcohol appears difficult. The National Institute on Alcohol Abuse and Alcoholism reported that approximately 90 percent of persons trying to quit drinking alcohol relapse at least once within four years of initiating treatment (1989). Relapse appears most common when persons are under stress or in environments previously associated with drinking (Carmona, 2022).

Interestingly, relapse rates of those addicted to alcohol are similar to those addicted to nicotine and heroin. This suggests some common underlying bio-psycho-social mechanisms.

Medication and Psychoactive Medication for Police Officers

Millions of persons take medication daily. Some take medication for chronic conditions, while others utilize medication to treat transitory illnesses or injury. Modern medications are the result of years of pharmacological research. They improve the quality of life for countless individuals. It should come as no surprise that some of these individuals are police officers.

Most police agencies have policies that regulate the use of medications. The *Model Policy on Standards of Conduct* published by the International Association of Chiefs of Police specifies officer responsibility in this area, "No officer shall report to work or be on duty as a law enforcement officer when his or her judgment or physical condition has been impaired by alcohol, medication, or other substances" and "Officers must report the use of any substance, prior to reporting for duty, that impairs their ability to perform as a law enforcement officer" (n.d. para.,3).

Medical condition and medication

If the medical condition requiring medication does not prevent the officer from working, the medications used to treat the condition sometimes can. The use of drugs such as muscle relaxants, sedatives, drugs with sedating side effects, and certain analgesics may require a period of medical leave. This is because these medications can impair an officer's ability to safely function. Medical leave based upon the use of medication usually remains in place until the condition is treated and the medication is discontinued, the medications are determined to no longer cause impairment, or the medications are adjusted so as to avoid impairment.

The use of other medications, such as blood thinners may not in themselves require medical leave. However, because of the dangers associated with the effects of anticoagulants, a modified duty assignment may become necessary. Modified duty assignments for officers taking high dosages of anticoagulants usually involve working on administrative tasks within police headquarters. By working inside and not in the field, the probability that an officer will be injured and bleed uncontrollably is reduced. Once the medication is discontinued or the effects of the medication no longer pose a risk, the officer can safely return to full duty.

In cases of medication-related leave, before return to full duty, agencies normally require that the medication-prescriber provide a document clearing the officer for full duty.

Psychoactive medication

An issue that sometimes arises for police officers is the use of psychoactive medications. Psychoactive medications are used primarily to treat psychological conditions. Depression, anxiety, and posttraumatic stress disorder are the most likely psychological conditions to affect working police officers, and the most likely to be treated with psychoactive medications.

When experiencing clinical levels of depression, anxiety, or PTSD some officers have no difficulty taking psychoactive medications. They are quite open about it. Other officers will take such medications, but only in secret. These officers often fear that they will be seen as weak, unreliable, emotionally unstable, or unable to do the job if their medication treatment becomes known. Still, other officers simply refuse to take psychoactive medications for a variety of personal or social reasons (chapter 9, *Psychopharmacology*).

Psychoactive medication and police officers: The facts

Working police officers have utilized psychoactive medications for many years without detriment. Like persons in every other occupation, they have benefitted from appropriate pharmacological treatment of depression, anxiety, and PTSD. This benefit is passed on to the department and the community through the officer's improved quality of service.

From a police administrator's and citizen point of view, think of this: who would you rather have responding to calls - a depressed, anxious, or PTSD police officer, or a police officer that is being successfully treated for these conditions? The choice seems clear. For officers, keep in mind that psychoactive medications have been used for many years and have been proven safe for working police officers.

Within the police culture, significant progress has been made in eliminating the stigma associated with psychoactive medications. While officers should not abandon questioning any healthcare provider that suggests a course of such medications, neither should they dismiss the idea solely out of self-generated conceptions of weakness, concerns about agency reprisal, or fear of peer ridicule.

Psychoactive medication bias

Want to check your bias regarding psychoactive medications? Consider this. Would you feel differently about your surgeons if you discovered just prior to undergoing surgery that they were being successfully treated with an antidepressant? Would it surprise you to know that many surgeons, physicians, nurses, and other health care workers regularly take such medications?

What about the pilot of your soon to depart plane? Would you feel differently if you knew that your pilot was being successfully treated with a medication for depression, anxiety, or PTSD?

Federal Aviation Administration

On April 5, 2010, the Federal Aviation Administration (FAA) reversed a long-standing ban on allowing commercial pilots to fly while taking psychoactive medication (Staton, 2010). Commercial pilots may now retain their flying status while taking specified *selective serotonin reuptake inhibitors* (SSRI) prescribed to treat major depressive disorder (mild to moderate) either single episode or recurrent episode, dysthymic disorder (now called *persistent depressive disorder*), adjustment disorder with depressed mood, and any non-depression related condition for which the SSRI is used (FAA, 2018). On a case-by-case application process, commercial pilots can fly if they are using and have been treated with a SSRI "for a minimum of 6 continuous months prior, the applicant has been clinically stable as well as on a stable dose of medication without any aeromedically significant side effects and/or an increase in symptoms" (ibid, 1). This change in FAA policy marks a major cultural shift in commercial aviation.

As of 2022, the FAA has approved the following SSRIs for use by commercial pilots: fluoxetine (Prozac), escitalopram (Lexapro), sertraline (Zoloft), and citalopram (Celexa). As new medications are developed and proven safe, this list will likely expand.

Psychoactive medication and psychological condition

The real issue is not that any person is taking psychoactive medication. The real issue is the status of the psychological condition for which the medication is being prescribed. A surgeon is a better surgeon when an underlying depression or anxiety condition is being successfully treated. An airline pilot whose depression is being successfully treated is a safer pilot than when the condition is untreated. The same is true for police officers. As retired police officer and psychologist Joel Fay stated, "As a retired cop I would much rather work with an officer on an antidepressant than an officer who should be on one, because a cop on an antidepressant is in control of his/her moods" (n.d., 1).

Minority and Women Police Officers

Being a good police officer has nothing to do with race or gender. Persons of minority and women have distinguished themselves as police officers for many years.

The history of minority police officers in America spans several decades. For the most part, it parallels the issues first brought to light during the civil rights movement of the 1960s and 1970s. Although a comprehensive discussion of minorities in American policing is well beyond the scope of this book, it is fair to say that minority police officers have confronted significant past obstacles - many of which still exist. It is also fair to say that they have contributed a great deal to the policing profession.

Like minorities, women of all ethnic backgrounds have made significant contributions to policing. However, best estimates reveal that women comprise just over 18 percent of the police officers in America (Zippia, 2022). This is an improvement over past estimates of 11 to 14 percent (Horne, 2006; Crooke, 2013). While women are making some headway into policing, their numbers remain strikingly low. Especially when you consider that women make up about 50.3 percent of the U.S. population (U.S. Census Bureau, 2012; Statistics Times, 2020). The *Status of Women in Policing: 2000* survey reported that "the gains for women in policing are so slow that, at the current rate of growth (the number of women in policing) ...will not reach equal representation or gender balance within the police profession for at least another 70 years, and many experts caution that time alone is not sufficient to substantially increase women's numbers" (Harrington, 2001, 4). Clearly, women remain underrepresented in policing.

Despite their recent limited gains and accomplishments, female officers continue to confront bias and harassment from some male officers. A 1998 study conducted by the International Association of Chiefs of Police concluded that sexual harassment of female officers still exists within the profession. Some instances of male officer behavior toward female officers have been so serious as to result in criminal charges, including sexual assault (Dwyer, 2021). Such behavior towards female coworkers cannot be tolerated. Officers that engage in harassing and assaultive behavior must be held accountable. They must be removed from the ranks of the nation's finest and criminally prosecuted when warranted.

In spite of these unfortunate circumstances, no one would seriously challenge the capabilities of women in policing based on gender. In modern police agencies women serve honorably at all ranks, from line officers to chiefs, sheriffs, and commissioners.

Lesbian, Gay, Bisexual, Transgender, Queer+ (LGBTQ+) Police Officers

There are thousands of police officers in the world. Some of them are LGBTQ+. Although countless LGBTQ+ officers have served admirably while keeping their personal lives private, many have now come out of the policing closet. These officers have been successful in their careers and report being tired of feeling that they have to keep a secret.

Once a taboo, being LGBTQ+ and a police officer has gained public acceptance in most quarters. There are organizations throughout the world supporting LBGTQ+ police officers and several police agencies actively recruit LGBTQ+ candidates.

It is difficult to estimate the percentage of LBGTQ+ police officers in the world. In America, anecdotal guesses range from 2 to 4 percent. This is in contrast to the estimated percentage of LGBTQ+ persons in the general population, thought to be somewhere between 1.2 percent to 10 percent. A recent Gallup poll placed the percentage of LBGTQ+ persons in the general population at 7.1, with more than half identifying as bisexual. About one in ten persons polled reported being married to a same-sex partner (Jones, 2022).

It is difficult to obtain accurate population statistics involving persons that identify as LGBTQ+ because many wish to maintain their privacy. For police officers, some remain private because they fear the reactions of their community and peers while others feel that their personal life is no one's business.

LGBTQ+ police organizations

Several organizations in major metropolitan areas have been developed to support LGBTQ+ police officers. One is the Gay Officers Action League (G.O.A.L.) established 1982 in New York City. G.O.A.L. was founded by Charles Henry "Charlie" Cochrane, Jr. (1943-2008) a sergeant with the New York City Police Department. He was the first openly gay NYPD police officer (goalny.org, 2022).

The G.O.A.L. New England chapter was started by Officer Preston Horton of Northampton, Massachusetts in 1991. In particular, G.O.A.L. and G.O.A.L. New England have supported their members struggling with LGBTQ+ issues, including coming out at work - "The difficulty varies from department to department. For example, in larger cities, it is, in my opinion much easier. The cities and their respective departments offer greater diversity within the department as well as within the communities they serve. However, even in smaller or more rural areas one must remember that this is New England and a distinctive part of the U.S. in that it is generally more accepted. Even from a political standpoint, both parties have been more or less more supportive over the years" said police officer and president of G.O.A.L. New England, Anthony Imperioso. He added, "Transgender issues need much work in terms of understanding and acceptance within society, even within the GLBTQ community itself and obviously law enforcement" (Walleser, 2022,1). Since its inception, G.O.A.L. chapters have arisen across the country and around the world.

Coming out and work environment

An openly gay officer of the Boston Police Department (BPD) reported that he believed it was easier for lesbian officers to come out than gay men. He attributed this to the idea that heterosexual male officers are more likely to have problems with homosexual male officers sharing department gymnasiums, locker rooms, and showers (personal communication, March 15, 2010). A lesbian Colorado police officer offered this explanation of the lesbian *coming out* phenomenon: "A lesbian officer is seen more manly, more like a traditional cop. A gay guy might be seen as effeminate, less like a traditional cop. So he'll keep it secret."

Relationship with coworkers

The BPD officer previously mentioned also stated that in his years as an "out" gay police officer, he had never been threatened or harassed by any of his coworkers (2010). More recently, a high-ranking openly gay Boston police officer reported having a similar experience. Throughout his more than twenty years of service, he had never been harassed, threatened, or felt discriminated against due to his sexual orientation. He recalled only one incident that occurred early in his career when a straight male coworker made an inappropriate remark. As to BPD in general, he reported that he was not aware of a single complaint filed by any person identifying as LBGTQ+ involving threats or harassment from coworkers due to their LGBTQ+ identification. And what of the coworker that made the inappropriate remark? Both have long-since moved past this occurrence and remain good friends (personal communication, July 20 & 22, 2022).

Boston Police Department

The Boston Police Department made history in 2015. That year, the BPD Police Academy graduated the first known openly gay couple. Boston police officers Jimmy Moccia and Shawn MacIver may be the first openly gay couple to ever to graduate from a major city police academy. Moccia commented to local news, "I think it's important to note that throughout the entire academy experience we were never afraid to be ourselves"..."I wanted people to get to know us. We didn't want to be known as 'the gay cops.' We're cops who just happen to be gay. There's so many other things we are. Yeah, gay's on the list, but it doesn't define us."..."And over the course of our training, we were welcomed by everyone" (Gelzinis, 2015,1).

LGBTQ+ and policing

Experience has shown that many persons identifying as LGBTQ+ are excellent police officers. Like race and gender, identifying as LGBTQ+ has nothing to do with being a good cop.

Minority status, gender, and personal LGBTQ+ identification

Although the minority status, gender, and personal LGBTQ+ identification of police officers may have social and cultural meaning to various persons, communities, or particular groups, *all* good police officers share similar characteristics.

Good police officers are characterized by honesty, integrity, compassion, community-mindedness, and professionalism. Good police officers serve and protect in accordance with the highest traditions of policing.

> "When all Americans are treated as equal, no matter who they are or whom they love, we are all more free"... Barack Obama

Appendix A

Peer Support Team Code of Ethical Conduct

As a member of an agency peer support team, I am committed to the highest standards of peer support. I knowingly accept the responsibility associated with being a member of a peer support team.

<u>Peer support team persons</u>:

- engage in peer support within the parameters of their peer support training.
- specify when they are functioning in their peer support role, and if uncertain whether an interaction is peer support, they inquire to clarify.
- keep themselves current in all matters of peer support confidentially.
- disclose peer support information only with appropriate consent, except in cases where allowed or mandated by law.
- clearly specify the limits of peer support confidentiality prior to engaging in peer support.
- make a reasonable effort to attend scheduled team meetings and programs of in-service training.
- make referrals to other peer support team members, their clinical supervisor, and others when appropriate.
- are careful providing peer support for persons with whom they have a troubled history. If the history cannot be overcome, they provide appropriate referral.
- comply with peer support team statutes, policies, and operational guidelines.
- do not utilize their peer support role for personal gain or advantage.
- do not engage in inappropriate behaviors with those for whom they are providing peer support.

- contact their clinical supervisor immediately with any perceived ethical issue or possible conflict of interest arising out of peer support.
- seek immediate clinical supervision and consultation in any circumstance that reasonably exceeds the assessment and parameters of peer support.
- reach out to others they know or suspect may benefit from peer support.
- make reasonable effort to respond to individual requests for peer support and to respond to critical incidents as needed.
- seek support from other peer support team members, their clinical supervisor, or other support personnel when stressed or otherwise in need of support.
- are committed to helping other peer support persons to become better skilled. They do this by readily sharing their knowledge and experience when it does not conflict with the standards of peer support confidentiality.
- endeavor to maintain a positive relationship with their clinical supervisor and other peer support team members, and make an effort to resolve any issues of conflict that may arise in these relationships.
- understand that they are perceived as role models and that their actions reflect upon the entire team.

(Digliani, J.A., 5/2015)

Appendix B

The Imperatives

1. **The Communication Imperative:** Persons will respond to the message they received and not necessarily the message that you intended to send.

2. **The Occupational Imperative:** Do not forget *why* you do *what* you do.

3. **The Relationship Imperative:** Make it safe!

The Reclamations

1. **Reclaim your Career.**

2. **Reclaim your Marriage.**

3. **Reclaim your Life.**

Appendix C

History of the FCPD/FCPS Peer Support Team and Office of Human Services - Personal Journey*

In 1986, the Fort Collins Police Department (FCPD), renamed *Fort Collins Police Services* (FCPS) later the same year, created its first ever peer support team. This small group was to be called the Traumatic Incident Team (TIT). While I liked the name, I was concerned about its acronym. As this team would be responsible for facilitating debriefings as well as providing peer support, the word "debriefing" was added.

The Traumatic Incident Debriefing Team (TIDT) was to be comprised of four police officers. As one of the four police officers that would comprise the team and author of much of the policy that created it, I was selected to serve as the TIDT coordinator. At that time no one could anticipate how the Traumatic Incident Debriefing Team would develop or how integral a part of FCPS it would become.

Work to develop a peer support team within the FCPS had started several years prior to 1986. FCPS staff was generally supportive of the idea of a peer support team; however, they remained concerned about several issues. One of the concerns was summarized by an FCPS division director who stated, "If we have a team like this, officers won't take their problems to their supervisors." I remember my response: "They don't take their problems to their supervisors now. We can give them someplace to go." Thoughts about this response later evolved into the TIDT motto. I still use it to describe the primary mission of peer support teams. Although it is bad grammar, it captures the essence of those committed to the concept of peer support, *"A police officer should never not have a place to go."*

Another staff concern involved team member confidentiality. In 1986, the state of Colorado did not include peer support teams in the law that prohibits testifying without consent. This meant that there were no statutory protections for the information exchanged in peer support interactions.

In an effort to provide some protection for peer support team interactions, the proposed FCPS policy included this statement, "Issues discussed during any peer support interaction involving a member of the Traumatic Incident Debriefing Team shall be considered confidential and not subject to questioning during an administrative/criminal investigation." If approved, this statement would provide some protection for TIDT members from internal investigators, but would it protect team members in the courts or from investigators who were not subject to FCPS policy? No one knew for certain. Despite this question, and with a willingness to explore new territory, then chief of police Bruce Glasscock on June 1, 1986, approved and signed into effect FCPS directive No. 58, *Traumatic Incident Policy*. This policy not only officially created the Traumatic Incident Debriefing Team, but also provided for team member confidentiality.

In 1986 the idea of peer support was relatively new to the field of policing. The FCPS endorsement of such a sweeping peer support team confidentiality standard was generally unheard of. Directive No. 58 demonstrated the significant commitment of FCPS staff to the principles of peer support.

Incidentally, the division director which I spoke of earlier, after observing the actions and results of the TIDT for a period of time, became one of its most ardent supporters. (Note: in 1986, an officer at the rank above lieutenant was designated *division director*. This FCPS rank has undergone several title changes since then, including, *deputy chief, commander,* and *captain*. Today (2022) at FCPS, an officer of this rank is designated *assistant chief*.)

In 1989, the Traumatic Incident Debriefing Team was renamed the *Critical Incident Team* (CIT). This name change was implemented because it seemed to be more descriptive of the team's mission and activities.

As CIT coordinator, I remained concerned about the provisions for peer support team confidentiality and relied primarily upon directive No. 58; however, several years had passed and there were no difficulties involving confidentiality. The CIT had doubled in size. Through its work, it had established credibility and had demonstrated its value. Personally, I was doing more individual counseling through CIT than ever before. The demand on my time for counseling became so great that late in 1989, I was granted one day out of each four-day patrol work cycle for peer support counseling with other police employees.

In mid-1989, with my graduate studies nearly complete, I intended to separate from FCPS. I was planning to depart at the end of the year. My plan was to establish a private practice limited to working with officers and their families. Although I had not submitted any formal communication to FCPS administration, my plans became known. I am not certain how this occurred, most likely via the grapevine. I was approached by staff with a proposal. It was proposed that I continue my career with FCPS. If I agreed, I would remain a police officer, reclassified as a technician, and be assigned to a full-time counseling position. I would also be permitted to design and develop the position within appropriate legal, ethical, and agency parameters. To this day, I remain grateful to have been provided such an opportunity. But I had already rented an office and planned on launching a private practice. After some consideration, I accepted the FCPS offer upon the condition that after one year the position be evaluated. If either FCPS or I were dissatisfied, I would depart and initiate my original plan.

So, with this agreement in place, I worked my 1989 New Year's Eve swing shift patrol assignment. The next day, January 1, 1990, I became the first Director of the newly created FCPS Office of Human Services (OHS).

The naming of the Office of Human Services and "Director" was a compromise. Administration personnel suggested "Coordinator" and "Office of Human Services." I preferred "Director" and "Office of Psychological Services." In the end, I won one and lost one.

My first challenge as Director of the Office of Human Services was to define the duties of the Office. While I was permitted a great deal of discretion, I always understood that my primary responsibility was providing counseling and support services for FCPS employees and their families.

As the OHS was earning its way into the FCPS organizational structure, I became licensed as a professional counselor. Shortly thereafter, I was licensed as a psychologist. As Director of OHS and the department psychologist, I clinically supervised the Critical Incident Team.

I remained the FCPS Director of OHS and CIT clinical supervisor until I entered private practice in August 2001. Following my departure, the FCPS Critical Incident Team was renamed Peer Support Team (PST).

The PST continues to provide support to FCPS employees and their families, as does the FCPS OHS.

* To preserve an obscure piece of Fort Collins Police Services history.

About the Author

Jack A. Digliani, PhD, EdD is a licensed psychologist and a former deputy sheriff, police officer, and detective. He served as a law enforcement officer for the Laramie County, Wyoming Sheriff's Office, the Cheyenne, Wyoming Police Department, and the Fort Collins, Colorado Police Services (FCPS). He was the FCPS Director of Human Services and police psychologist for the last 11 years of his FCPS police career. While in this position he provided psychological services to employees and their families, and clinically supervised the FCPS Peer Support Team. He has received several commendations from the FCPS and various other law enforcement agencies for his work in police psychology.

Dr. Digliani also served as the police psychologist for the Loveland Police Department and Larimer County Sheriff's Office (Colorado). During his service he provided psychological counseling services to department members and their families. He was also the clinical supervisor of the agencies' Peer Support Teams. He has worked with numerous municipal, county, state, and federal law enforcement agencies. He specializes in police and trauma psychology, group interventions, and the development of police peer support teams.

Dr. Digliani is the author of *Reflections of a Police Psychologist, Contemporary Issues in Police Psychology, Law Enforcement Peer Support Team Manual, Law Enforcement Critical Incident Handbook, Law Enforcement Marriage and Relationship Guidebook*, and several other publications. He is a contributor-writer of Colorado Revised Statute (CRS) 13-90-107(m) *Who may not testify without consent*, the statute and paragraph which grants law enforcement and public service peer support team members specified confidentiality protection during peer support interactions. He is also the principal author of the peer support section of the *Critical Incident Protocol* of the Eighth Judicial District of Colorado. Portions of his Trauma Intervention Program have been incorporated into CRS 16-2.5-403, *Peace officer-involved shooting or fatal use of force policy* (2019).

In 1990, he created the *Psychologist And Training/Recruit Officer Liaison* (PATROL) program, a program designed to support police officer recruits and their families during academy and field training.

Dr. Digliani developed the Freezeframe method of critical incident debriefing. He also created the "2-and-2", Option Funnel versus Threat Funnel, Level I and Level II peer support, Life-by-Default/ Life-by-Design, Proactive Annual Check-in, and the Comprehensive Model for Police Advanced Strategic Support (COMPASS). COMPASS is a career-and-beyond psychological health and wellness strategy for police officers.

In 2013, Dr. Digliani developed the conceptions of primary and secondary danger. He then created the "Make it Safe" Police Officer Initiative, a 12-element strategy designed to reduce the secondary danger of policing and thereby reduce the number of police officer suicides.

In 2015, Dr. Digliani crafted the *Peer Support Team Code of Ethical Conduct*. He developed the *Peer Support Team Utilization and Outcome Survey* in 2017, a survey specifically designed to assess the use and efficacy of agency peer support. The survey was utilized in peer support team research projects conducted in 2018 and 2022.

Dr. Digliani is a guest lecturer in forensic and police psychology at Colorado State University.

References

Aamodt, M.G., & Werlick, N. (2001). Police officer suicide: frequency and officer profiles. In Shehan, D. (Ed.) *Law Enforcement and Suicide*. Quantico, VA: Federal Bureau of Investigation.

American Heart Association.(2022).https://www.heart.org/en/healthy-living/healthy-eating/eat-smart/sodium/how-much-sodium-should-i-eat-per-day

American Psychiatric Association. (1952). *Diagnostic and statistical manual of mental disorders*. Washington, DC: Author.

American Psychiatric Association. (1968). *Diagnostic and statistical manual of mental disorders* (2nd ed.). Washington, DC: Author.

American Psychiatric Association. (1980). *Diagnostic and statistical manual of mental disorders* (3rd ed.). Washington, DC: Author.

American Psychiatric Association. (1987). *Diagnostic and statistical manual of mental disorders* (3rd ed., revised). Washington, DC: Author.

American Psychiatric Association. (1994). *Diagnostic and statistical manual of mental disorders* (4th ed.). Washington, DC: Author.

American Psychiatric Association. (2000). *Diagnostic and statistical manual of mental disorders* (4th ed., text revision). Washington, DC: Author.

American Psychiatric Association. (2013). *Diagnostic and statistical manual of mental disorders* (5th ed.). Washington, DC: Author.

American Psychiatric Association. (2022). *Diagnostic and statistical manual of mental disorders* (5th ed., text revision). Washington, DC: Author.

American Psychological Association. (n.d., para.,3). *Psychologists in public service.* http://search.apa.org/search?query=sections.

American Psychological Association. (2013b). *Posttraumatic stress disorder.*https://www.psychiatry.org/File%20Library/Psychiatrists/Practice/DSM/APA_DSM-5-PTSD.pdf.

American Psychological Association. (February 14, 2022). *What's the difference between stress and anxiety.* Retrieved from https://www.apa.org/topics/stress/anxiety-difference.

Anton, E., Marti, J., Kwatra, M. M., Bohner, H., Schneider, F., Inouye, S. K. (2006). Delirium in older persons. *New England Journal of Medicine,* 354: 2509-2511.

Associated Press. (2015). https://nypost.com/2015/01/06/man-shot-dead-by-cops-left-suicide-note-telling-officers-i-used-you/.

Burch, K. (2021). *How many days a person can survive without food and water.* https://www.insider.com/guides/health/diet-nutrition/how-long-can-you-go-without-food.

Artwohl, A. & Christensen, L. W. (1997). *Deadly force encounters: what cops need to know to mentally and physically prepare for and survive a gunfight.* Boulder: Paladin Press.

Avram, M. M. (December 2004). Cellulite: a review of its physiology and treatment. *Journal of Cosmetic Laser Therapy, 6* (4), 181-185.

Beck, A.T., Rush, A.J., Shaw, B.F., Emery, G. (1979). *Cognitive Therapy of Depression.* The Guilford Press.

Calories in Protein, Fat and Carbohydrates. (n.d., para.,1). http://www. caloriesperhour.com/tutorialgram.php.

Cannon, W. B. (1915). *Bodily changes in pain, hunger, fear and rage: an account of recent researches into the function of emotional excitement.* New York: Appleton.

Cannon, W. B. (1932). *The wisdom of the body.* New York: W. W. Norton. Carr, K. F. (2003). *Critical incident stress debriefings for cross-cultural workers: harmful or helpful?* Retrieved from http://www.mmct.org/critical incident stress.php.

Carmona, M. (2022). *Alcohol abuse, alcohol relapse statistics.* https:// www. therecoveryvillage.com/alcohol-abuse/alcohol-relapse-statistics/.

Centers for disease control and prevention. (2009). *Body mass index.* http://www.cdc.gov/healthyweight/assessing/bmi/adult bmi/index. html.

Centers for disease control and prevention. (2022). https:// www. cdc.gov/suicide/facts/.

Cordingley, G. (2005). *Walter Freeman's lobotomies at Athens State Hospital.* http://www.cordingleyneurology.com/lobotomies.html.

Cosmopoulos, M. B. (ed.). (2007). *Experiencing war: trauma and society from ancient Greece to the Iraq war.* Chicago: Ares Publishers.

Crooke, C. (2013). *Women in law enforcement.* https://cops.usdoj. gov/ html/dispatch/07-2013/women_in_law enforcement. asp.

Da Costa, J. M. (January 1871). On irritable heart; a clinical study of a form of functional cardiac disorder and its consequences. *The American Journal of the Medical Sciences* (61), 18-52.

Digliani, J. A. (2015). *Contemporary issues in police psychology.* Bloomington:Xlibris.

Digliani, J. A. (1992). *Guidelines for conducting a police critical incident debriefing.* Unpublished manuscript.

Digliani, J. A. (2013). *"Make it Safe" Police Officer Initiative.* Unpublished manuscript. Later published in *Contemporary issues in police psychology (2015).* Bloomington:Xlibris.

Digliani, J. A. (1986-2023). *Police peer support team training program.* Unpublished manuscript. Later published in *Contemporary issues in police psychology* (2015). Bloomington: Xlibris.

Dobbins, R. (2008). *Do what is right even when no one is looking.* http:// www.af.mil/news/story.asp?id=123081361.

Dwyer, T.P. (2021). *Police Liability and Litigation.* https://www. police1.com/ columnists/terry-dwyer/Dwyer, T.P.

Ellis, A. (2004). *Rational Emotive Behavior Therapy: It Works for Me--It Can Work for You.* Amherst, NY: Prometheus Books.

Environ International Corporation. (2002). *What America drinks.* National Health and Nutrition Examination Survey.

Fay, J. (n.d.). *A few thoughts about the use of medications for law enforcement officers.* Joelfay.com/medication-and-law-enforcement. html.

Freud, S. (1920). *Beyond the pleasure principle.* In J. Strachey (Ed.& Trans.), Standard edition of the complete psychological works of Sigmund Freud (Vol.18, p. 27). London: Hogarth Press.

Freudenberger, H. J. (1974). Staff burnout. *Journal of Social Issues, 30*(1), 159-165.

Freudenberger, H. J. & Richelson, G. (1980). *Burn out: the high cost of high achievement.* New York: Bantam Books.

Frothingham, M. B. (2021). *Fight, flight, freeze, or fawn: what this response means.* https://www.simplypsychology.org.

Geldmacher, D. S. (2003). *Contemporary diagnosis and management of Alzheimer's dementia.* (2nd ed). Charlottesville: Handbooks in Healthcare.

Gelzinis, P. (2015). *Gay BPD cadets step out of the shadows.* https:// www. bostonherald.com/2015/06/16/gelzinis-gay-bpd-cadets-step-out-of-shadows/.

Goodwin, J. (1987). The etiology of combat-related post-traumatic stress disorders. In T. Williams (Ed.), *Post-traumatic stress disorders: a handbook for clinicians.* (pp. 1-18). Cincinnati: Disabled American Veterans.

Gorman, S. & Gorman, J. M. (2022). *We still don't know how antidepressants work.* https://www.psychologytoday.com.

Gottman, J., & Silver, N. (1999). *The Seven Principles for Making Marriage Work.* Three Rivers, Random House.

Grant, J.E. (2018) *Current Psychiatry*, February, p.34.

Griffin, S. E. (2006). Fats & Cholesterol: out with the bad, in with the good. *Harvard School of Public Health Newsletter,* Oct 31.

Halliday, D., Resnick, R., & Krane, K. S. (2001). *Physics.* New York: John Wiley & Sons.

Harrington, P., et al (2001). *Equality denied: The status of women in policing:2000.* http://www.womenandpolicing.org/PDF/2000%20 Status%20 Report.pdf.

Hersh, K. & Borum, R. (1998). Command hallucinations, compliance, and risk assessment. *Journal of the American Academy of Psychiatry and the Law,* (26), 353-359.

Honig, A. L. (September/October 2007). Facts refute long-standing myths about law enforcement officers. *National Psychologist,* 16(5).

Honig, A.L., & Sultan, S.E. (December 2004). Under fire—reactions and resilience: what an officer can expect. *The police chief.* International association of chiefs of police.

Horne, P. (September 2006). Policewomen: their first century and the new era. *The police chief.* International association of chiefs of police, 73, 9.

International Classification of Diseases (2018). *Complex posttraumatic stress disorder.* World Health Organization.

International Association of Chiefs of Police (2010). *Model policy on standards of conduct.* Retrieved from http://www.theiacp.org.

Jones, J. M. (2022). *What percentage of Americans are LGBT?* https://news. gallup.com/poll/332522/percentage-americans-lgbt. aspx.

Johnson, A. (December, 2015). *Beverages can add hundreds of extra calories a day.* https://www.premierhealth.com.

Keller, M. B., McCullough, J. P., Klein, D. N., Arnoe, B., Dunner, D. L., Gelenberg, A. J., Markowitz, J. C., Nemeroff, C. B., Russell, J. M., Thase, M. E., Trivedi, M. H., Zajecka, J. (18 May 2000). A comparison of nefazodone, the cognitive behavioral-analysis system of psychotherapy, and their combination for the treatment of chronic depression. *New England Journal of Medicine, 342,* 1462-1470.

Kirsch, I. (2009). *The emperor's new drugs: Exploding the antidepressant myth.* London: The Bodley Head.

L.A. Times (2007, January 14). *Woman dies after being in water-drinking contest.* https://www.latimes.com/archives/la-xpm-2007-jan-14-me- water 14-story.html.

Lebow, J. (2005). *Handbook of clinical family therapy.* Hoboken, NJ: John Wiley and Sons.

Lefkowitz, M. R. & Fant, M. B. (n.d., para., 1). *Women's life in Greece and Rome*. http://www.stoa.org/diotima/anthology/wlgr/ wlgr-romanlegal120. shtml.

Lewin, K. (1935) *A dynamic theory of personality: Selected papers*. New York: McGraw-Hill.

Lieberman, S. & Bruning, N. (1990). *The real vitamin & mineral book*. New York:Avery Group.

Lindemann, L. (2021). *What's the average survey response rate?* https: //pointerpro.com/blog/average-survey-response-rate/#how-to-calculate-response-rate.

Maffetone, P. (2000). *The Maffetone method*. Camden, ME: Ragged Mountain Press.

Malcom, A. (1972). *The pursuit of intoxication*. New York: Washington Square Press.

McCoy, S. & Aamodt, M. (2009). *Police officers divorce rates not as high as many think*. http://www.runet.edu/NewsPub/ December09/1217 divorce. html.

McNiel, D. E., Eisner, J. P., & Binder, R. L. (October 2000). The relationship between command hallucination and violence. *Psychiatric Services*,51:1288-1292.

Meichenbaum, D. (1993). Stress inoculation training: A twenty year update. In R. L. Woolfolk and P. M. Lehrer (Eds.), *Principles and practices of stress management*. New York: Guilford Press.

Mitchell, J. T. (2004). *Crisis Intervention and Critical Incident Stress Management: A defense of the field*. http://www.icisf.org/ articles/ Acrobat Documents/CISM Defense of Field.pdf.

Mitchell, J.T. (1983). When disaster strikes . . . the critical incident stress debriefing process. *Journal of Emergency Medical Services,* 8(1): 36-39.

Mitchell, J. T. & Everly, G. S. (1995). *Critical incident stress debriefing: An operations manual for the prevention of trauma among emergency service and disaster workers.* (2nd ed.). Baltimore: Chevron.

Moberg, J. L. & Aamodt, M. G. (2007). *The use and effectiveness of the insanity plea by serial killers.* http://maamodt.asp.radford.edu/ Research Forensic/SPCP 2007Moberg&Aamodt-NGRI.pdf.

Mohandie, K., Meloy, J. R., & Collins, P. I. (2009). Suicide by cop among officer-involved shooting cases. *Journal of Forensic Sciences,*54 (2):456-462.

Moncrieff, J., Cooper, R. E., Stockmann, T., Amendola, S., Hengartner, M. P., and Horowitz, M. A. (2022). *The serotonin theory of depression: a systematic umbrella review of the evidence.* https:// www.nature.com.

National Academies of Science, Engineering, and Medicine (2004). *Dietary reference intakes for water, potassium, sodium, chloride, and sulfate.* https://www.nationalacademies.org.

National Center for PTSD (2022). *Types of debriefing following disasters.* http://www.ptsd.va.gov/professional/pages/debriefing-after-disasters.asp

National Center for PTSD (2022). *How common is PTSD in veterans?* https://www.ptsd.va.gov/understand/common_veterans.asp.

National Institute of Mental Health. (2021). *Suicide prevention.* https://www.nimh.nih.gov/health/topics/suicide.

National Institute of Mental Health. (2010). *What medications are used to treat depression?* http://www.nimh.nih.gov/health/ publications/

mental-health-medications / what-medications-are-used-to-treat-depression.

National Institute on Alcohol Abuse and Alcoholism. (October, 1989). No. 6, PH 277.

NPR, (2005). *A lobotomy timeline.* http://www.npr.org/templates/story/ story. php?storyId=50145 76& ps=rs.

Null, Gary (2006). Obsessive-compulsive disorder. *Get Healthy Now.* Seven Stories Press.

O'Hara, A. F. & Violanti, J. M. (2013). *Police suicide: a comprehensive study.* http://www.policesuicidestudy.com/.

Pavlov, I. P. (1927). *Conditioned reflexes: an investigation of the physiological activity of the cerebral cortex.* Translated and edited by *G. V. Anrep.* London: Oxford University Press.

Parekh, R. (2018). *What is mental illness?* https://www.psychiatry.org/ patients-families/what-is-mental-illness.

Perine, T. (May 26, 2021) The law enforcement suicide data collection: The FBI's new data collection on officer suicide and attempted suicide. *Police Chief Online.*

Perlmutter, A. (2022). *If serotonin does not cause depression, what does?* https://www.psychologytoday.com/us/blog/the-modern-brain/ 202207/if-serotonin-doesn't-cause-depression-what-does.

Pierre, J. (2018). *Do antidepressants work? Yes, no, and yes again!* https://www.psychologytoday.com/us/blog/psych-unseen/201802/ do-anti depressants-work-yes-no-and-yes-again.

Povenmire, H. (1995). The Sylacauga, Alabama meteorite: the impact locations, atmosphere trajectory, strewn field and radiant. *Abstracts of the Lunar and Planetary Science Conference,* (26), p.1133.

Psychology Today (n.d.). *Denial.* https:// www.psychologytoday. com/us/ basics/denial.

Psychology Today (n.d.) *Rationalization.* https://www. psychologytoday. com/us/basics/rationalization.

Reiser, M. (1982). *Police psychology: collected papers.* Los Angeles: LEHI Publishing.

Reschenthaler, G. (2002). *House passes Reschenthaler, Trone public safety officer support act.* https://reschenthaler.house.gov/.

Restak, Richard (2000). Fixing the Brain. *Mysteries of the mind.* Washington, D.C.: National Geographic Society.

Rosen, G.M., Spitzer, R.I., & McHugh, P.R. (2008). Problems with the PTSD diagnosis and its future in DSM 5. *British Journal of Psychiatry,192,* 3-4.

Ross, C A. (2006). The sham ECT literature: implications for consent to ECT. *Ethical Human Psychiatry and Psychology,* 8 (1): 17-28.

Rubinstein, M. (2016). *Not guilty by reason of insanity: Getting away with murder?* https://goodmenproject.com.

Schultz, E. A. & Lavenda, R. H. (2006). *Core concepts in cultural anthropology.* New York: McGraw-Hill.

Selye, H. (1974). *Stress without stress.* New York: Signet.

Serna, J. (2015) https://www.latimes.com/local/crime/la-me-0107-suicide-by-cop-20150107-story.html.

Slawinski, T. T. and Blythe, B. T. (2004) *When doing the right thing might be wrong: research questions the value of critical incident stress debriefings.* http://www.cmiatl.com/news article55.html.

Smith, K. (2022). *Hundreds of police officers sign up for Texas mental health program.* https://www.officer.com.

Smith, S. (2003). *Treating schizophrenia: medication versus therapy.*

Smith, D. (2012) *Anxiety; it's still the 'age of anxiety.' Or Is It?* The New York Times, January 15, 2012.

Spence, Deborah L., and Jessica Drake. (2021). *Law Enforcement Suicide: 2020 Report to Congress.* Washington, DC: U.S. Department of Justice.

Sokolove, B. (September, 2022). Personal email.

Statistics Times. (2020). https://www.statisticstimes.com/ demographics /country/us-sex-ratio.

Staton, T. (2010). *FAA OKs four antidepressants for pilot use.* http:// www. fiercepharma.com/story/faa-oks-four-antidepressants-pilot-use/2010-04-05.

Stratton, J. G. (1984). *Police passages.* Manhattan Beach, CA: Glennon Publishing.

Suleman, R. (2020). A brief history of electroconvulsive therapy. *The American Journal of Psychiatry.* https://ajp.psychiatryonline. org/ doi/ 10.1176/appi.ajp-rj.2020.160103.

Taylor, G. J. (March 2001). Relicts from the birth of the solar system. *PSR Discoveries.*

True, W.R., Rice, J., Eisen, S.A., Heath, A.C., Goldberg J., Lyons, M.J., & Nowak, J. (1993). A twin study of genetic and environmental contributions to liability for posttraumatic stress symptoms. *Archives of General Psychiatry, 50* (4), 257-264.

U.S. Census Bureau (2012). *An overview of the U. S. population.* http:// www.infoplease.com/ipa/A0004925.html.

Van Zandt, C. (1993). Suicide by cop. *The police chief, 7,* 24-30.

Villalvazo, P., Fernandez-Prado, R., Sanchez Niño, M., Carriazo, S., Fernández, B., Ortiz, A., Perez-Gomez, M. (2022). *Clinical Kidney Journal,* Volume 15, Issue 12, 2169-2176.

Violanti, J.M. (1992). *Police retirement: The impact of change.* Springfield, Illinois: Thomas.

Violanti, J.M., and Steege A. Policing. (2021). *Law enforcement worker suicide: an updated national assessment.* 44(1):18-31. doi:10.1108/ PIJPSM-09-2019-0157. Epub 2020 Oct 21. PMID: 33883970.

Vukicevic, M. & Fitzmaurice, K. (2008). Butterflies and black lacy patterns: the prevalence and characteristics of Charles Bonnet hallucinations in an Australian population. *Clinical and Experimental Ophthalmology, (36),* 659-65.

Walleser, L. (2022). *New England supports LBGTQ public safety professionals.* https://www.therainbowtimesmass. com/g-o-a-l-new-england-supports-lgbtq-public-safety-professionals.

Wambaugh, J. (1975). *The choirboys.* New York:Delacorte Press.

Weg, A. (2022). *FDA approves first fact-acting oral drug for clinical depression that works in 1 week.* https://www. prevention.com.

Werder, P. & Rothlin, P. (March 2007). *Diagnosis boreout—How a lack of challenge at work can make you ill.* Germany: Redline Wirtschaft.

Willett, W. C. & Skerrett, P. J. (2005) *Eat, drink, and be healthy: the Harvard Medical School guide to healthy eating.* New York: Free Press.

Williams, D. (2006). *Manic depression.* http://www.Peaceandhealing. com/ depression/manic.asp

Wolpe, J. (1969). *The practice of behavior therapy.* New York: Pergamon Press.

Woo, J. M., Okusaga, O., Postolache, T. T. (2012). Seasonality of suicidal behavior. *Int Journal of Environ Res Public Health.* 9:531–47.

Worden, J. M. (1982). *Grief counseling and grief therapy: a handbook for the mental health practitioner.* New York: Springer.

World Health Organization. (2014). *Preventing suicide: A global imperative.* World Health Organization.

Zimbardo, P., Sword, R.M., & Sword, R.K.M. (2012). *The time cure.* San Francisco, CA: John Wiley and Sons, Inc.

Zippia. (2022). *Police officer demographics and statistics in the US.* https://www.zippia.com/police-officer- jobs/demographics/.

Zisook, S., Byrd, D., Kuck, J., & Jeste, D. V. (October 1995). Command hallucinations in outpatients with schizophrenia. *Journal of Clinical Psychiatry,*56(10),462-465.

Index

Printed in the United States
by Baker & Taylor Publisher Services